The UNITED NATIONS EMERGENCY FORCE

NUMBER TWO

COLUMBIA UNIVERSITY STUDIES IN INTERNATIONAL ORGANIZATION

EDITORS

LELAND M. GOODRICH AND WILLIAM T. R. FOX

The UNITED NATIONS EMERGENCY FORCE

By GABRIELLA ROSNER

1963 · Columbia University Press · New York and London

To my Mother and Father

COLUMBIA UNIVERSITY STUDIES
IN INTERNATIONAL ORGANIZATION

The United Nations Emergency Force, by Gabriella Rosner, the second in the series, was made possible by a grant from the Rockefeller Foundation. The first was *Controls for Outer Space and the Antarctic Analogy,* by Philip C. Jessup and Howard J. Taubenfeld.

This series of monographs is not intended to provide a systematic coverage of the field of international organization nor is it anticipated that volumes will appear with any set regularity. The value of the contribution which the monograph makes to knowledge and understanding of the role of international organization and its functioning in the world in which we live will be the dominant consideration in determining inclusion.

The series is published under the joint editorship of Leland M. Goodrich and William T. R. Fox, with Andrew W. Cordier and Louis Henkin acting in an advisory capacity.

FOREWORD

This book by Miss Rosner on the United Nations Emergency Force represents the first effort to write a comprehensive account of the creation, organization, functions, status and operation of the Force from all existing unclassified documents.

The Force came into being at the very height of the Suez crisis in the first days of November, 1956. There was no opportunity for relaxed planning over an extended period of time. It is a tribute to the late Secretary-General Dag Hammarskjold that the creation of such a force, together with the determination of its legal status, the character of its operations, and its effectiveness in action could have been achieved with such speed and relative perfection.

UNEF was charged by the General Assembly with a dual role "initially to secure and supervise the cease-fire and withdrawal of armed forces from Egyptian territory and later to maintain peaceful conditions in the area by its deployment along the Egyptian-Israeli armistice demarcation line in the Gaza area and to the south along the international frontier. This dual role determined the size, organization, equipment and deployment of the Force."

While Mr. Hammarskjold was carrying on the negotiations with the governments for the achievement of the cease-fire and the withdrawal of forces, his difficult task was facilitated and the compliance of the governments of the withdrawing forces was eased by the role played by the Force in the areas of withdrawal.

There were strong political pressures for an interpretation of the Force as well as for its use which did not correspond with the strict legal concepts and the firm adherences to principles which the

Secretary-General felt should be elaborated and adhered to if the
Force was, in fact, to play its proper role in an atmosphere of extreme tension and intense conflict of interest. For example, there
was the view that the Force should be recognized as an extension
of the British-French thesis that action by them in Egypt was aimed
at the separation of Egyptian and Israeli forces. This view was not
accepted by the General Assembly nor by the Secretary-General.
There was a view that the Force might be used as a political and
military instrument to hasten withdrawal. This, too, was rejected
by the Secretary-General with the support of the General Assembly.
Finally, there was the view that the position of the Force on Egyptian soil should not require the consent of the Egyptian government.
This, too, was rejected by the Secretary-General, and he was supported in his judgment by the General Assembly. In this connection,
he argued that the action taken in the Suez crisis was not taken
under Chapter 7—the peace enforcement provisions of the Charter
—nor was it taken by the Security Council. It was taken by the
General Assembly which has only powers of recommendation. Furthermore, Egypt, as a sovereign State would have the right to accept
or reject the Force, and, therefore, consent was necessary.

The determined adherence of the Secretary-General to the importance of principles and to the development of legal formulae in
the creation and operation of this new mechanism in international
life caused him to be criticized as excessively legalistic in his approach. It is of interest that subsequently all members of the United
Nations recognized the validity and soundness of his approach.

The principles elaborated by the Secretary-General for UNEF
centered mainly upon an effort to establish and secure recognition
of the international character of the Force. The Force was established by the General Assembly on the basis of principles reflected
in the structure and the Charter of the United Nations itself. The
Commanding Officer of the Force was appointed by and was responsible to the United Nations and his authority was so defined as to
make him fully independent of the policies or the control of any

one nation. The functions of the Force were described as exclusively international in character in that they related to armed conflict among states and the purpose of the Force was to facilitate compliance with resolutions relating to the conflict adopted by the General Assembly. Its role was circumscribed by the principle that there was "no intent . . . to influence the military balance in the present conflict and, thereby, the political balance affecting efforts to settle the conflict." Nor was the Force to be "used so as to prejudge the solution of the controversial questions involved." Thus, there was a clear demarcation between the role of the Force on one side and the area to be reserved for diplomatic negotiation and for further action by the General Assembly. Furthermore, the principle of good faith was embodied on the side of both Egypt and the United Nations with respect to interpretation of the purposes of the Force. Thus, on the question of the withdrawal of the Force, the interest of the government concerned was to be balanced with the right of the General Assembly to review the need for the continuation of the Force in carrying out its mandate.

The United Nations reserved to itself the authority to decide on the composition of national military elements in the Force but it recognized that the host country in giving its consent could not be indifferent to its composition. In this connection, the Force did not include units from any of the permanent members of the Security Council nor did it include elements from any country which, because of its geographical position or for other reasons, might be considered as possibly having a special interest in the situation which had called for the operation.

The presence of a United Nations Force on the soil of a sovereign state also called for an elaborate legal agreement determining the rights, privileges, and immunities of the Force and of its members in relation to the host state.

The United Nations Emergency Force is still in being. It has served effectively for over six years and there is no indication that it will be brought to an early end.

The experience in regard to UNEF was of great value in connection with the pressing need of organizing a similar force in the Congo in July, 1960. On the practical side of logistics and supply, of the recruitment of units, of field headquarters organization, as well as in the field of legal concepts and of the principles determining the relationship of the Force to the host country in the performance of its duties, the experience of UNEF was of great value.

The future of para-military forces in the service of the United Nations is not yet clear, but the need is evident. The financial difficulty in support of ONUC * indicates the necessity of devising measures for training between crises which are the least expensive. This might imply that a program for the training of officers at United Nations headquarters in UNEF and ONUC experiences and of planning for the future might be combined with national initiatives, such as those already undertaken in the Scandinavian countries, whereby units of armed forces are specifically earmarked for training in United Nations principles, methods, and procedures for para-military action in crisis areas. In any case, there is widespread recognition of the need of such para-military force in support of all the techniques of negotiation undertaken by the United Nations in dealing with a threat to the peace.

In Miss Rosner's comprehensive analysis of both the practical and legal aspects of UNEF, she presents the facts with fullness and clarity and engages in interpretations and conclusions which are the result of her extensive reflections on a vital aspect of international organization.

ANDREW CORDIER

Dean, School of International Affairs

Columbia University
in the City of New York
February 13, 1963

* The French initials for the United Nations Force in the Congo.

ACKNOWLEDGMENTS

For the discerning advice and continuing interest of the many people who helped me in the preparation of this volume, I would like to express my grateful appreciation.

My warmest thanks, particularly, are extended to Professor Leland M. Goodrich who first introduced me to the field of international organization and guided me throughout my graduate studies. His instruction and counsel, always stimulating and enriching, were invaluable to this study. I am deeply grateful, too, for his constant encouragement and interest.

I take this opportunity to express my gratitude to Dean Andrew Cordier who gave me the benefit not only of his first-hand knowledge and experience, but also his generous support. My sincere thanks go furthermore to Professor William T.R. Fox for his very valued criticism and guidance. His instruction has always been a source of great stimulus. Mr. William M. Jordan of the United Nations Secretariat read the manuscript and made numerous helpful suggestions. I appreciated very much his advice and kindness.

I should like to thank the Rockefeller Foundation for the generous support which made possible the completion and publication of this book. I am, moreover, indebted to Mr. Oscar Schachter, Mr. W. W. Cox, and Mr. F. Blaine Sloan of the United Nations Secretariat who in conversations provided me with information and perspective by which I have benefited considerably.

Elizabeth Korbonski proofread the galleys and provided many editorial suggestions; Hazel Weinberg constructively criticised some of the writing; Miss Phyllis Holbrook of the Columbia University

Press edited the manuscript and extended patient aid in the many tasks of publication; and the staff of the international law library of Columbia University, particularly Mrs. Florence Zagayko, granted me most courteous assistance: I thank them for their help.

My deep gratitude goes to my mother and father: they have provided much encouragement and many kindnesses in the course of preparing this book. And lastly, to Kenneth Lande: a thousand thanks!

GABRIELLA ROSNER

New York City
March 1963

CONTENTS

The UNITED NATIONS
EMERGENCY FORCE

INTRODUCTION

The greatest prayer of man does not ask
for victory but for peace.

DAG HAMMARSKJOLD

A new "weapon for peace"—an international security force—was created by the United Nations in the autumn of 1956. For the first time in history, a force of this type worked toward the peaceful settlement of a dangerous dispute. Efforts to achieve this goal had been made many times in the past: always they had failed.

When the General Assembly in emergency special session on November 5 and 7, 1956, brought into being the United Nations Emergency Force (UNEF) to help resolve a severe crisis in the Middle East and stem the invasion of Egypt by the troops of Britain, France, and Israel, it was a swift and improvised action. UNEF was designed as a temporary police force operating with the consent of Egypt and the cooperation of contributory states. It was primarily assigned the task of supervising withdrawal of non-Egyptian troops from Egyptian territory and promoting compliance with United Nations resolutions. In its years of service, however, the Force has been concerned with a great number of far-reaching duties and responsibilities, and has also been recognized as an important contribution to international organization's technique of peacekeeping.

Indeed UNEF, although "a new and in many ways unique experiment by the United Nations in a type of operation which previously it had not been called upon to conduct," [1] represents the prototype of a small police force which the international community might well find useful at other times of crisis. It was the continuing success of the Emergency Force which encouraged the establishment on July

14, 1960, of the United Nations Force for the Republic of the Congo. The Congo operation leaned heavily upon UNEF's experience, and similar future enterprises might certainly draw lessons from it as well. Dag Hammarskjold himself declared that

. . . the organization of the United Nations Force in the Congo was considerably facilitated by the fact that it was possible for the Secretary-General to draw on the experience of the United Nations Emergency Force in Gaza and on the conclusions regarding various questions of principle and law which had been reached on the basis of that experience.[2]

It is thus not only for the results achieved but also for the hopes aroused that the "spirit" of UNEF has spread.

The results achieved are notable. With the help of the Force, a local war in the Middle East was brought to an end, a menacing situation was stilled, quiet and reasonable stability became possible in the Suez Canal area and on the Egypt-Israel frontier. The risk of active interference in the area by the Soviet Union and the United States was eliminated. Creation of UNEF—a new tool of peaceful settlement—was a positive step in United Nations "preventive diplomacy."

The special need and the special possibilities for what Secretary-General Dag Hammarskjold called United Nations "preventive diplomacy" were clearly demonstrated in the Suez crisis of 1956. This diplomacy aims at keeping newly arising conflicts outside the sphere of power-bloc differences, or, in the case of conflicts already within this sphere, at localizing the area of hostilities. It proposes to fill a power vacuum between the main blocs, if such should exist. It seeks to prevent military initiative by either of the "super-powers." During the crucial months of agitation in the Middle East, it entailed compromise between use of strong, condemnatory methods to achieve peaceful settlement and mild policies of pacification and conciliation.

The story of UNEF has not been told. How was the Force created

and how did it play its part in preventive diplomacy? What were
its legal basis, its functions and powers, financial and administrative organization? What precedents did UNEF establish? If the
experience of the United Nations Emergency Force were not built
upon, declared Lester Pearson of Canada, it would always be necessary to "go back again to the situation in which we found ourselves
last November [1956], when everything had to be improvised, when
there was no precedent for making units available, no administrative and financial procedure, and no organization to which the
Secretary-General could turn in the task given him by the Assembly
of putting a United Nations force into a dangerous and delicate
situation." [3]

UNEF's experiences may provide insights to an important question for the United Nations: Would the maintenance or restoration
of international peace and security be substantially furthered by
the creation of a standing UN military force?

It has been conjectured that, had the United Nations possessed
a peace force before the time of the Anglo-French invasion of
Egypt, that invasion might never have taken place. "Countries like
Britain and France, sensitive to the moral judgment of mankind,
require persuasive pretexts when they resort to force to gain their
ends. Without such pretexts, they are unlikely to take action which
the world—including many of their own people—will condemn." [4]
In 1956, the "pretext" of the United Kingdom and France was that
the United Nations was incapable of effective action in halting the
fighting between Israel and Egypt and protecting the Suez Canal.
Would these pretexts have been persuasive, however, "if a U.N.
police force had been standing by, ready to perform those tasks?" [5]

The world has erected a ring of mighty defenses against aggression and developed safeguards to protect the peace. Alliances and
counter-alliances, treaties of mutual assistance, national arsenals of
nuclear weapons, policies of deterrence and massive retaliation, international organizations of wide scope and purpose, all stand in a
powerful effort to deter military action. In November 1956, the

United Nations added a highly useful instrument to the world's stock of peacekeeping equipment. It made available "an intermediate technique between merely passing resolutions and actually fighting." [6]

Chapter One

THE POLITICAL BACKGROUND

Achievement of international security through the mechanism of a multinational police force is a concept scarcely peculiar to the postwar world. Throughout modern history attempts to oppose conflict by international military means have been promoted. Throughout modern history a search for an international order supported by lawful force has taken place.*

During these 300 years since the peace of Westphalia the effort has been to develop concepts and institutions for the world similar to those long accepted as a matter of course for national states and for our domestic society—namely, an established and organized community; rules of conduct or a system of law binding on all within the community; courts and other machinery for the adjudication and settlement of disputes; and policemen, sheriffs, militia, and, if necessary, even armies, to enforce the law and maintain peace and security.[1]

Yet during the autumn of 1956, the Secretary-General in drafting his plans for the United Nations Emergency Force, and the Secretariat staff in preparing for the execution of his recommendations, had sparse particular knowledge upon which to draw. An international police force, matching in nature, type, and function the one envisaged in Mr. Hammarskjold's plan, had previously never existed.[2] And, although the idea of a multinational military group—with either peace enforcement or peacekeeping duties—had been proposed many times in the past and had been implemented in practice at irregular intervals, the world of 1956 had no such force at its disposal.

* See Appendix.

The United Nations Emergency Force, then, came into being in direct response to the outbreak of war in the Middle East on October 29, 1956. At that time, "one of the festering sores of world politics came to a temporary head and burst," [3] as Israel, France, and the United Kingdom launched their attack upon Egyptian territory. Members of the United Nations promptly and vigorously tried to check the military action and the use of force in international affairs.

Might has never been the source of right, but the United Nations was founded on a new principle, expressly accepted by all the Members of the United Nations on their signature of the Charter, namely, that, except in cases of collective action undertaken in accordance with the provisions of the Charter, no country might secure its rights, however legitimate, by the use of force.[4]

The United Nations General Assembly proposed to stop hostilities without delay, to localize the conflict, and to prevent further military moves in the region. To aid in the attainment of these ends, UNEF was born.

The eruption of hostilities in the Middle East climaxed a series of critical events concerning the area which had followed swiftly one upon the other during the summer of 1956. By November the United Nations faced a grave crisis in Egypt.

This troubled situation had its source and history in a myriad of political, economic, and legal problems stemming back many decades and involving intricate questions of nationalism, self-determination, and historic rights. Egyptian restrictions on shipping in the Suez Canal and in the Gulf of Aqaba, as well as generally tense relations between Israel and the Arab States, played a significant role. More immediately, however, the Israeli military attack was aimed at removing the bases of guerrilla raiders in the Gaza Strip. From the British and French points of view, Egyptian nationalization of the Suez Canal Company and Egyptian encouragement of Algerian nationalism were at the heart of the problem. Yet intervention in Egypt on the part of Britain and France was intended, officially, "to separate the belligerents [Israel and Egypt] and to guarantee freedom of transit through the [Suez] Canal by the ships of all nations. . . ." [5]

ARAB-ISRAELI TENSIONS

Since 1949 a precarious armistice had existed between Israel and her Arab neighbors. No permanent peace settlement had been concluded and violations of the armistice agreements by all parties were commonplace. In effect, the armistice machinery for settling disputes peacefully was in a constantly threatened position: Egypt maintained a blockade on Israeli shipping in the Suez Canal and the Gulf of Aqaba; her economic boycott of Israel caused much hardship for that country; *fedayeen* raids from Egypt into Israeli territory, followed by violent reprisal action on the part of Israel, became more and more serious during 1955 and 1956. Tension in the Middle East mounted steadily.

Discordant relations between Israel and the Arab States had been continuous since the creation of the state of Israel in 1948. The Arab world had never been reconciled to the presence of the Jewish nation in its midst and had remained at war with Israel. Its position was that Israel usurped Arab territory by force; hence the Israeli presence in the Middle East was that of the unjust conqueror, with an aim of further territorial expansion for the purpose of accommodating new immigrants from every land of the world. Israel's actions had driven thousands of Palestinians to impoverished exile. An Arab spokesman has said:

It is the nature of the Zionist movement itself—of which Israel is a prolongation—to try to expand and expand so that more space can be acquired to gather in the so-called exiles from many lands, and it is that movement which, in many countries, exerts an influence which ofttimes goes far beyond measure. [6]

On its side, Israel remained convinced of its historic and legal right to a Jewish homeland in Palestine and sought, above all, a stable relationship with the countries surrounding her. But the inhabitants of Israel remained nervously poised for encounter with what they believed would be the "second round"—the Arab ambition of driving the Jews into the sea and "restoring Palestine to its rightful owners." [7]

In theory the armistice agreements, separately concluded by Israel between February 24 and July 20, 1949, with each of her neighbors —Egypt, Lebanon, Jordan, and Syria—provided for an end to the hostilities which began in 1948 and set up machinery to prevent their recurrence. [8] But the negotiation of an ultimate peace and the settlement of fundamental questions of a nonmilitary nature were postponed. [9] In the years following the armistice settlement, the deferred political issues and the rivalry they engendered represented fearful sources of Arab-Israel animosity. [10]

The economic boycott of Israel by the Arab League states also gained intensity with the years. [11] Formally instituted immediately after the establishment of the Israeli state, the boycott soon covered many aspects of economic and commercial life. [12] Regional boycott offices were established and strict rules were applied. Refusing to deal with foreign commercial and industrial firms that had business with Israel, the Arabs exerted pressure on many companies to abandon commerce with the new state. Airline companies were not permitted to include Israel in routes passing through Arab lands, and foreign trading vessels were forbidden entry to Arab ports if they had stopped in Israeli harbors en route. [13]

But blockade restrictions by Egypt in the Gulf of Aqaba and the Suez Canal were those most seriously felt by Israel and were the cause of much concern for many years. By closing the two waterways to Israeli trade, Egypt denied Israel contact with the Indian Ocean and the Far East, except by means of the extended sea lane through the Mediterranean and around Africa. The Egyptian government justified these restrictions by maintaining that the state of war between Egypt and Israel had continued to exist ever since March 15, 1948, despite the General Armistice Agreement with the Israeli state on February 24, 1949. Egypt argued that from this state of war were derived certain rights of belligerency, such as the right of visit, search, and seizure. A shipping inspection service was set up, a Prize Court was established, and a black list of oil tankers was prepared.[14] Furthermore, in agreement with Saudi Arabia, the government of Egypt occupied the islands of Tiran and Sanafir in the Red Sea at the entrance to the Gulf of Aqaba and erected a number of military installations in the region to prevent commerce to and from the Israeli port of Elath.[15] Such restrictions provoked a series of grave incidents in the Gulf of Aqaba.[16]

Before Israel's attack on Egypt in October 1956, Israel complained often to the Security Council regarding Egypt's restrictive measures.[17] Time and again the Egyptian defense was rejected by a majority of Council members as unfounded. On September 1, 1951, the Security Council passed a resolution which, among other things, called

upon Egypt to terminate the restrictions on the passage of international commercial shipping and goods through the Suez Canal wherever bound and to cease all interference with such shipping beyond that essential to the safety of shipping in the Canal itself and to the observance of the international conventions in force.[18]

The resolution noted the report of the Chief of Staff of the United Nations Truce Supervision Organization [19] to the Council on June 12, 1951. In this document, it was emphasized "that action taken by Egyptian authorities in interfering with passage of goods destined for Israel through the Suez Canal must be considered an aggressive action." [20] Lamenting the fact that the 1951 resolution had not been complied with, many delegates, in 1954, again condemned Egypt's actions, but the situation remained essentially unchanged. Israel thus remained faced with a continuation of the problem—another source of serious anxiety for her vis-à-vis the Arab States.[21]

Mutual hatred and distrust between Arabs and Jews gave rise to increasingly belligerent border violations. Since 1948 hundreds of incidents had occurred in which exchanges of fire took place between military outposts of the two sides and between border patrols which had crossed the demarcation lines. Infiltration across boundaries became more frequent and aroused heated passions. Determined to stop the infiltrators at all costs, Israel, led by her Premier, David Ben-Gurion, adopted a fierce policy of retaliation which developed into well-organized military raids against Arab settlements in Arab territory.[22] Indeed, the Arabs were convinced that a "study of the aggression and incidents on the border . . . will show that it is Israel which has constantly been the aggressor, that it is the Israel army which has constantly penetrated into neighboring Arab States. No Arab army has ever entered Israel or trespassed the armistice lines." [23]

The thirty-seven mile frontier between Israel and the Egyptian-controlled Gaza Strip was the scene of special difficulties. During 1955, Israel complained more and more frequently of hostile raids into Israel by *fedayeen* or armed bands operating in the Gaza Strip. It was Israel's contention that these bands were officially sponsored by the Egyptian authorities to carry out a war of terror against Israel.[24] As a result, tension on the border was high during 1955 and 1956.

The Secretary-General during this time had acted energetically to halt a number of military moves and dispositions by Israel and Egypt around the sensitive El-Auja region—considered the gateway to invasion. The Armistice Agreement between the two countries had demilitarized this zone but, to observers, both nations seemed to have violated its provisions. On March 20, 1956, the United States called a meeting of the Security Council to consider the status of compliance with the Armistice Agreement. Mr. Hammarskjold was asked to survey the compliance situation, which he understood to mean "re-establish compliance" to the greatest possible extent.[25] In his report of May 9, the Secretary-General declared that a "chain of actions and reactions" had occurred in the Middle East which, unless broken, would lead to war.[26] He sought to lift the cease-fire provision out of the Armistice Agreement and give it a special sanctity—make of it an obligation independent of the Agreement. Violation of other terms of the Agreement would not justify a violation of the cease-fire.

With the governments concerned giving the Secretary-General assurances that they would observe the cease-fire clause unconditionally, subject only to a self-defense reservation, this effort on the part of the Secretary-General was generally considered a great success. It resulted in a temporary decrease of tension and the consideration of specific measures for preventing further border clashes and incidents in the Middle East. Officials in the Western capitals were emboldened to edge the parties toward a settlement. In a draft resolution submitted to the Security Council, the British, for example, formulated a preambular clause which, they hoped, would serve as the basis for mutually acceptable agreements.[27] But sharp Arab protests, backed by the Soviet Union, resulted in its deletion.[28] Thus, the hopes which had been kindled were short-lived. The resolution which was finally accepted by the Council was merely an endorsement of the Secretary-General's action in trying to secure compliance with the Armistice Agreement.[29]

Indeed, Israel feared once more that its national security was gravely threatened. This fear mounted when President Eisenhower, in the spring of 1956, failed to persuade President Nasser, of Egypt, to turn his efforts toward a peace settlement. On July 19, 1956, the Secretary-General visited Jerusalem to talk with Israeli Prime Minister Ben-Gurion about Israeli limitations on the movement of UN observers in El-Auja.[30] The Israeli leader maintained that the Armistice Agreement was indivisible. He felt that Egypt's refusal to accept Article I, which committed both sides to refrain from undertaking, planning, or threatening aggressive acts against the other, freed Israel from complying with the other terms of the Agreement. "Hammarskjold," Joseph Lash reports, "was in the middle of trying to break out of this dangerous deadlock when the event occurred which British Prime Minister Sir Anthony Eden said transformed everything in the Middle East." [31] Nasser nationalized the Suez Canal. Then, on October 29, 1956, Israeli forces moved into the Sinai Peninsula—Egyptian territory.

Spokesmen of the Israeli government declared the *fedayeen* raids to be the immediate reason for the military action. Speaking in the Security Council, Ambassador Eban declared:

At this morning's meeting I defined the objective of the security measures which the Israel defense forces have felt bound to take in the Sinai Peninsula in the exercise of our country's inherent right of self-defense. The object of those operations is to eliminate the Egyptian *fedayeen* bases from which armed Egyptian units, under the special care and authority of Mr. Nasser, invade Israel's territory for purposes of murder, sabotage and the creation of permanent insecurity to peaceful life.[32]

Two days after the Israeli invasion, Britain and France joined the contest by sending a squadron of bombers under an Anglo-French command against Egyptian military targets.

BRITAIN, FRANCE, AND NATIONALIZATION OF THE SUEZ CANAL

The British and French military action against Egypt also had an entangled and a complex history. Since the Arab world extended from the Persian Gulf to the Atlantic, and the Arab States controlled not only the Suez Canal but the world's largest oil supplies, a constant courting of the Arab world by all the great powers had taken place throughout the postwar years.

The British, for example, had hoped to place their relations with Egypt on a permanently friendly basis in July 1954 by agreeing to withdraw their garrisons from the Suez Canal area and by encouraging Arab claims for frontier revisions in Palestine. France likewise sought to conciliate the postwar surge of Arab national feeling and, like Britain, was supported in this endeavor by the United States. Washington, indeed, was more than eager to convince these Middle Eastern states of U.S. friendship and to outbid the Soviet Union in its concern for the Arab world. The Soviet Union—through the instrumentality of Czechoslovakia—had begun to make deliveries of modern armaments to Egypt, thereby not only increasing Arab power but championing the Arab cause against Israel, which was represented by Soviet propaganda as an instrument of Western imperialism.

The British and French attitudes toward the ebullience of Pan-Arabism nonetheless began, with time, to differ from those of the Soviet Union or the United States. In France, resentment toward the Arab States grew in steady proportion to the Arabs' moral and material support of the Algerian nationalist movement. In Britain, President Nasser of Egypt was increasingly viewed as a hostile figure whose actions might well endanger freedom of passage through the Suez Canal—a matter of urgent British interest. The British looked with considerable alarm at Egyptian influence in Jordan and Syria, at the growing isolation of Iraq from the rest of the Arab world under the impact of Egyptian propaganda, and at the effect of that propaganda on the young Arab nationalists of the Persian Gulf. The United States continued to woo the Egyptian President, although Washington became more and more unhappy with Nasser's Czechoslovak arms deal of September 1955. Was this not, Washington asked, a sign of Egyptian subservience to Moscow? It is against the background of these divergent attitudes, then, that the crisis over Suez emerged.[33]

In a speech at Alexandria, July 26, 1956, President Nasser announced Egyptian nationalization of the Suez Canal Company. Egypt, he declared, would assume complete control of the Suez Canal Company's assets and obligations in return for which she would promise compensation to all shareholders.[34] Revenues from the Canal would be used to finance the projected building of the Aswan High Dam. President Nasser's venture in this direction came after the United States and the United Kingdom withdrew their offers to help finance the Dam project.[35]

Egypt's act of nationalization produced not only intense reactions in London and Paris, where important national interests were felt to be at stake, but in the world at large.[36] The Suez Canal Company's concession [37] was not due to expire until November 17, 1968. The British government owned 44 percent of the Company's shares and over 25 percent of the remainder was owned by private share-holders in France. The Canal was a vitally strategic link in Britain's communication with her empire and all of Europe was heavily dependent upon the oil transported through the Canal from the Middle East. The interested parties were not prepared to let a change in the *status quo* go unchallenged.

Attempts at negotiation, following Nasser's action, met with failure. A London conference of the twenty-four nations most directly concerned with the Suez Canal was held during August 16–23 without Egyptian participation. At this conference, United States Secretary of State John Foster Dulles presented a plan which was intended to place operation of the Suez Canal Company in the hands of an international board, the status of which was to be defined in a subsequent convention. Eighteen nations accepted the American proposal, but Egypt rejected it outright, as did the Soviet Union, India, Indonesia, and Ceylon.[38] A committee of five, under the chairmanship of Prime Minister Menzies of Australia, was then set up to approach the Egyptian government and initiate additional discussions; this further essay at negotiation also failed.[39]

On September 12, Prime Minister Eden told the House of Commons of French and British plans to organize, with provisional U.S. support, a Suez Canal "users' association" which would employ its own pilots, collect tolls, and give Egypt "appropriate payment" for its members' ships passing through the Canal. In the event of Egypt's refusal to cooperate, members of the "users' association," Eden said, would "be free to take such further steps as seem to be required, either through the United Nations or by other means, for the assertion of their rights." [40] Despite Nasser's rejection of the idea as "an association for waging war," a second London conference met from September 19 to 21 and on October 1, a Suez Canal Users' Association was inaugurated.[41]

Events subsequently shifted to the United Nations where the Security Council took up the matter: a complaint against Egypt for terminating international control of the Suez Canal had been presented by England and France; Egypt had asked the Council to consider French and British threats to the peace.[42] More than ever now, the problem was one for the world community to consider and solve.

After an initial round of statements in the Security Council, informal talks were held between the parties in the UN corridors and in the Secretary-General's office. With Hammarskjold's help, six principles which should govern a settlement of the Suez issue were agreed upon.[43] While these principles were acceptable to all members of the Council, the operative part of an Anglo-French draft resolution suggesting their implementation was vetoed by the Soviet Union on October 13. Secretary of State Dulles, heartened by the acceptance of the principles, urged the Secretary-General to continue his efforts for a negotiated settlement. The Secretary-General, too, was encouraged and viewed the resolution as a valuable starting point. Prime Minister Eden, however, remained dissatisfied.

In the days thereafter, political explosions reverberated around the world. Swift in its impact, resounding in its implications, the Hungarian revolution broke forth on October 23. Concurrently, anti-French riots erupted throughout Algeria, Tunisia, and Morocco. And six days later, while France in the Security Council accused the Egyptian government of furnishing military aid to the rebels of Algeria, the Israeli Army thrust deeply into Egyptian territory in the direction of the Suez Canal.

Almost immediately, on October 30, an Anglo-French ultimatum was issued to Israel and Egypt calling for cessation of fighting within twelve hours and withdrawal of all troops from a ten-mile radius of the Suez Canal area. In order to assure free passage through the Canal, Egypt was asked to accept temporary British and French occupation of key positions at Port Said, Ismailia, and Suez.[44] The ultimatum was forthrightly rejected by Egypt, though accepted by Israel. Also on October 30, the United States called for an immediate meeting of the Security Council to consider "The Palestine Question: steps for the immediate cessation of the military action of Israel in Egypt." [45] A United States sponsored resolution calling upon Israel to leave Egypt without delay and asking all Member States to "refrain from the use of force or threat of force" and "from giving any military, economic or financial assistance to Israel so long as it has not complied with this resolution," was vetoed by the United Kingdom and France on the same day. [46] A similar resolution, omitting recommendations to Members to refrain from force, was sponsored by the Soviet Union and again met defeat by means of the Anglo-French veto.

When at dusk on the evening of October 31 bombers under British-French Command began to raid military targets in Egypt, tension throughout the world became severe. Events had moved fast—dangerously fast. Israel had moved into Egypt, the British and French governments had sent Egypt and Israel an urgent ultimatum to cease fire which had been rejected by Egypt, and the Security Council had failed to find a solution to the problem. The Anglo-French attack on the Egyptian air force was in progress less than twenty-four hours after the vetoes in the Security Council.

In defending the United Kingdom's military action, Prime Minister Eden told the House of Commons of his conviction that the international waterway had to be promptly protected:

We have no desire whatever, nor have the French Government, that the military action that we shall have to take should be more than temporary in its duration, but it is our intention that our action to protect the Canal and separate the combatants should result in a settlement which will prevent such a situation arising in the future. If we can do that, we shall have performed a service not only to this country, but to the users of the Canal.

It is really not tolerable that the greatest sea highway in the world, one on which our Western life so largely depends, should be subject to the dangers of an explosive situation in the Middle East which, it must be admitted, has been largely created by the Egyptian Government along familiar lines. I would remind the House that we have witnessed, all of us, the growth of a specific Egyptian threat to the peace of the Middle East. . . .[47]

But the British and French aim in ordering military action was not only to protect the international waterway and separate the combatants, but to force President Nasser's hand into compromising on the Canal dispute. The leaders of the two nations may also have hoped to prevent the Egyptians from achieving mastery of the Arab world through a series of palace revolutions in other Middle Eastern states and from leading a united Arab crusade not only against Israel but against the "colonial" West. The United Kingdom and France would no doubt have liked to see the downfall of Colonel Nasser. But Eden professed to fear that, without rapid action on Britain's part, the war would be extended by the intervention of other Arab States:

The chief danger, especially for us, was that the conflict would spread. A localized war between Israel and Egypt, while troublesome, should not be highly dangerous internationally. The same could not be said of a war which spread to include Syria and Jordan, with Iraq morally compelled to take a hand too. . . . Two events could be counted on to encourage Jordan and Syria to inaction, swift Israeli military success and the knowledge that British and French forces were on the way and would be used to localize the dispute. If that restraint was to be effective it must be applied at once. Twenty-four hours might well be too late, forty-eight certainly would.[48]

Charges of collusion between Israel, France, and Britain were loudly voiced. Speculation on this question became more and more widespread during the early weeks of November, but official denials of collaboration were rigorous.[49] Even more widespread and outspoken, however, was criticism of the Anglo-French military action itself. Public and official opinion in Britain was sharply divided.[50] (In France, somewhat milder discord existed in government circles.) [51] India, Pakistan, Burma, and most of Asia denounced the move with sharp admonitions.[52] And the United States government reacted with almost unprecedented shock and dismay:

> This city [Washington], which has seen a good many extremes in political behaviour, has never witnessed such an exhibition of pique and anger as the Anglo-French-Israeli action against Egypt has touched off.
>
> At one moment, the highest American policy makers actually played with the astonishing idea of ordering the American Sixth Fleet to oppose the Anglo-French landings on the Egyptian coast.[53]

A fundamental difference had indeed developed between the allies in regard to their Middle Eastern policy and their attitude toward Gamal Abdel Nasser. The British and French viewed the Egyptian President as a belligerent anti-Western leader who in time would wear away any influence the free world still possessed in the Arab realm. Nasser's fall from political power as soon as possible would thus be a triumph for the anticommunist alliance.[54] Washington, likewise, would have wished to bring down the nationalistic President of Egypt, but preferred to achieve this aim by steady, if slow, economic pressure. United States officials believed that the United Kingdom and France, by using military force against Nasser, had seriously weakened Western denunciations of Soviet imperialism at the very moment when the peoples of Eastern Europe were rising up against Russian control. James Reston reported at the time:

> Nothing could have caused more dismay in Washington than the coordinated decision of London and Paris to resort to force in defiance of what the United States Government had always regarded as the main principles of British foreign policy in the post-war years.
>
> Britain and France fought alongside the United States to create an international organization in 1945 at San Francisco for the specific purpose of persuading nations not to resort to the use of force to achieve national objectives no matter how fundamental. Yet here were the British and French Governments taking action against Egypt not only in opposi-

tion to United States policy but in defiance of the principles of the United Nations.[55]

Eden, then, while not anticipating strong American support for his Suez venture, had certainly underestimated the strength of American opposition to an operation conducted in complete disregard of U.S. policy. The United States government was certain that the reaction of the Arab world to the Anglo-French invasion would be severe. The Americans feared that critical oil lines might be sabotaged, thereby precipitating a major economic and political crisis in Western Europe. Sherman Adams states that when President Eisenhower met with Secretary of State Dulles, Secretary of Defense Wilson, Admiral Radford, Allen Dulles, Herbert Hoover, Jr., and various other staff members on October 29, a good deal of discussion arose on "the military moves that would have to be made in the Mediterranean." While the President did not contemplate direct United States intervention at Suez, he did envisage that "our naval forces would be placed in a position to evacuate American citizens if that was necessary." And all the participants in the conference "agreed that if Russia came openly to Nasser's assistance, a war was inevitable." [56]

Fear was thus immediately voiced by government officials and members of the press, both in the U.S. and abroad, that the Soviet Union would attempt interference in the situation and that the conflict would spread. At the United Nations the Soviet Union proposed that the Security Council, acting under Article 42 of the Charter, authorize the USSR and the United States to send "naval and air forces, military units, volunteers, military instructors and other forms of assistance" to Egypt.[57] In similar notes to the United Kingdom and France, the Soviet Union stated that these countries might face "some stronger power" if they did not halt their invasion.[58] President Eisenhower was informed by letter of Moscow's belief that fighting in Egypt "contains danger of turning into a third world war." [59] Warnings, interpreted to mean Soviet intention to aid Egypt, multiplied steadily: at a Moscow news conference Premier Bulganin stressed Soviet possession of nuclear rocket weapons; on November 7, it was reported that Russian "volunteers" were ready to join the Egyptian forces.

Whether these threats were seriously meant or were merely intended to incite fear remains speculative. The alarms undoubtedly had their effect and evoked great concern in Western circles. In the early days of November the United States government informed the Soviet government of its determination to oppose any effort by the USSR to intervene by force in the Middle East.[60] This policy statement was repeated in the days ahead. The actual fear of a large war involving Soviet military might intensified the feeling, not only in the United States but throughout the world, that hostilities must be swiftly ended and foreign forces withdrawn from Egypt. Faced with the lack of unanimity of the permanent members, the Security Council turned to the General Assembly for an answer to the problem.[61]

Chapter Two

CREATION OF THE FORCE

By establishing the United Nations Emergency Force in response to the military invasion of Egypt by Israel, France, and the United Kingdom beginning October 29, 1956, the General Assembly adopted a compromise course between actions of "pure coercion" and "pure conciliation" [1] to restore peace. Several courses of procedure were open to the Assembly in settling the crisis: First, there was the possibility of utilizing collective sanctions, as provided for in the "Uniting for Peace" resolution, of branding the invaders as "aggressors," and of recommending the use of collective military forces to expel Israel, Britain, and France from Egyptian territory. Second, there was the possibility of negotiation within the framework of the United Nations, of attempting to obtain the withdrawal of foreign troops from Egypt through measures of conciliation and accommodation. Third, there could be a combination of military measures and conciliation, a combination which became a reality, with the consent of the nations concerned, in the creation of an emergency international UN force. The force was not to be a combat army with military objectives. It was not to *enforce* a withdrawal of troops but merely to *secure* the cessation of hostilities and compliance with United Nations resolutions. No aggressor was named.

The Assembly began consideration of the matter on November 1, the day following the veto by France and the United Kingdom of the Soviet draft resolution in the Security Council calling for a cease-fire and the withdrawal of Israeli forces. As a result of the negative votes of Britain and France, the Security Council had decided "to call an emergency special session of the General Assembly, as provided in General Assembly resolution 377 (V) of 3 November 1950, in order to make appropriate recommendations." [2]

The situation before the Assembly was, in many ways, unique and past crises afforded little guidance. In some respects, the Korean situation in June 1950 seemed to contain elements similar to those prevalent in the Middle Eastern crisis.[3] At both times there were open and deliberate military attacks: Israel's push into Sinai and the North Korean invasion across the thirty-eighth parallel into South Korea. During both periods, no organized international forces were available to repel the invaders and restore international peace and security. The United Nations in 1956, as in 1950, was called upon to deal with a situation in which intricate military machinery had already been set into motion. In both situations, special interests of Great Powers were involved.

But the Korean case was nonetheless a singular one in the annals of United Nations history, attended by circumstances which made quick and effective action by the Security Council possible. No mitigating conditions were present to relieve the North Korean attack from being branded a breach of the peace; absence of the Soviet representative from Council meetings when deliberation of the Korean question was in progress prevented stifling veto action; agreement between the Western powers as to what should be done to push back the North Korean attack, combined with the fact that United States armed forces—equipped and trained for action—were in the close vicinity of Korea, promoted speedy and authoritative decisions on collective military measures.

This extraordinary assemblage of circumstances did not exist in the Middle Eastern situation. Many states felt that although Israel's attack was overt and deliberate, it contained ingredients of defensive action against Egypt's provocations and threats. There was considerable sympathy with Israel's grievances against Egypt and general recognition that the United Nations had failed for many years to relieve the outstanding sources of tension in the Middle

East. Accordingly, José Vincente Trujillo of Ecuador stated in the
Assembly:

I can explain, though I do not justify, Israel's aggression. From the
beginning, Israel's history has been one of struggle. It is surrounded by
a group of peoples hostile to it . . . on grounds of religion, language and
culture; it has to fight, and it has fought bravely. . . .

So that although it has committed an act which we do not approve,
even if we can explain it, it is fighting for its life and for an ideal, the
ideal of being an independent country, however small; the ideal of being
a State and of giving fit expression to the intellectual gifts with which its
great race has been endowed.[4]

And the Chinese delegate, later seconded by the representative from
Colombia, emphatically declared that "it would be very difficult and
unfair to say that one party . . . alone, bears the whole responsibility for the recurrence of conflict in the Middle East. The
responsibility is two-sided, and the restoration of peace in that
region does require the cooperation of all parties."[5] There was thus
a certain reluctance on the part of some delegations palpably to
condemn the Israeli attack and to name Israel as an aggressor.

Some sympathy was also felt in the Assembly for the Anglo-
French action. The Suez Canal, it was recognized, represented vital
interests to Western Europe, interests which, the Australian delegate,
E. Ronald Walker, maintained, had to be protected:

The declared objectives of the United Kingdom and France in this matter
are not to wage war, but to prevent some of the consequences of war,
and to prevent the development of the conflict between Israel and Egypt,
and, in particular, to safeguard the lives and property of the nations using
the Suez Canal. Their objectives have been stated to be to prevent the
Canal itself from becoming a battle line between Israel and Egypt, a
development which would deny the use of this international waterway
to the whole world. Their objective is to interpose forces between Egyptian and Israel forces.[6]

Even Secretary of State Dulles, sternly condemnatory of the resort
to force by America's allies, spoke of serious provocations and ad-

mitted not to be "blind to the fact that what has happened within the last two or three days has emerged from a murky background." [7]

Again differing from the circumstances of the Korean war was the fact that the unity of the Western allies during the autumn of 1956 was in a state of disarray. Agreement in the Security Council proved impossible. Great Britain and France, hopeful of strengthening their hand in the Suez Canal negotiations and eliminating Egyptian support of the Algerian rebel movement, had plunged determinedly into Egypt. The move was viewed with solemn surprise and dismay by the United States government; for, not only was the United States opposed to this use of force, but it had been kept totally ignorant of Anglo-French intentions. "The United States," declared President Eisenhower, "was not consulted in any way about any phase of these actions. Nor were we informed of them in advance." [8] Prime Minister Eden later maintained that

such consultation was not possible within a matter of hours; it must take days at least. Nor was there any chance that all concerned would take precisely the same view of what action must follow the consultation. As a result there would be attempts to modify our proposals, to reach some compromise between divergent points of view and, before we knew where we were . . . no effective action would be possible. [9]

In explaining his military decision, Eden pointed out that although the "safety of transit through the Canal" was a "matter of survival" for Britain and for all Europe, it was merely "of concern to the United States":

If anyone says that on that account we should have held up action until agreement could be reached with the United States as to what to do I can only say that this would have been to ignore what everyone here and in the United States knows to have been different approaches to some of these vital Middle Eastern questions. They know it. We know it. Of course, we deplore it, but I do not think that it can carry with it this corollary, that we must in all circumstances secure agreement from our American ally before we can act ourselves in what we know to be our vital interests. [10]

But President Eisenhower and Secretary of State Dulles voiced strong disapproval of the policy adopted by their allies,[11] condemned the resort to force by Britain, France, and Israel, which "can scarcely be reconciled with the principles and purposes of the United Nations to which we have all subscribed," [12] and found themselves curious bedfellows with the Soviet Union in opposing the actions taken. Nevertheless, the United States had no intention of initiating or supporting collective military measures against the invading states.

James Reston reported on November 4 that, in effect, Washington's ire against the British, French, and Israelis for their planned and secret defiance of U.S. policy had become somewhat tempered. Gradually, United States officials adopted the view that America's independent policy toward Asia and Africa was a justifiable but shortsighted one. Sherman Adams declares:

While the British were holding out in the Middle East in the face of growing fuel and money shortages at home, their plight was being discussed in many anxious meetings in Washington. The American Government found itself in the strange anomaly of trying to punish publicly her best, but errant, friend while privately sitting up late at night attempting to devise means of getting that same friend out of the straits she had gotten herself into.[13]

Also unwilling to support strong coercive action by the United Nations were the older Commonwealth countries and the Western European members of the Assembly. Although expressing concern over the methods used in the crisis, these states could not bring themselves to denounce Anglo-French objectives in harsh terms. They felt deep consternation at the split that had occurred between the Western anticommunist countries [14] and were generally anxious to restore unity and peace by means of negotiation and political settlement of larger issues. This was the conciliatory approach to the Middle Eastern situation. "I should have liked," said Sir Leslie Munro, of New Zealand, ". . . to have heard some response to the constructive suggestions of the United Kingdom in regard to the desirability of a conference to negotiate a lasting settlement of the problems which have thrown the Middle East into turmoil." [15]

A greater number of states in the Assembly, however, including the communist bloc and Afro-Asian nations, outspokenly declared their strong opposition to the military measures initiated in Egypt, desired open condemnation of Israel, the United Kingdom, and France as "aggressors," and were anxious to establish an immediate cease-fire and to secure a withdrawal of forces with no concern for face-saving or the larger issues involved. Profound anxiety was felt that two of the major powers in the United Nations had resorted to force and committed a breach of the peace. Several of the new Asian nations referred to the Anglo-French action as "a continuation of the tradition of colonialism." [16] Supported by his East European colleagues, the Russian delegate, A. A. Sobolev, urged the Assembly

to condemn the armed attack by the United Kingdom, France and Israel against Egypt as an act of aggression incompatible with the purposes and principles of the United Nations; to demand . . . the immediate cessation of hostilities and the withdrawal of . . . armed forces . . . to appoint a United Nations commission to supervise the carrying out of the recommendations of the . . . General Assembly.[17]

Going still further in proposing a policy of "pure coercion," the Arab delegates demanded not only condemnation of the military action but "the application of sanctions against Israel for its consistent aggression and continued violations" and, in case an immediate cease-fire and withdrawal of forces were not effected, "provision for United Nations assistance to Egypt, the aggrieved party." [18]

But neither this extreme policy of coercion nor the milder proposals for conciliation were fundamentally regarded as practical or suitable to a settlement of the crisis. A policy of coercing Britain, France, and Israel into obeying Assembly injunctions was extremely hazardous.[19] Faced with a refusal to obey, the Assembly would have had either to accept meekly an open defeat or to recommend vigorously the application of sanctions against the invading states.

Not only were many delegates, especially those from Europe and the Commonwealth, strongly opposed to sanctions, but the United States undoubtedly would not have lent support to military measures against its NATO allies. Moreover, the Western anticommunist powers would have been strongly opposed to Russian or communist expeditionary forces in the Middle East, even under United Nations auspices.

The adoption of a policy of mere conciliation also did not seem appropriate to the case at hand. Peace had been severely ruffled in the Middle East; yet the United Nations was unrelentingly committed to preservation and restoration of tranquillity in all parts of the world. The territorial boundaries of Egypt had been openly violated by three other states; yet all Members of the United Nations had solemnly pledged to refrain from the use of force against the territorial integrity or political independence of any state. These principles and commitments were at the heart of the world organization; they could not lightly be ignored. Finding it impossible to accept the military moves in Egypt as *faits accomplis* and, consequently, to recommend only conciliatory measures of negotiation and deliberation, desiring positive action to deal with the situation but reluctant in part to propose harsh, condemnatory sanctions, several delegations in the Assembly looked about for an intermediary policy, a "middle road" between the paths of coercion and conciliation.

It was Lester Pearson, Canadian Minister of External Affairs, who first came forward with a suggestion which seemed to combine the elements of policy needed for the occasion:

. . . instead of indulging then or since in gratuitous condemnation we expressed our regret and we began to pursue a policy, both here by diplomatic talks and diplomatic correspondence, and later at the United Nations, which would bring about peace in the area on terms which everybody would accept. Our policy, then, in carrying out these principles was to get the United Nations into the matter at once; to seek through the United Nations a solution which would be satisfactory to all sides.[20]

The Assembly had adopted a United States draft resolution, on November 2, urging a cease-fire, withdrawal of all forces behind the armistice lines, observance of the armistice agreements, and abstention on the part of Member States from introducing military goods in the area of hostilities.[21] The resolution was approved in a vote of 64 in favor, 5 opposed, and 6 abstentions. Among those abstaining was Lester Pearson, who told the Assembly that its resolution lacked a vital provision for UN action toward a peace settlement. To allow Egyptian and Israeli forces to resume their old positions in an unchanged atmosphere of distrust and hatred would lead once more to a military explosion. Pearson proposed that the Secretary-General be authorized by the Assembly "to make arrangements with Member States for a United Nations force large enough to keep these borders at peace while a political settlement is being worked out—a truly international peace and police force." [22]

Joseph P. Lash reports that Ambassador Pearson had informed the Secretary-General of the type of force he envisaged, but Hammarskjold had seriously doubted that the moment was propitious for efforts to obtain a lasting peace settlement.[23] When in the early morning of November 3, however, the American delegate, Ambassador Lodge, informed Pearson of U.S. support for a United Nations force and later showed him a draft resolution requesting the Secretary-General to submit a plan for such an operation, Lester Pearson decided to go ahead. He outlined his plan in detail to Hammarskjold and the Secretary-General's special assistant, Andrew Cordier. "Hammarskjold, who had been depressed, was persuaded of its workability and discussion turned to how it should be gotten under way." [24] That evening the preparatory work had been done: support had been found in Hans Engen of Norway, Arthur Lall of India, and Francisco Urrutia of Colombia. The government of Egypt had been consulted and the Commonwealth countries had been kept informed.

On November 3, the fighting had not ended and the Assembly's cease-fire resolution had not been observed, but the British and

French representatives informed the Secretary-General of their willingness to stop military action upon the satisfaction of the following conditions: acceptance by Egypt and Israel of a United Nations Force to be stationed between their armies to keep the peace; maintenance of such a Force until satisfactory political arrangements were reached in regard to Arab-Israeli problems and the Suez Canal; agreement by both combatants to accept stationing of limited Anglo-French troop detachments in the area of hostilities until such time as the UN Force was effectively constituted.[25] Although the Assembly found these conditions, or any conditions, quite inacceptable,[26] the communications of England and France nevertheless indicated that a compromise between coercion and conciliation, an acceptable median action which would be consistent with Charter principles and with the views of the parties concerned was undoubtedly possible. Acting upon such a diagnosis, Pearson pursued his earlier suggestion by introducing a draft resolution [27] in the Assembly requesting the Secretary-General to submit a plan within forty-eight hours for the setting up, "with the consent of the nations concerned," of an emergency international force "to secure and supervise the cessation of hostilities" in accordance with the terms of the November 2 resolution. The Assembly's reaction was almost immediately positive.[28] It was adopted by a vote of 57 to 0, with 19 abstentions.[29]

That night and the following day continued to be long and arduous for the Secretary-General and his staff, as well as for the Assembly delegates. It was the evening when the Red Army had started its final tank and artillery onslaught in Hungary. The Assembly's discussions on the Middle East ended at three o'clock in the morning. Wearily, the UN diplomats and the Secretary-General convened in the Security Council to deal with the tragic events unfolding in Budapest. At dawn Hammarskjold went to his offices to continue drafting his plans on a UN force.

His initial pessimism and doubts overcome, he embraced Pearson's idea with his customary energy, enthusiasm, and imagination. Even before the

Assembly vote he had sounded out several delegations . . . Saturday night Hammarskjold received word from President Nasser he could not accept contingents from NATO powers. He put in a call to Urrutia, who had flown to Washington. Would he come right back to New York? . . . By 9 A.M. Pearson and Engen had come in and soon after that, Lall. Hammarskjold had a working paper ready for them to discuss.[30]

Later the same day, November 4, the Secretary-General submitted his first report [31] to the Assembly on the plan for an emergency international United Nations force. Indicating that he had consulted with delegates from Member States throughout the day regarding possibilities of contributions to the projected force, Hammarskjold was able to specify that Colombia and Norway had already agreed to participate in it. He proposed establishment without delay of a United Nations Command, drawing for its skeleton staff upon the United Nations Truce Supervision Organization; he recommended Major General E. L. M. Burns, Commander-in-Chief of the United Nations Truce Supervision Organization, to be Chief of the new command and suggested that the general be quickly authorized to recruit officers "drawn from countries which are not permanent members of the Security Council."

Although several delegates desired further deliberation before the vote, approval of the Secretary-General's suggestion was extended by the Assembly in its resolution of November 5 which established "a United Nations Command for an emergency international Force to secure and supervise the cessation of hostilities in accordance with all the terms of the General Assembly resolution 997 (ES-I) of 2 November 1956." [32] This resolution, it will be remembered, had urged "that all parties now involved in hostilities in the area agree to an immediate cease-fire and, as part thereof, halt the movement of military forces and arms into the area"; had urged Egypt and Israel "promptly to withdraw all forces behind the armistice lines, to desist from raids across the armistice lines into neighboring territory, and to observe scrupulously the provisions of the armistice agreements"; had recommended that no military goods be introduced into the area by any Member State; had urged "that, upon the cease-fire being effective steps be taken to reopen the Suez Canal and restore freedom of navigation." These resolutions of November 2 and November 5 furnished the fundamental basis and directive for the future operations of UNEF.

The delegate from Colombia, Francisco Urrutia, summarized well what seemed the prevailing feeling toward the creation of an international force at that time:

We believe that in order to re-examine this problem, to find a new approach to it and to arrive at a comprehensive solution, the first requirement is the restoration of peace; there can be no kind of conciliation and no kind of settlement while there is war. As means of restoring peace we have suggested two basic principles. The first is that we offer Israel a guarantee, the guarantee of an international force which will be able to forestall real or illusory dangers and at all events the dangers which according to Israel existed along its borders. Secondly, in return for this guarantee, we ask Israel that when the United Nations forces arrive it should withdraw its forces to the territory where it has lawful jurisdiction or, in other words, from territories which are outside Israel's jurisdiction and have, for one reason or another, been occupied by Israel's forces.[33]

The same principles were to be applicable to the United Kingdom and France: they too, were to be offered the guarantee of a force and they, too, were to leave Egypt forthwith. Upon Israeli acceptance of a cease-fire and withdrawal of forces, the United Kingdom and France would, indeed, no longer be able to justify their presence in Egypt and would be required to withdraw. Primary and overriding as an objective was the objective of peace.

But there existed several conflicting opinions in the Assembly on the nature and function of the proposed force which the Secretary-General, in preparing a more detailed plan, was required to take into consideration. On the one hand, the three invading nations, supported by Australia and New Zealand, envisaged the new organ as an instrument of pressure on the Egyptian government; the force, they felt, should not be allowed to leave Egyptian

soil until desirable political settlements had been achieved; satisfaction of some of their demands would thus be a prerequisite to
withdrawal. Indeed the presence of Anglo-French-Israeli troops
in Egypt represented bargaining power to these states in their
negotiations with Nasser over Suez and Palestine. With their troops
in control of the Canal and Sinai, the governments of Britain, France
and Israel felt that they would be in a better position to extract
from the Egyptian President a settlement favorable to their interests. A political price would be paid by Nasser for the withdrawal
of non-Egyptian forces, and, in the eyes of the English and French,
this price would be equally high if the occupation force was made
up of UN soldiers or of their own troops.[34]

On the other hand, this approach was sharply inconsistent with
the views of Egypt, the Arab States, and their supporters. These
nations saw the proposed force merely as a temporary measure to
insure observance of a cease-fire and peaceful withdrawal of the
Anglo-French-Israeli troops. An occupation force was certainly not
to be envisaged. The tasks of the UN soldiers would have to be very
different from those of the invading armies. And the bargaining
positions of the British, French, and Israeli governments in their
disputes with Egypt were not to be improved by their use of force
in violation of the Charter.

The Egyptian view had powerful support. Not only had the
Assembly stipulated that "consent of the nations concerned" was
needed to create the force, thus giving Egypt veto power over its
entry into Egypt, but the two super-powers were fundamentally,
though for different reasons, in agreement with Egypt. Indeed, although United States ire had abated, Washington was opposed to
any concessions, any inordinate demonstration of friendliness toward
the two allies and Israel before they agreed to remove their forces
from Egypt. Any show of sympathy, it was believed, would decidedly turn the Arab nations against the United States, the only
Western country still commanding respect in the Middle East at
that time.[35] These attitudes had an unmistakable influence on the
concept of the UN police force.

Threading his way among the various strands of Assembly opinion and basing his analysis on the previous resolutions, the Secretary-General on November 6 tendered a "second and final report" [36] to the Assembly in which he set forth the fundamental principles to govern the Force, its functions, size, organization, financing and recruitment. It was on the basis of principles presented in this report that Israel, France, the United Kingdom, and Egypt unconditionally accepted a cease-fire.[37] Hammarskjold envisaged a temporary Force, "the length of its assignment being determined by the needs arising out of the present conflict," with a chief officer appointed by the United Nations and ultimately responsible to the General Assembly or the Security Council or both. The full determination of the Force's tasks and legal basis was left open, but it was clearly stated that "there is no intent in the establishment of the Force to influence the military balance in the present conflict and, thereby, the political balance affecting efforts to settle the conflict." The Force was to be a neutral one and not a diplomatic instrument of pressure to enhance the bargaining positions of the invading states. This point was essential to the entire UN operation. It reflected well the majority Assembly opinion and ensured not only Egyptian consent, but the active cooperation of Member States.

Although para-military in nature, the United Nations Emergency Force was not to have military objectives but was to function solely on the basis of consent of the nations concerned; and it was not to be "guided by the needs which would have existed had the measure been considered as part of an enforcement action. . . ." Hammarskjold pointed out that the questions of size, organization, and financing of the Force required further study. Annexed to the report, however, were letters of Member governments to the Secretary-General offering assistance: the governments of Canada, Colombia, Denmark, Norway, Pakistan, and Sweden had expressed their willingness to contribute troops to the new organ.

The Secretary-General thus indicated that in his conception of the nature of the Force, the elements of coercion and conciliation were to be fundamentally combined. Consent was an essential feature of the entire scheme; nonetheless, UNEF itself was directly responsible to the United Nations. *Enforcement* of UN resolutions was certainly not envisaged; yet the Force was to be "more than an observers corps" and its essential function, to *secure* the cessation of hostilities and a withdrawal of forces, was decidedly military in character. It was to be a truly international force, created and supervised by the majority of nations in the world: "the basic political decisions of the Assembly, of course, constitute the fundamental law of this whole operation." [38]

Endorsing the second report of the Secretary-General by an overwhelming vote on November 7,[39] the Assembly invited Hammarskjold "to continue discussions with Governments of Member States concerning offers of participation in the Force. . . ." In addition, the Chief of Command, after consultation with the Secretary-General, was requested to proceed forthwith with the full organization of the Force and an Advisory Committee was established "to undertake the development of those aspects of the planning for the Force and its operation not already dealt with by the General Assembly and which do not fall within the area of the direct responsibility of the Chief of Command." [40] All regulations and instructions which might be considered essential to the effective functioning of the Force were to be issued by the Secretary-General after conferring with this committee.

The role of the Secretary-General and his staff in the creation of UNEF was outstanding. Before any decisions regarding the Force were taken by the Assembly, Hammarskjold had held exploratory talks with Lester Pearson. Thereafter, on November 4, it was the Secretary-General's task to prepare a plan for UNEF, a task which, although undertaken in close consultation with delegates of Member States, nonetheless signified that the General Assembly was delegating a remarkable degree of power to its chief administrative officer. Furthermore, Hammarskjold was asked to negotiate with Member States regarding their contributions, to settle the conditions under which these contributions were to be made, to help Major General

Burns organize UNEF, and to issue rules and regulations governing its functioning, subject only to consultation with the Advisory
Committee. Responsibility for negotiating and making arrangements
with Britain, France, and Israel in regard to the cease-fire, the
withdrawal of foreign troops from Egypt and the entry of UNEF
contingents was also assigned to the Secretary-General. Dag Hammarskjold and his staff were clearly, then, to be not only the major
architects of the Emergency Force but the chief administrative and
executive officers as well. These important tasks assigned to the
Secretary-General were to become significant once more when the
Security Council four years later decided "to authorize the Secretary-General to take the necessary steps, in consultation with the
Republic of the Congo, to provide the Government with such military assistance, as may be necessary. . . ." [41] In 1960, Hammarskjold benefited considerably from the earlier experience in setting
up the Emergency Force.

A great number of states came forward with offers to participate
in UNEF (see Chapter V). As a result, the Secretary-General
was able to notify Egypt almost immediately after the passage of
the November 7 resolution that the UN Force was ready. For
several days, however, the Egyptian government withheld per-
mission for entry of the Force into its territory: clarification was
desired of the exact nature and character of the new enterprise—
especially since Britain, France, and several other states had described the projected operation as a weapon of political pressure
on Egypt. This was the first time in history that an international
peace force was to enter sovereign territory. What would this force
be like and what would it do? On November 14, however, the host
government formally agreed to the entry of the Emergency Force.[42]
And two days later, Dag Hammarskjold flew to Cairo to discuss
important matters—UNEF's deployment, its composition, functions,
and legal characteristics—with Egyptian officials.

Meanwhile, in order to arrange the effective mobilization of the
Emergency Force, the Secretary-General's staff directed by Andrew

Cordier and Ralph Bunche was quickened to action. With the assistance of military attachés from the participating states, this informal council of Secretariat officials faced a myriad of administrative, legal, and practical detail. "Every conceivable problem was discussed as it arose: clothing, air transport, equipment, inoculations, badges, discipline, pay, rations, postal arrangements, headquarters organization, supplies." [43] Much improvisation was necessary; but the Force was ready in a remarkably short time. In the early morning of November 15, eight days after the Assembly's resolution endorsing the Secretary-General's second report, the first group of United Nations soldiers landed in Egypt. A UNEF company entered Port Said on November 21 and by mid-December, the United Nations Force was fully operating in the Suez Canal area.

Chapter Three

LEGAL BASIS

In the resolutions of the General Assembly pertaining to the United Nations Emergency Force no reference is made to its legal basis. However, despite this omission, despite the innovating nature of this para-military organ and the fact that UNEF was hastily created for a temporary period of time, the Force, in the minds of its supporters, is constructed upon a solid legal foundation.

General authority for UNEF is to be found in the Charter of the United Nations, particularly in those provisions relating to the functions and powers of the General Assembly, the rights and duties of Member States, and the general principles of international law. Particular sources of UNEF's legal authority are a number of understandings between Member States and the Secretary-General and various agreements concluded between Hammarskjold and the Egyptian government.

UNEF AND THE CHARTER

It is clear that the Charter in Article 24 gives the Security Council primary responsibility for the maintenance of international peace and security and for initiating collective measures in case of a threat to or breach of the peace. It is also clear that the Council, in order to discharge its responsibilities successfully, possesses the power to establish and control an international military force under Chapter VII of the Charter. The early history of the United Nations showed, however, that frequent use of the veto in the Security Council resulted in deadlock and inaction. The permanent members of the Security Council, moreover, were unable to come to an agreement regarding the principles to govern the use of military forces by the UN.* And so United Nations Members found it necessary to develop alternative procedures within the framework of the Charter not only for collective military action but also for other means to restore or maintain peace.

Primary responsibility for peace certainly belongs to the Council; but Article 24 of the Charter certainly does not bestow exclusive jurisdiction. The overriding purpose of the entire organization and all its organs is the maintenance or restoration of international peace and security.[1] Articles 10 and 11 of the Charter give the General Assembly broad powers of discussion, consideration and recommendation with regard to any question within the scope of the Charter, and any question relating to the maintenance of international peace and security; and, by the terms of Article 14, the General Assembly may

recommend measures for the peaceful adjustment of any situation, regardless of origin, which it deems likely to impair the general welfare or friendly relations among nations, including situations resulting from a violation of the provisions of the present Charter setting forth the Purposes and Principles of the United Nations.

These Charter articles are sufficiently broad to authorize the General Assembly to recommend, as well, that its Members use certain military measures for the maintenance of international peace and security. Although United Nations action in the Spanish and Greek cases (which were brought to the Assembly's attention in 1946 and 1947 respectively)[2] seemed to imply that the Assembly in truth possessed this authority, no categorical assertion of such competence was made until the discussions preceding the adoption of the "Uniting for Peace" resolution in the autumn of 1950.

Member States cited Articles 10, 11, and 14 of the Charter as the basis of the Assembly's power and "residual responsibility" to maintain or restore peace by collective means. It was recognized,

* See Appendix.

however, that although wide powers of recommendation certainly belonged to the Assembly, this organ was not competent, in the realm of collective measures, to make binding decisions. Putting its views into explicit formulation, the General Assembly in the "Uniting for Peace" resolution stressed the Assembly's own responsibilities for maintaining peace and resolved that if the Council was prevented by the veto from discharging primary responsibility in the security field when a threat to the peace, breach of the peace, or act of aggression appeared, the Assembly itself

. . . shall consider the matter immediately with a view to making appropriate recommendations to Members for collective measures, including in the case of a breach of the peace or act of aggression the use of armed force when necessary, to maintain or restore international peace and security. If not in session at the time, the General Assembly may meet in emergency special session within twenty-four hours of the request therefor. . . .[3]

Accordingly, six years later, when the Assembly met in special emergency session after the Security Council had failed to reach a decision on the means of settling the crisis in the Middle East and when the Assembly established a UN Command for an emergency international force, it was utilizing its broad powers under Articles 10, 11, and 14 to discharge a "residual responsibility" (that remains to it after the Security Council has failed to discharge its primary responsibility). The General Assembly was exercising a power which it has claimed for itself under the "Uniting for Peace" resolution.[4] In his report on UNEF of November 6, 1956, the Secretary-General emphatically referred to the fact that the Force would function "on the basis of a decision reached under the terms of the resolution 377 (V) 'Uniting for Peace'. . . ."[5] While the Emergency Force was hardly the armed force contemplated in the "Uniting for Peace" resolution, that is, an armed force to be used against an aggressor or a force whose use the Assembly could recommend in case of a breach of the peace or act of aggression, "its validity seems to be based on the premise that the right to establish such a smaller force is implicit in the right to establish a large fighting force." [6]

Furthermore, in the Secretary-General's words, UNEF was to be considered as a "subsidiary organ of the General Assembly," [7] for it had been "established in accordance with Article 22 of the Charter." [8] Article 22 specifically permits the General Assembly to establish "such subsidiary organs as it deems necessary for the performance of its functions." The primary functions and powers of the Assembly are set out, as we have seen, in Articles 10, 11, and 14 of the Charter and elaborated in the "Uniting for Peace" resolution. Establishment of UNEF and approval of the principles to govern the organization and tasks of the Force fall within the scope of these powers. But creation of the Emergency Force is authorized by Article 22 as well, for the Assembly has evidently considered the Force necessary to the satisfactory fulfillment of its functions —the restoration of peace and tranquillity in the Middle East.[9]

In the past the Assembly had created over a hundred subsidiary organs, varying in their function, duration, membership, and scope of power and authority.[10] Thus, there had been study committees which prepared reports and analyses for consideration by the General Assembly.[11] There had been political commissions and organs, possessing active political responsibilities. Some of these organs were assigned duties of investigation (e.g., the UN Commission to Investigate Conditions for Free Elections in Germany); some were concerned with the establishment of a new government (e.g., as done in Libya and Eritrea); others functioned as mediators and conciliators (e.g., the United Nations Mediator in Palestine); and still others assisted in negotiations between governments (e.g., the Good Offices Commission which dealt with the question of the treatment of people of Indian origin in the Union of South Africa).[12] A number of the political bodies had actually been given a certain degree of authority to make decisions without referring to the General Assembly.[13] In addition, the Assembly had constructed organs of administrative assistance with duties in the financial, budgetary, and administrative realm; operational agencies to administer relief, rehabilitation, and assistance programs; judicial bodies; and other organs which do not fall readily into the above categories.

Although, in practice, the Assembly had always assumed its right to create a large number of subsidiary organs with varying functions, the limits on this right had been debated in various connections. And it may perhaps be argued that the subsidiary organs envisaged in Article 22 of the Charter should be limited to committees or commissions with limited functions and aims outside the military realm—organs which would aid the Assembly in its deliberative, investigating tasks.[14] During the discussions on the establishment of the Interim Committee [15] and the Collective Measures Committee,[16] objections were raised by some delegations to the effect that, by creating these committees, the Assembly was seeking to arrogate to itself powers which properly belonged to the Security Council. The majority of delegates felt, however, that when faced with the inability of the Council to fulfill its primary task of maintaining peace and security, the Assembly itself had a duty to exercise its own "residual responsibility of recommendation" in this field.

Again, in the debates [17] prior to the establishment of the United Nations Palestine Commission, the question arose whether the Assembly was acting within its powers in setting up an organ to exercise the functions of government.[18] The delegates who objected to the commission declared that grants of legislative, executive, and administrative powers to the commission would exceed the powers of the Assembly under the Charter. Legislative authority and control of life in Palestine, it was argued, belonged to the people of that region, not to the General Assembly. But the commission's supporters upheld the competence of the Assembly to establish such a subsidiary organ. They pointed to its powers under Articles 10 and 14, whereby the Assembly may make recommendations on any questions or matters within the scope of the Charter, including those affecting peace.

Thus, as previous discussions on the question indicate, the entire concept of a subsidiary organ has never been decisively defined. Hans Kelsen states that such bodies are

. . . auxiliary organs established for the purpose to assist the organ competent to establish them. If an organ is competent to establish a "subsidiary" organ, it may establish it for the performance of some or of all its functions; but only for the performance of "its" functions, that is to say, the functions assigned to it by the Charter.[19]

His statement makes clear the view that the competence of the Emergency Force indisputedly may not go beyond the competence of the organ which established it. The General Assembly cannot confer upon the Force any powers which it does not itself possess.

In the case of the Emergency Force, however, did the Assembly grant its subsidiary organ extra-legal powers? Did UNEF's authority to enter Egypt in order to help maintain quiet and secure compliance with the terms of Assembly resolutions exceed the Assembly's authority under Articles 10, 11, and 14? [20]

Were UNEF merely an observer corps, the question could easily be decided in the negative. The Force, however, has definite military duties—maintaining order, supervising the armistice, patrolling the borders, indeed "*securing* compliance with the terms of Resolution 997." In fact, while no enforcement functions were envisaged for UNEF, *securing* compliance may actually entail a small measure of enforcement. The line between securing compliance and enforcing compliance is in reality perhaps rather thin. The problem becomes more confusing when we consider the Secretary-General's view that UNEF's Chief of Command "should be responsible ultimately to the General Assembly *and/or the Security Council*" and that, moreover, the possibility must not be excluded "that the Security Council could use such a Force within the wider margins provided under Chapter VII. . . ." [21] In addition to this, UNEF is alternately referred to by the Secretary-General as a "subsidiary organ of the General Assembly" [22] and as a "subsidiary organ of the *United Nations.*" [23] These factors might lead to the questionable conclusion that the power and authority of the Emergency Force as a *subsidiary organ* of the General Assembly exceed those of the Assembly.

What must be kept in mind, however, is that consent has been an essential part of the entire UNEF scheme of things (see pp. 46–59). The Force is dependent upon and circumscribed not only by the consent of Members of the Assembly, but by that of the "states concerned," including the host state, Egypt. Unconditional agreement by the parties to a cease-fire was prerequisite to the operation of the Emergency Force. Likewise, the invading countries agreed voluntarily to withdraw their troops from Egyptian territory. Enforcement action on the part of United Nations soldiers has never been taken at any time. Since the establishment and functioning of the Force have thus been based upon the acceptance by Member States of the Assembly's resolutions, or, in other words, their consent was absolutely required, the Force may not be said to have enforcement authority—nor indeed any authority which exceeds that of the Assembly. "The Force has no rights other than those necessary for the execution of the functions assigned to it by the General Assembly and agreed to by the country or countries concerned." [24]

Moreover, it might be remembered that the Assembly may allot to a subsidiary organ certain *functions* which the Assembly itself, due to its nature, can hardly perform, provided of course that this organ is essential to the general functioning of the Assembly and provided that the *authority* of the subsidiary organ does not go beyond that of the Assembly's authority.

In 1954 the International Court of Justice upheld the power of the Assembly to establish a tribunal competent to render judgments binding on the United Nations. The Court's advisory opinion on "Effect of Awards of Compensation made by the United Nations Administrative Tribunal" [25] made clear that the Assembly was acting within its jurisdiction by creating the UN Administrative Tribunal under Article 22, although the "Assembly itself could hardly act as a judicial organ—considering the arguments of the parties, appraising the evidence produced by them, establishing the facts and declaring the law applicable to them." [26] This subsidiary organ was, therefore, given certain functions to perform by the Assembly which the principal organ was unsuited to handle itself.[27]

It is also interesting to note in this connection a significant statement by the Court in its advisory opinion on "Reparations for Injuries Suffered in the Service of the United Nations":

Under international law, the Organization must be deemed to have those powers which, though not expressly provided in the Charter, are conferred upon it by necessary implication as being established to the performance of its duties.[28]

Although the Force was to be possessed of different functions than those performed by the General Assembly, all United Nations Members nonetheless considered at the time of the birth of the Emergency Force that the Assembly was empowered to bring it into being; they felt indeed that the creation of the new subsidiary body was essential to the discharge of the major organ's peacekeeping responsibility. No Member State voted against the November 4 resolution; those states which had serious reservations were content to abstain and to voice their objection in the debates.[29] UNEF was thus an outstanding precedent: the authority to create a security force was assumed by the Assembly as an interpretation of its own powers. Furthermore, inherent in this interpretation is the use of its authority in the future, extending as far as the possible creation of a permanent para-military organ.

The overwhelming majority of states in the Assembly have continued to accept the United Nations Emergency Force as a legal operation, established on the basis of the Charter and international law. But, the Soviet Union has taken the stand that creation of the Force by the General Assembly was an illegal act. Although abstaining and consequently not voting against resolutions 1000 and 1001 (ES-I), the USSR delegate has expressed the opinion that these resolutions in effect accepted the conditions which Britain and France had demanded: the maintenance of their troops in Egypt until the United Nations Assembly had constituted its own military force. Such a procedure was inadmissible, V. V. Kuznetsov declared, for British and French forces had come to Egypt in direct violation of the Charter, and as a result could not demand any conditions from the United Nations. Furthermore,

The General Assembly resolution on the basis of which it is now proposed to form this Force is inconsistent with the Charter. Chapter VII of the Charter empowers the Security Council, and the Security Council only, not the General Assembly, to set up an international armed force and to take such action as it may deem necessary, including the use of such a force, to maintain or restore international peace and security.

The resolution on the creation of an international armed force is also inconsistent with the purposes for which the United Nations Charter permits the creation and use of an international force. The Charter envisages the use of such a force to help a State victim of aggression to repel the aggressor and to defend such a State against the aggressor.

But the resolution 1000 (ES-I) of 5 November 1956 and the plan for its implementation . . . provide for the use of an international force for quite another purpose than that of repelling aggression against Egypt. The plan provides for the introduction of the international force into Egyptian territory and the transfer of a large part of that territory, including the Suez Canal zone, to its control.

No one can fail to see that the occupation of the Suez Canal zone by an international force really means removing the Canal from Egyptian administration—and that, as we all know, was one of the purposes of the United Kingdom and France in launching aggressive operations against Egypt.[30]

The reasoning of the Soviet representative was thus composed of political as well as legal elements. On the one hand, Kuznetsov maintained that the Security Council alone, acting under Chapter VII of the Charter, has the power to create an international armed force.[31] He failed, however, to mention the tasks and powers of the

General Assembly and its right of recommendation under Chapters IV and VI of the Charter. On the other hand, interpreting the resolutions as a provision for transfer of control over the Suez Canal to UNEF, and fearing that such a move would bring about a solution of the entire question favorable to the United Kingdom and France, the Soviet Union seemed to see the resolutions in its own light and to object to them on political grounds. Certainly, the Soviet stand on the legal basis of UNEF has been equivocal. There has been no unrestrained and continuing attack on the Force by the Soviet government (although members of the Soviet bloc have refused to pay their assessments for UNEF's expenses). On November 7, 1956, the Polish delegation seemed to approve the creation of UNEF: "In our opinion, the action proposed by the draft resolution, namely, the establishment for the first time, of an emergency international force of the United Nations, constitutes a very important step. This action should be very carefully planned and observed." [32] A Soviet delegate in 1959 even expressed hope that UNEF might "prevent any further extension of the aggression." [33]

THE ROLE OF PARTICIPATING STATES

While the Assembly had the power to establish an international police force, it could not, in practice, achieve its aim without contributions to the Force from Member States. In the Secretary-General's second report on UNEF, he stated that the Force "would be limited in its operations to the extent that consent of the parties concerned is required under generally recognized international law." [34] Clarification of the term, "with the consent of the nations concerned," had already been demanded by a number of states during the discussion [35] preceding adoption of the Canadian draft resolution of November 3.[36] Arthur Lall, the delegate from India, understood these words "to mean with the consent of the nations which will contribute to an emergency international United Nations force" and assumed "that countries which are engaged in hostilities will not be members of the emergency force." [37] Upholding this interpretation, the sponsor of the resolution, Lester Pearson, remarked:

What we had in mind was that the Secretary-General, in submitting a plan to the United Nations, should not include in that plan for an international force the name of any country without the consent of that particular country. That may seem an obvious point, but our own experience in the past has shown that it is just as well to make it quite clear, because it has happened that on armistice commissions Governments have been named at international meetings not only before they had agreed but even before they were consulted on the subject, and these words are intended to make it doubly sure that will not happen on this occasion.[38]

Thus, members of the United Nations were reaffirming this basic fact: although the Assembly could *recommend* to its Member States that they contribute to the Force, it could not *bind* a state to comply with this request. Hence, for a practical implementation of UNEF, the consent of Member States to contribute troops and matériel to the Force was also an essential prerequisite.

Nevertheless, it may be argued that, after the Assembly had specifically established a United Nations Command for a police force, had invited "the Secretary-General to continue discussions with Governments of Member States concerning offers of participation in the Force," and had requested all Member States "to afford assistance as necessary to the United Nations Command in the performance of its functioning," [39] Member States had a strong moral, if not legal, duty to ensure that UNEF was actually constituted.[40] Member States must give due consideration to all Assembly recommendations.[41] They have solemnly pledged not only "to fulfill in good faith the obligations assumed by them in accordance with" the Charter, but also to "give the United Nations every assistance in any action it takes in accordance with the present Charter. . . ." [42] The Secretary-General, moreover, has stated that although decisions of the General Assembly, legally, are only recommendations, "they introduce an important element by expressing a majority consensus on the issue under consideration." This element

. . . leaves scope for a gradual development in practice of the weight of the decisions. To the extent that mere respect, in fact, is shown to General Assembly recommendations by the Member States, they may come more and more close to being recognized as decisions having a binding effect on those concerned, particularly when they involve the application of the binding principles of the Charter and of international law.[43]

In any case, offers to assist in the setting up of UNEF were swiftly forwarded. The Secretary-General's first report of November 4 indicated that Colombia, Norway, and New Zealand had already agreed to participate in the Force. Thereafter, at least twenty-four other countries, on their own initiative, tendered contributions of one kind or another.[44] Several of these nations, however, made their offers of aid dependent upon express understandings and reservations. The government of Sweden stated its understanding as follows:

The Swedish Government presume that the task of the Force should be limited to the objective set out in the above-mentioned resolutions of 4 and 5 November [resolutions 998 (ES-I) and 1000 (ES-I)], and that it should not imply that the Force should remain on watch duty in the area for an unspecified period of time, or pending the solution of the political questions affecting that area.

Further, the Swedish Government presume that the Swedish unit shall not be stationed in foreign territory without the consent of the State concerned, and that the costs involved will, to a considerable extent, be borne by the United Nations in accordance with a specific agreement to be concluded for that purpose with the United Nations.[45]

The context and conditions of participation in UNEF by the government of India were thoroughly discussed by the delegate from that country and the Secretary-General, and received the following explicit formulation:

1. The Emergency Force is set up in the context of the withdrawal of Anglo-French forces from Egypt and on the basis of the call to Israel to withdraw behind the armistice lines.

2. The Force is not in any sense a successor to the invading Anglo-French forces, or in any sense to take over its functions.

3. It is understood the Force may have to function through Egyptian territory. Therefore, there must be Egyptian consent for its establishment.

4. The Force is a temporary one for an emergency. Its purpose is to separate the combatants, namely, Egypt and Israel, with the latter withdrawing as required by the resolution.

5. The Force must be a balanced one in its composition.

6. The agreement would be in principle and the position in regard to actual participation is reserved until the full plan is before us.

It is understood that the size of Indian participation is about a battalion strength.

It is also understood that transport, including airlift and all facilities, will be provided by or through the United Nations.[46]

One of the understandings stated by the Finnish government was that the assignment of its unit would be for a limited time only and "therefore determined exclusively by the needs arising out of the present conflict in the area in question." [47]

Letters from Member States to the Secretary-General contained these reservations, as well as offers of contributions to the Emergency Force. These letters constituted legal acceptance of participation in UNEF by the Member States. The Secretary-General apparently consented to the reservations as representing the individual conditions under which the respective units would operate.[48] Moreover, informal arrangements between the Secretary-General and the ten contributing states were formalized in an agreement, effected by an exchange of letters, which purported to be legally binding on the participating nations and on the Organization:

It is the intent that this letter together with your reply accepting the proposals set forth herein shall constitute an agreement. . . . It is also intended that it shall remain in force until such time as your national contingent may be withdrawn from the Force. . . .[49]

The Secretary-General explained in his letter that UNEF's effective functioning required some continuity of service of national contingents, and he therefore requested assurances that units would not be withdrawn "without adequate prior notification." On his part, Hammarskjold pledged that, were circumstances to render participation of a contingent in the Force no longer necessary, "the Secretary-General undertakes to consult with your Government and to give adequate prior notification concerning its withdrawal." [50]

Accordingly, it may seem that a participating state is entitled to withdraw its soldiers at will if the condition of "adequate prior notification" is fulfilled. In the three cases of withdrawal that have occurred,[51] notice was given sufficiently in advance to avoid embarrassment and replacements were obtained without difficulty by increasing the size of one or more remaining contingents. But the issue of unilateral recall of military units is not altogether without controversy. Does each contributing state retain complete control over the troops which it has furnished to UNEF? [52] If Egypt were to withdraw consent to the Force, would a participating state have the right to recall its troops? Is each contributor entitled to determine unilaterally and authoritatively when the emergency situation has ended, when UNEF's tasks have been completed, and when it shall withdraw its national contingent?

The replies to these queries remain ambiguous. To some extent, they depend upon specific reservations made by the states donating forces to UNEF in their agreements with the United Nations. Unless a state has explicitly reserved to itself the right to determine when UNEF's job is finished, it would seem consistent with the spirit of the Charter and of the "Uniting for Peace" resolution to leave to the *Assembly* the determination of not only when collective action by the emergency police force is necessary but also when its usefulness has ended.[53] But it is chiefly political and not only legal factors (especially since the latter remain essentially undefined) which will probably determine the actions of the host state and of contributing nations under varying circumstances.

THE ROLE OF THE HOST STATE

The General Assembly, then, was legally empowered by a two-thirds vote of its members to establish UNEF, provide for its financing, and, with the consent of the contributing states, supervise its organization and composition. Deployment of the Force, however, was not in the Assembly's hands; Hammarskjold and Member States were singularly forceful on this point:

While the General Assembly is enabled to *establish* the Force with the consent of those parties which contribute units to the Force, it could not request the Force to be *stationed or operate* on the territory of a given country without the consent of the Government of that country.[54]

The delegate from Israel was expressly concerned with this issue as soon as the suggestion for creation of a police force was raised in the Assembly:

The first and crucial legal problem which arises is that of the sovereignty of States in the context of the consent required for the implementation of this project. The consent required is not merely or primarily the consent of the States invited to participate in the force, but chiefly the consent of those States upon the territory of which it is proposed to station these forces. It would seem to my delegation to be axiomatic under the law of the Charter that the stationing of any force in a territory under Israel's jurisdiction or control is not possible in law without the Israel Government's sovereign consent and that this principle would of course apply to the territory of any other State under whose jurisdictional control it was proposed to station these forces. . . . If this question of sovereign consent were not clarified, then a precedent would be created whereby a majority of the General Assembly could decide to station forces in the territory of any State irrespective of its prior consent.[55]

And, indeed, modern international law would seem to substantiate this opinion.

The obligation imposed by international law upon a State not to exercise its power, in the absence of a permissive rule to the contrary, within the territory of another State is the counterpart of the right of the State to maintain the inviolability of its territory. States are entitled to regard as violations of international law breaches of their territory committed by foreign military or naval authorities.[56]

Sovereignty, then, would forbid the entry of foreign forces without approval into territory under the sovereign's jurisdiction, unless, of course, such forces were dispatched by the Security Council "within the wider margins provided under Chapter VII of the United Nations Charter." [57] The need to have Egyptian consent to the stationing of UNEF troops on territory subject to Egyptian sovereignty has not been denied by the Assembly at any time.

The government of Egypt gave its consent to the Emergency Force in principle when it accepted the Assembly's resolution 1000 (ES-I) establishing a UN Command for an emergency international force.[58] It desired clarification and interpretation of the relevant General Assembly resolutions, however, before the entry of the Force into Egypt. A number of conversations took place between representatives of the Egyptian government and the Secretary-General. Hammarskjold then reported to UNEF's Advisory Committee upon the interpretations which had been made. The Advisory Committee approved these interpretations and recommended dispatch of the Force to Egyptian territory. Egypt likewise found the Assembly's resolutions, as interpreted by the Secretary-General, acceptable and therefore the first transport of UNEF soldiers took place without any other formal agreements.[59]

Feeling, however, that the presence and functioning of UNEF in Egypt as well as continued cooperation between the UN and the Egyptian government required "a firmer foundation," the Secretary-General on November 16 to 18, 1956, visited Cairo for personal discussions with the Egyptian authorities. Certain questions of principle were resolved at that time and were summarized in an "Aide-memoire on the basis for the presence and functioning of the United Nations Emergency Force in Egypt," [60] a document which after approval by the Assembly on November 24 [61] constituted an understanding between the United Nations and Egypt. Later, other agreements were developed on the basis of this understanding. The relevant principles governing the presence and functioning of UNEF were stated in the Aide-memoire as follows:

1. The Government of Egypt declares that, when exercising its sovereign rights on any matter concerning the presence and functioning of UNEF, it will be guided, in good faith, by its acceptance of General Assembly resolution 1000 (ES-I) of 5 November 1956.

2. The United Nations takes note of this declaration of the Government of Egypt and declares that the activities of UNEF will be guided, in good faith, by the task established for the Force in the aforementioned resolutions [resolutions 997, 1000, 1001 (ES-I)]; in particular, the United Nations, understanding this to correspond to the wishes of the Government of Egypt, reaffirms its willingness to maintain UNEF until its task is completed.

The Aide-memoire envisaged joint exploration by the Secretary-General and Egypt of concrete aspects of the functioning of UNEF, including the question of its stationing and that of its lines of communication and supply. Hence, on February 8, 1957, Dag Hammarskjold, after consultation with the Advisory Committee, negotiated and concluded an Agreement on the Status of the Force with the government of Egypt. Both the Aide-memoire and the Agreement are particularly significant in UNEF's legal architecture.

Brought into being by an exchange of letters and approved by the Assembly on February 22,[62] the Agreement on the Status of the Force contained provisions dealing with questions of criminal and civil jurisdiction, privileges and immunities, settlement of disputes, taxation, customs, the use of facilities, and other legal matters.* It was deemed to have taken effect from the date of the arrival of the first elements of the Force in Egypt and to remain in force until UNEF's departure from Egyptian territory.

When the question of deployment of UNEF in Gaza was discussed, the Secretary-General reiterated his view that "use of military force by the United Nations other than that under Chapter VII

* For a detailed account of the Agreement, see Chapter VI.

of the Charter requires the consent of the States in which the force is to operate." [63] He made clear that a widening of UN responsibility in the Gaza area, beyond responsibility for the refugees, "would have to be based on agreement with Egypt"; and, although the Assembly "would be entitled to recommend the establishment of a United Nations administration and to request negotiations in order to implement such an arrangement, it would lack authority in that recommendation, unilaterally, to require compliance." [64]

Egypt never expressly agreed to United Nations activity in Gaza. In a statement to the Assembly on February 22, 1957, the Secretary-General implied, however, that Egyptian consent to UNEF's operation in the Gaza Strip may be assumed:

The Secretary-General states with confidence that it is the desire of the Government of Egypt that the take-over of Gaza from the military and civilian control of Israel—which, as has been the case, in the first instance would be exclusively by UNEF—will be orderly and safe, as it has been elsewhere.

It may be added with equal confidence that the Government of Egypt . . . has the willingness and readiness to make special and helpful arrangements with the United Nations and some of its auxiliary bodies, such as the United Nations Relief and Works Agency for Palestine Refugees and UNEF.[65]

A number of important matters concerning the Force were thus conclusively regulated by the Secretary-General and Egypt. Other matters, however, were never firmly decided and their legal status remains obscure. Important, in this regard, is the question of Egypt's right to place conditions of various kinds on UNEF's operation and composition. After Egypt gave her consent to the establishment of the Force and its entry on her jurisdictional domain—consent which was unequivocally and unconditionally given—did she retain a power of veto over any other matters pertaining to UNEF? [66]

Again the answers to such questions are speculative and vary widely. There is reason to believe that some diplomatic bargaining took place during which Egypt surrendered certain points and won others—won especially in the realm of "rejecting participation in the Force of contingents from Pakistan, and in restricting the Canadian participation to certain types of personnel." [67] Louis B. Sohn observes that in those

> cases in which the consent of the "host" state is required, such consent might be conditional and though it has been argued that the "host" state should not be allowed to dictate to the United Nations what should be the composition of the Force, in practice it may refuse its consent unless it is guaranteed that the Force will be composed of contingents or nationals of certain states, or that contingents or nationals of some states will be excluded from the Force.[68]

On the other hand, Lester Pearson, "author" of the Emergency Force idea, has constantly maintained that neither Egypt nor any other government may determine what contributions or whether any contributions would be made by a Member State to the Force. This was a matter for the United Nations alone to decide. Egypt's right to consent to the admission of the United Nations Force on its territory did not, according to Pearson, imply the necessity of consent to admission of, or right to reject, *separate* units or elements of that Force.

Nevertheless, Secretary-General Hammarskjold indicated that Egypt was consulted in regard to UNEF's composition, although in principle the right of veto was denied; for, in principle, by agreeing to the Assembly's resolution of November 5, Egypt undertook to admit the Force as constituted by the Secretary-General and his staff, acting in consultation with the Chief of Command.

Although there is no decisive evidence to indicate how much, if any, pressure Egypt brought to bear upon the Secretary-General in regard to arrangements concerning the Canadian and Pakistani offers of assistance, a certain amount of negotiation occurred before the Force was finally organized. The Secretary-General's summary report of October 9, 1958, certainly lends support to this conclusion. Yet, Hammarskjold was careful to point out that if a severe disagreement between Egypt and the UN had occurred, it would have been referred to the Assembly for solution. He asserted the United Nations' right of final decision:

The choice of the contingents for the Force, while subject to the decision of the United Nations alone, is nevertheless of major concern also to the country in which the Force operates. Thus, the United Nations must give most serious consideration to the views of the host Government on such matters without, however, surrendering its right to take a serious difference, should one develop, to the political level for resolution. In the experience of UNEF, this latter course has not been necessary, since no impasse has ever developed in this area. A balanced composition was always sought in the selection of units.[69]

This principle was applied once more to the formation of the United Nations para-military force for the Congo. During the course of the Congo operation the host government made sharply critical statements on the employment of non-African troops in ONUC. But, the Secretary-General maintained that the standard of universality was applicable and upheld the principle that since the Force was a UN body, the Organization would have final authority as to the component units.[70]

In regard to the functions of the Force, Egyptian consent has been necessary insofar as these functions depend on UNEF's deployment. Again, however, there are veiled elements to the problem:

To the extent that the movements of the United Nations Force are supposed to follow from the duties of the Force in relation to the cease-fire and the withdrawal, the matter . . . has been regarded as non-controversial, as it is covered by Egypt's general consent while, on the other hand, as regards activities of the United Nations Force which would extend beyond what is covered by this consent, an additional consent has been considered as necessary. . . .

The question which is not yet fully clarified is how far in the practical cases under consideration the duties of the Force go, and how far, therefore, certain arrangements for the Force are covered or not by the consent given by Egypt as qualified by its assurance of interpretation in good faith of the basic decisions of the General Assembly.[71]

The following question has also arisen and has been left obscure: Is Egypt entitled to withdraw consent to UNEF, after having expressly approved entry of the Force on its territory and after having made no effort specifically to reserve the right to decide the time of withdrawal? On the one hand, Egypt itself has claimed that UNEF must leave the territory of the "host" country whenever that country should so request:

. . . as must be abundantly clear, this Force has gone to Egypt to help Egypt, with Egypt's consent; and no one here or elsewhere can reasonably or fairly say that a fire brigade, after putting out a fire, would be entitled or expected to claim the right of deciding not to leave the house.[72]

On the other hand, the Secretary-General pointed to the understanding between Egypt and the United Nations, constituted by the Aidememoire of November 20, 1956, as the basis for mutual and reciprocal consultation on all important matters such as withdrawal of consent:

The consequence of such a bilateral declaration is that, were either side to act unilaterally in refusing continued presence or deciding on withdrawal, and were the other side to find that such action was contrary to a good-faith interpretation of the purposes of the operation, an exchange of views would be called for towards harmonizing the positions. This does not imply an infringement of the sovereign right of the host Government, nor any restriction of the right of the United Nations to decide on the termination of its own operation whenever it might see fit to do so. But it does mean a mutual recognition of the fact that the operation, being based on collaboration between the host Government and the United Nations, should be carried on in forms natural to such collaboration, and especially so with regard to the questions of presence and maintenance.[73]

In practice, it would seem, were Egypt to demand withdrawal of the Force from her territory or from a certain area therein, the Secretary-General would so inform the Advisory Committee on the United Nations Emergency Force, which would determine whether the matter should be brought to the attention of the Assembly.[74]

It is submitted, however, that from a strictly legal point of view,

Egypt's acceptance of UNEF without specific reservations regarding her right to call for withdrawal at will binds the Egyptian government to complete fulfillment of its agreement with the UN and precludes unilateral termination.[75] Likewise, the United Nations is required to uphold its part of the agreement until such time as the Assembly decides that the emergency situation has ceased and the functions of the Force have been completed. The cablegram of November 5, 1956, from the Egyptian government to the Secretary-General accepting resolution 1000 (ES-I), the Aide-memoire of November 20, 1956, and the exchange of letters between the Secretary-General and Egypt on arrangements concerning the status of the United Nations Emergency Force, represent valid international agreements which may be terminated only by (a) fulfillment of the provisions of the agreement; (b) agreement of the parties; (c) implication, for example, the conclusion of a subsequent agreement covering the same subject matter or one wholly inconsistent with the earlier treaty; or (d) denunciation by one party and acquiescence by the other.[76]

Hence, one of the following conditions must be met before UNEF can leave Egyptian territory: (a) a General Assembly decision that UNEF's tasks "to secure and supervise the cessation of hostilities in accordance with all the terms of General Assembly resolution 997 (ES-I) of 2 November 1956" have been completed; [77] (b) agreement between the Egyptian government and the United Nations; (c) conclusion of a subsequent agreement by Egypt and the UN wherein specific stipulations regarding withdrawal of the Force from Egypt would be enunciated; these stipulations would clearly supersede the former agreements between the parties; or (d) denunciation of the constituted agreements by either Egypt or the United Nations and agreement thereto by the other party.

Of course, from a practical standpoint, Egypt's continuing consent is necessary to the successful operation of the Emergency Force, for, in the face of violent opposition on the part of Egypt, the contributing states would, no doubt, withdraw their forces. Moreover, it is unlikely that the Secretary-General could, as a practical matter, regardless of the legal principles involved, assume responsibility for ordering the Force to withstand military action on the part of the host state.[78]

It is interesting to note that the situation of the United Nations force in the Congo is somewhat different in this respect.[79] Although ONUC, like the Emergency Force, operates with the consent of the host state, it was created by the Security Council, not the General Assembly, and in the course of its establishment, Chapter VII was invoked by Council members and the Secretary-General.* Indeed, the Council's resolution on the Congo of August 9, 1960, called upon all Member States, in accordance with Articles 25 and 49 of the Charter, to accept and carry out the decisions of the Security Council and to afford mutual assistance in fulfilling measures decided upon by the Council.[80] ONUC, then, is a subsidiary organ of the *Council,* and as a result of this legal basis its functions and powers were more easily widened than were those of UNEF. ONUC, for example, has been empowered by the Council to use force in the achievement of certain of its aims (see Chapter IV).

THE ROLE OF BRITAIN, FRANCE, AND ISRAEL

Consent to the establishment of UNEF by those states which had initiated hostilities in Egypt was not required for the legal authority of the Force. This, as least, seems to have been the prevailing opinion among Member States, but again the question is not unequivocal. The views of commentators differ. The Secretary-General declared that "UNEF as a practical operation was made possible only by the concurrence, in one form or another, of the parties to the conflict in its establishment by the General As-

---

* Upon the request of the Congo government, the Security Council on July 19, 1960, authorized the Secretary-General to send troops under UN auspices into the Congo. This action followed a week of strife and violence in that country, triggered by the refusal of the Congo troops to obey their officers, a general administrative collapse in the new nation, and the re-entry of Belgian forces into the area.

sembly." [81] Agreeing with Hammarskjold, C. Chaumont takes the view that "the consent of the nations concerned" required by resolution 998 (ES-I) included the consent of Britain, France, and Israel. In effect, all three "consented to the creation of the Emergency Force and their consent in this instance was particularly important, since establishment of the Force seemed to be their condition for ending the conflict itself." [82] Charles P. Noyes's comments on this point are diametrically opposed: "Israel's consent was in no legal sense a requisite to the establishment or operation on Egyptian territory of UNEF. Nor was the consent of the United Kingdom or France." [83]

Whether UNEF's creation was a "precondition" to the Anglo-French-Israeli cease-fire and withdrawal is also unclear. On the one hand, Hammarskjold indicated that such a precondition existed,[84] while, on the other, he noted that "the General Assembly did not make the cease-fire dependent upon the creation or the functioning of UNEF." [85]

Israel declared that there existed a direct relationship between the creation of UNEF and the withdrawal of British, French, and Israeli troops: the note sent to the Secretary-General on November 8 stated that "the Government of Israel will willingly withdraw its forces from Egypt immediately *upon the conclusion of satisfactory arrangements* with the United Nations in connection with the emergency international force." [86] In the Assembly, Abba Eban made this point unmistakably plain:

The General Assembly will observe that in our conception the process of withdrawing Israel troops from Egyptian soil is integrated with the plans for the United Nations Force. We believe that this is a legitimate interpretation. Indeed, if we study the jurisprudence under which the United Nations Force was established, we find that it had an accepted relationship to the procedure for effecting the withdrawals. This was clear from the address by the Secretary of State for External Affairs of Canada, who, as the author of the concept of the United Nations Force in this General Assembly, speaks with a special authority in this as in other matters. There is what he called "a relationship . . . between the withdrawal of the forces . . . and the arrival and the functioning of the United Nations Force." [87]

In direct contrast, A. A. Sobolev, the Soviet delegate, maintained:

The Secretary-General . . . loses touch with reality, when "looking back" to events of the recent past. He affirms in his report [A/3694] that the Emergency Force was established at the request of the United Kingdom, France and Israel as a pre-condition for their agreement to a cease-fire. To assert that the presence of the United Nations Emergency Force in Egyptian territory was a pre-condition for the withdrawals from Egypt of the Anglo-French and Israel forces means, at the very least, to disregard General Assembly resolutions and to encourage those who at the time propagated the idea that the United Nations Force was a kind of substitute for the Anglo-French and Israel occupation armies.[88]

Whatever one's opinion on the legal situation, however, it seems clear, as Noyes has pointed out, that Anglo-French and Israeli consent to a cease-fire, to withdrawal, and to UNEF provided the basis, from the point of view of *practical diplomacy*, for the establishment of the Force in its present form and size and with its present functions.[89] It is very dubious indeed that UNEF could have acted effectively without such cooperation. The Force does not possess enforcement powers. UNEF soldiers could hardly have served a useful military purpose had Israel, for example, refused to leave Sharm el Sheikh or had Egypt one day decided to carry on a full war of annihilation against Israel. In such circumstances, UNEF would be effective only if endowed with a new, extended mandate.

Israel's position vis-à-vis UNEF has, of course, been particularly important, since her territory is contiguous to that of Egypt and since she is a party to the Armistice Agreements which the United Nations is bound to uphold. The functions and operation of the Emergency Force have, therefore, not only been dependent upon Israel's willingness to cooperate with the Force, but also upon her attitude to the Armistice Agreement with Egypt of February 24, 1949. Without the consent of *both* parties to this Agreement, the UN cannot change the situation created by the armistice, cannot place the Force in a region which may violate the terms of the Agreement or place duties on UNEF contrary to its provisions. On February 2, 1957, however, without having obtained Israel's consent thereto, the Assembly considered that "the scrupulous maintenance of the Armistice Agreement requires the placing of the United Nations Emergency Force on the Egyptian-Israel armistice demarcation line. . . ." [90]

Israel has consistently refused to accept UNEF on her territory. One reason for this reluctance is fear that an international police force would better prevent her own large-scale retaliatory actions against Egypt than it would *fedayeen* activity. Moreover, Israel is gravely concerned for her territory; her desire and will to preserve all of it is a passionate goal. With international military troops on her territory, Israel's apprehension that the world community may one day attempt an imposed peace settlement with reduced boundaries would mount. She seems afraid to risk such a situation. The precariousness of the armistice settlement (underlined by Arab insistence upon a state of belligerency), the perpetual refusal of the Arab States to recognize the state of Israel, their constant threat to Israeli security which developed along with Arab nationalism, and the uncertainty of great-power support for Israel have made the small Jewish nation especially sensitive to its *territorial* and military sovereignty. "In a certain sense, Israel is a military state: there isn't room on her territory for armed forces . . . other than her own." [91]

Despite personal efforts on the part of the Secretary-General, Prime Minister Ben-Gurion has not been persuaded to permit UNEF border patrols on the Israeli side of the demarcation lines.[92] Agreement, it seems, would only occur if the Arab theory and practice of belligerency were revoked and a final peace settlement were instituted. That the United Nations, however, respected Israel's wishes confirms the legal principle upon which the Emergency Force is based and which had been formulated in regard to Egypt: UNEF cannot operate on a nation's territory without the latter's freely given consent.

Thus, a number of principles relating to the legal basis of a multinational military organ created by the General Assembly have been clarified by the experience of the United Nations Emergency Force. Certainly, the legal basis of UNEF is a solid one. Stemming from Charter provisions, which were interpreted by the "Uniting for Peace" resolution, it is given expression in specific agreements between the United Nations and the Member States concerned. As a Force essentially different from the one envisaged in Chapter VII of the Charter, UNEF is dependent upon contributions from member governments and upon the consent of the state in whose territory it functions. The General Assembly has no authority to use military personnel and matériel of Member States contrary to their wishes. Nor may the Assembly infringe upon state sovereignty by stationing military units on the territory of a Member State without the consent of the government in question. Should the Assembly, in the future, decide to establish a military force of the UNEF-type or a permanent international police force, it would, presumably, be required to follow these basic rules.

The experience of the Emergency Force has helped to illuminate the authority of the Assembly in regard to creation and use of military forces and has provided valuable precedents for practical arrangements which need to be instituted. The indispensability of the host state's consent in a police operation outside the framework of enforcement action

creates a problem, as it is normally difficult for the United Nations to engage in such an operation without guarantees against unilateral actions by the host Government which might put the United Nations in a questionable position, either administratively or in relation to contributing Governments.[93]

But, as the Secretary-General has pointed out, experience dictates that the formula employed in relation to the Egyptian government for UNEF seems an adequate solution to this problem. Egypt agreed that, when exercising its sovereign right with regard to the presence of the Force, it would be guided, in good faith, by the Assembly's resolutions on UNEF. The United Nations likewise declared its willingness, in maintaining UNEF, to act, similarly, in good faith. Such an arrangement has proved a satisfactory one. Moreover, as the Secretary-General stated, it is doubtful "that any Government in the future would be willing to go beyond the declaration of the Government of Egypt with regard to UNEF." [94] In Hammarskjold's view, the UN, also, should not commit itself beyond the point established for UNEF in relation to Egypt. Both observations seem fundamentally sound. And arrangements between the United Nations and the government of the Congo in 1960 have embodied these principles.[95]

In regard to the recruitment of participating states, Hammarskjold again endorsed the UNEF example, but his emphasis upon consultation with the host state seems unwise. He himself recognized that when the view of the host government is taken as one of the most serious factors in a recruitment policy, it is likely to mean that the host's serious objections against participation by a particular country in the UN operation will determine the action of the Organization.[96] Such a course of events might well lead to undue interference by the host state in the entire procedure and might prevent the force not only from being under the sole authority of the United Nations but from truly representing the will of the international community. However, in order to limit the scope of possible differences of opinion, the formula applied to UNEF regarding composition would be valuable for any future international military force outside the framework of Chapter VII of the Charter: exclusion of the permanent members of the Security Council and of any state which might be considered as possibly having a special interest in the situation calling for the operation.

The United Nations military action in the Middle East has brought to light a number of important legal questions which have not been resolved and which remain highly controversial. For example, the question to what extent Member States are obliged morally and legally to contribute to a police force, once that force has been established by the Assembly and once the states in question have consented to its establishment, has not been clearly answered. Also undecided is the problem of the contributing state's right unilaterally to withdraw its contingent without express UN authority. And, requiring solution, above all, is the issue of withdrawal of the force from the theatre of operation and of the host state's prerogative in this realm. These are points which demand decision in principle. Unresolved, they may create serious practical difficulties and may jeopardize the entire concept of an international military police.

Chapter Four

FUNCTIONS AND POWERS

By early 1963, the United Nations Emergency Force, although temporary in character, attained the status of an accepted organ of the General Assembly to which has been entrusted, in the many years of its functioning, a wide variety of tasks and responsibilities. Designed to meet a particular need in an acute crisis, UNEF was the product of much improvisation; thus the demands upon it which arose from specific situations could not, of course, all have been foreseen. But, in most instances, the Force seems to have had little difficulty in adapting itself to the changing tasks and developing situations with which it has been confronted.

The powers and duties of the United Nations Emergency Force were generally delineated in the Assembly's resolutions of November 2 and November 5, 1956, but more extensive interpretation was required. In his early report setting forth the principles of the Force, the Secretary-General indicated that UNEF's functions, upon the establishment of a cease-fire, would be

to enter Egyptian territory with the consent of the Egyptian Government, in order to help maintain quiet during and after the withdrawal of non-Egyptian troops, and to secure compliance with the other terms established in the resolution of 2 November 1956.[1]

The new United Nations Force, declared Hammarskjold, "obviously should have no rights other than those necessary for the execution of its functions, in cooperation with local authorities." The concept of the Force was unique:

It would be more than an observers' corps, but in no way a military force temporarily controlling the territory in which it is stationed; nor, moreover, should the Force have military functions exceeding those necessary to secure peaceful conditions on the assumption that the parties to the conflict take all necessary steps for compliance with the recommendations of the General Assembly.[2]

To secure the cessation of hostilities, supervise the cease-fire, ensure orderly withdrawal of forces, police border areas for the purpose of preventing commando raids, and oversee total observance of the Armistice Agreement was expressly UNEF's responsibility.*

The United Nations Emergency Force has been variously pictured as "an accident of history," [3] "a plate-glass window," [4] and "a symbol of the world's interest in avoiding further hostilities." [5] The Secretary-General called it "a unique and pioneering peace effort" [6] and "an instrument of mediation and conciliation." [7] Trujillo of Ecuador described UNEF as a "new form of army, which is going not to fight but simply to supervise and guarantee the effectiveness of the resolutions of the General Assembly." [8] The United Kingdom delegate, Allan Noble, in the course of Assembly debate stated that "the United Nations Force has responsibilities for ensuring against a resumption of hostilities in any form." [9] And Juan Carbajal Victorica, the Uruguayan representative, cogently remarked, "it is the 'we' of the world-wide Organization that is acting in this Force within the framework of the national 'I's'—which sometimes behave in the manner of the 'moi' of Louis XIV." [10]

These descriptions indicate that UNEF is, in essence, an unprecedented enterprise—neither an army in the traditional sense, nor merely an observer corps without any military power. It does not correspond to an occupation group or a punitive expedition or, indeed, a diplomatic instrument designed to solve the military or political problems in a troubled area. At full strength, it continues to flourish as an effective cog in UN peace machinery: more than five thousand "soldiers of peace" from many different lands "united

---

* The entire existence of the Force is intimately connected with the Assembly's resolution of November 2, 1956 (see pp. 28–31). Hence, UNEF's limits as well as its authority were broadly set.

by the amalgam of their primary task—to preserve peace in the Middle East." [11]

A number of important qualities and principles underlie the very nature of UNEF and are significant in determining its functions and authority. These traits, fundamental to the Force, have been defined by the Secretary-General on the basis of Assembly resolutions and have been described by Member States in the course of Assembly discussions. UNEF, first of all, must be envisaged as a temporary operation, set up on an "emergency" basis. Its length of assignment is to be determined by "the needs arising out of the present conflict." [12] It has been established to facilitate fulfillment of a number of Assembly resolutions; presumably, should the Assembly consider that this task has ended, the Emergency Force would no longer have any reason for existence. The majority of UN Members seem to predicate conclusion of UNEF's mission upon fulfillment of *all* the terms of the resolution of November 2; only the Soviet Union, seconded by its allies, has conceived of the situation in more limited terms and declared that once the United Kingdom, France, and Israel had withdrawn their armed forces from Egypt's territory there was no longer a need for a United Nations international police force. The USSR and associated nations, fearful that UNEF might assume functions of "occupation," were forceful in their insistence that the Emergency Force leave Egyptian soil as soon as possible.[13] Nevertheless, complete agreement has existed between all the Assembly members on this principle: the Force shall not be used, without a new mandate, for any other purpose than the one envisaged when the Force was created. In its present form, UNEF is not to be viewed as permanent United Nations machinery.

A second fundamental trait of the United Nations Emergency Force is its international character as a subsidiary organ of the UN. Ultimately, it stands responsible only to the General Assembly which "has wished to reserve for itself the full determination of the tasks of this emergency Force and of the legal basis on which it must function in fulfilment of its mission." [14] The authority of its chief officer is fully independent of the policies of any one nation. Likewise, UNEF itself is not subject to interference by any one country. It represents an *international* force with international loyalties and its role is to remain politically neutral in the Middle Eastern conflict: "there is no intent in the establishment of the Force to influence the military balance in the present conflict and, thereby, the political balance affecting efforts to settle the conflict." [15] Its task is, in essence, to help bring about the *status juris* existing before the Anglo-French-Israel invasion of Egypt:

The United Nations cannot condone a change of the *status juris* resulting from military action contrary to the provisions of the Charter. The Organization must, therefore, maintain that the *status juris* existing prior to such military action be re-established by a withdrawal of troops, and by the relinquishment or nullification of rights asserted in territories covered by the military action and depending upon it.[16]

The Emergency Force's objective in the Middle East, as interpreted by the Secretary-General, was hardly intended to solve substantive issues; for, although many members of the Assembly hoped to achieve settlement of some of the outstanding sources of friction in the area, they did not in their resolutions envisage such a basic task for the Emergency Force. And Hammarskjold merely stressed that the "basic function of the United Nations Emergency Force, to help maintain quiet, gives the Force great value as a background for efforts toward resolving such pending problems, although it is not in itself a means to that end." [17]

Also characteristic of the Force is the clear assumption that it would not be used for enforcement action, functioning as it does under the terms of an Assembly recommendation and not a Council decision. The Secretary-General did not exclude the possibility of using UNEF within the wider margins provided under Chapter VII of the Charter, should the Security Council so decide. Yet, in its existing form as an Assembly creation, the setting up of the Force should not be guided by the needs which would have existed had the measure been considered as part of an enforcement action directed against a Member country. There is an obvious difference between establishing the Force in order to secure the cessation of hostilities, with a withdrawal of forces, and establishing such a Force with a view to enforcing a withdrawal of forces.[18]

The functions of the Emergency Force in the Middle East were designed to be substantially different from those of the UN forces organized to repel the North Korean attack and to restore international peace and security under the Security Council resolutions of June 25 and 27, 1950. UNEF is decidedly military in organization but it does not employ strictly military methods in achieving its objectives: indeed, it is not clear whether UNEF soldiers, except for purposes of self-defense, have the right to make use of their firearms.[19]

Because of its para-military nature, UNEF has been compared with the United Nations Truce Supervision Organization (UNTSO).[20] Established under the Armistice Agreements, UNTSO was expected, among other things, to prevent incursions and raids across the armistice demarcation lines. Since UNEF, too, has been entrusted with such duties, appropriate liaison was established between the two organizations, and consideration was given to the extent to which the Force might assume responsibilities so far carried by the United Nations Truce Supervision Organization.[21]

While UNEF and UNTSO cooperate closely with one another,[22] and while both organizations possess certain para-military features in common, the Secretary-General has nonetheless observed that the objective entrusted to the Emergency Force "could not be achieved through an organization smiliar in kind to UNTSO or to the Egyptian-Israel Mixed Armistice Commission. . . ."[23] These bodies had been created under different circumstances and during earlier periods of time to serve other and narrower needs. The function of the Truce Supervision Organization is not only to observe and maintain the cease-fire in Palestine which the Security Council had ordered, but to service the Mixed Armistice Commission (MAC)—bilateral machinery established under the Egyptian-Israel General Armistice Agreement of 1949. The MAC helps to execute the terms of the Agreement and is entrusted with such functions as the investigation of incidents and complaints. UNEF, on the contrary, is obliged to direct and administer the cessation of hostilities brought about by the Israeli-British-French invasion of Egypt in November 1956, secure and supervise the withdrawal of forces, and seek observance of the provisions of the General Armistice Agreement between Egypt and Israel. As a result, UNEF has a wider and different role to play in the Middle East than has the Truce Supervision Organization. It is a police and patrol force rather than an observer corps.

In the Secretary-General's discussions with delegates of Member States, the characteristics and functions of the Emergency Force were further explored and clarified. Pertinent questions dealing with the conditions and circumstances under which UNEF would operate were raised by the permanent representative of India. An agreement was reached between the Secretary-General and India whereby it was understood that UNEF would be "set up in the context of the withdrawal of Anglo-French forces from Egypt and on the basis of the call to Israel to withdraw behind the armistice lines"; that the Force "is not in any sense a successor to the invading Anglo-French forces, or is in any sense to take over its functions"; and that its "purpose is to separate the combatants, namely, Egypt and Israel, with the latter withdrawing as required by the resolution." [24] Assurances such as these were desired by the Indian government to dispel doubts engendered by the earlier Anglo-French conditions for a cease-fire,[25] by the ambiguity and lack of detail in the Assembly's resolutions, and by Israel's declaration that the Armistice Agreement no longer held any legal validity.[26] The Indian formulations help to clarify the exact nature and character of the UN Force.

THE EMERGENCY FORCE IN ACTION

UNEF's practical job in the early phase of its operation was to ensure quiet by mere United Nations presence. UN soldiers reported upon the observation of the cease-fire, policed the zone between the opposing forces, and guaranteed order while taking over from the Anglo-French-Israeli troops, following the successive stages of their withdrawal from the Suez Canal area and the Sinai Peninsula. The British and French had wanted the Force to be stationed along the Canal, after their own withdrawal and pending a settlement of the Suez question. Backed by the Soviet Union, Egypt firmly opposed such a move; it would violate UN assurances that UNEF would not be used in any way to affect the political balance in the Middle East.

At midnight of November 6, the cease-fire was instituted. Nine days later, the first units of UNEF troops entered Port Said. The United Kingdom and France, through their delegates speaking in the Assembly on November 23 and 24 respectively, made known their willingness to withdraw their troops as soon as the UN Force "becomes effective and competent to discharge its functions." [27] Quoting Mr. Pearson, the Israel delegate asserted that there is "a relationship . . . between the withdrawal of the forces . . . and the arrival and functioning of the United Nations Force." [28] Accordingly, each invading state, despite considerable protest,[29] made the "effective" functioning of UNEF a prerequisite to withdrawal of their forces.

It was on December 3 that Britain and France publicly confirmed their belief that an effective police force was arriving in Egypt and, in consequence, instructed their Allied Commander, General Keightley, to negotiate with the Commander of UNEF regarding a timetable for withdrawal.[30] Thus, between November 15 and December 22, the day when Anglo-French troops left the Suez Canal area, UNEF soldiers, operating mainly in the vicinity of Suez, were required to act as a shield between the Anglo-French and Egyptian forces through occupation of a buffer zone. The Force patrolled the streets of Port Said and Port Fuad in order to ensure quiet and peaceful relations between the civilian population and the troops of Britain and France. At the same time, it maintained a safety cordon around the areas in these cities where the invading forces were engaged in their final stage of withdrawal.

UNEF made arrangements for and undertook supervision of the exchange between Egypt and the Anglo-French Command of hundreds of prisoners, detainees, and internees. Investigation of complaints and inquiries on the part of both the invaders and the invaded regarding matters of cease-fire violation, smuggling, and missing personnel was undertaken by the UN soldiers. They guarded British and French ships working on the salvage operation of the Suez Canal, trucked food supplies, set up checking points, detected stray mines, and brought currency to the occupied area in order that normal activities could be resumed. Administration of public utilities, finance, communications, fuel and food distribution, legal affairs, safety, health, and damage claims was surrendered to the Emergency Force by the withdrawing armies and turned over to the Egyptian authorities. Similar duties devolved upon the Force in the Sinai Peninsula where centered the second period of UNEF activities, from December to March 1957.[31]

THE PROBLEM OF THE SUEZ CANAL

Withdrawal of French and British troops from Egypt was successfully accomplished in December 1956. Thereafter, UNEF's role in regard to the Suez Canal waned. Thereafter, "resolution" of the entire "Suez question" occurred almost by default.

During the early days of the fighting, the Suez Canal had become blocked by sunken ships and destroyed bridges. On December 3, the British and French governments noted that the UN Secretary-General had accepted responsibility for clearing the Canal and that "free and secure transit" would be "re-established through the canal when it is clear." The Secretary-General had undertaken to "promote as quickly as possible negotiations with regard to the future regime of the canal on the basis of the six requirements set out in the Security Council resolution of 13 October" (see Chapter I).

Clearance operations by a UN salvage fleet began January 1. By March 9, 1957, the first commercial vessel was able to pass through the waterway. Then, on April 24, a Declaration on the Suez Canal was deposited and registered with the UN Secretariat by the Egyptian government.[32] According to its provisions, Egypt declared that (1) free and uninterrupted navigation for all nations within the limits of and in accordance with the provisions of the Constantinople Convention of 1888 would be afforded and maintained; (2) any increase beyond 1 percent in the current rate of tolls within any twelve months would be the result of negotiations and, failing agreement, would be settled by arbitration; (3) the Canal would be operated and managed by the autonomous Suez Canal Authority established by the government of Egypt on July 26, 1956; all tolls would be payable in advance to this Authority and, in turn, the Authority would pay the Egyptian government 5 percent of all the gross receipts as royalty; the Authority would also establish a Suez Canal Capital and Development Fund into which 25 percent of all gross receipts would be deposited.

The Declaration contained specific provisions for legal redress. Complaints of discrimination or violation of the Canal code, the Declaration stated, would be resolved, through the Suez Canal Authority, by reference of the complaining party to an arbitration tribunal composed of one nominee chosen by the complainant, one chosen by the Authority and a third to be chosen by both. In the event of disagreement on the third arbitrator, the President of the International Court of Justice, upon the application of either party, would make the selection. The arbitration tribunal would render decisions by majority vote which would be binding upon the parties. Questions of compensation and claims in connection with the nationalization of the Suez Canal Maritime Company were to be referred to arbitration in accordance with the established international practice. In addition, any dispute or disagreement arising in respect of the Constantinople Convention of 1888 or the new Declaration would be settled in accordance with the UN Charter. And differences arising between the parties to the Constantinople Convention in respect of the interpretation or the applicability of its provisions, if not otherwise resolved, would be referred to the world Court. Egypt pledged to take the necessary steps to accept the compulsory jurisdiction of the International Court of Justice. She asserted that her Declaration, with the obligations therein, constituted an international instrument, deposited and registered with the United Nations Secretariat.

Debate on the Egyptian Declaration took place in the Security Council at the end of April, 1957. Many Council members continued to question whether the Canal was properly insulated from the politics of any one nation. They pointed out that Egypt had not formally accepted the compulsory jurisdiction of the International Court of Justice (as promised in her Declaration). They were apprehensive that Egypt would feel free to amend or withdraw the obligations assumed in her Declaration. Britain, France, Australia, Cuba, Colombia, and China felt that an additional treaty should be negotiated to supplement the Declaration, one which could not be revoked or modified without the consent of all the signatories. "As the declaration is decreed unilaterally," said the French delegate, "it can be modified or nullified in the same way." And, Henry Cabot Lodge asserted that the Egyptian Declaration "does not fully meet the six requirements of the Security Council. . . ." Indeed, "there is no assurance that the six requirements will in fact be implemented. . . ." Therefore, "any de facto acquiescence by the United States must be provisional . . . United States vessels will be authorized to pay Egypt only under protest. . . ." [33]

But the U.S. government provisionally accepted Egypt's Declaration on Suez. Prime Minister Macmillan announced that his government would no longer advise British shipowners to avoid using the Canal. The Security Council adjourned without a decision on the course of action to be followed. Compulsory jurisdiction of the International Court of Justice in respect of the Constantinople Convention and the Egyptian Declaration on Suez of April 24, 1957 was subsequently accepted by Egypt on July 22, 1957. In November, Eugene R. Black, President of the International Bank for Recon-

struction and Development, went to Cairo to mediate the question
of Egyptian compensation for shareholders of the nationalized Suez
Canal Company. Shortly thereafter, the U.S. Department of State
made known the release of about one-quarter of the $40 million of
Egyptian assets in the United States which were frozen in 1956.
And, on January 1, 1958, the Bank of England released £20 million
from the blocked account of the Bank of Egypt. The question of
nationalization of the Suez Canal seemed no longer to be an area of
great friction and dissent in international politics.

While Anglo-French troop evacuation from Egypt was completed
on December 22, 1956, the withdrawal of Israeli forces occurred
more slowly and more doubtfully, and difficulties in Egypt continued. The government of Israel reaffirmed its undertaking to withdraw. But it sought a "method of withdrawal which would make a
renewal of the conflict or acts of war almost unthinkable." [34] Vigorous pressure was exerted upon Israel from many sides. The Assembly
reiterated its request for complete withdrawal of Israel's troops behind the armistice demarcation line, and the Secretary-General made
continuous efforts to secure compliance with the Assembly's demands. Nevertheless, Israel had not, by the end of January, withdrawn its troops from the Gaza Strip or the Sharm el Sheikh area
along the Gulf of Aqaba.

Israel declared that these regions represented problems of special
complexity, touching Israel's security at its most sensitive point.

They cannot be treated lightly, without danger to international peace and
security. In each case, a change in the existing situation without simultaneous measures to prevent the renewal of belligerency would lead to
a possibility, nay even a certainty, of tension and hostility.[35]

THE PROBLEM OF GAZA

The Gaza Strip forms a narrow, rectangular area of land, approximately six miles in width, extending north from the Egyptian
frontier for twenty-six miles along the Mediterranean coast. It was
occupied by Egypt at the time of the conflict following the establish-

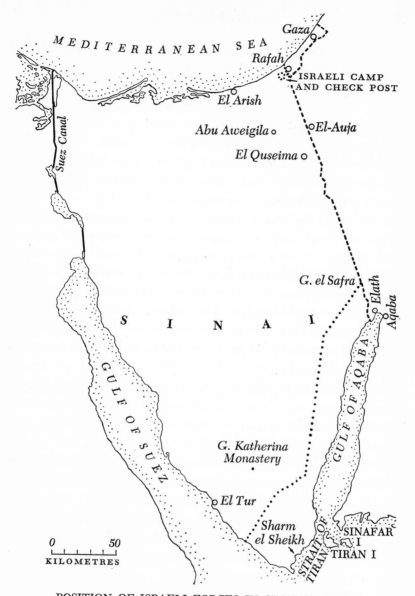

POSITION OF ISRAELI FORCES IN SINAI BY 1957

The dotted line indicates line to which Israeli forces remaining in Egypt had withdrawn as of January 22, 1957. The forces remained in the Gaza Strip and below there in a camp and check post. Elsewhere, the Israeli forces were behind the Armistice Demarcation Line.

The dash line indicates Armistice Demarcation Line.

ment of the State of Israel, but its sovereign status has never been authoritatively defined. By the terms of the Armistice Agreement between Egypt and Israel, the Gaza Strip fell to the jurisdiction of Egypt, and, as a result, that country has administered Gaza since 1949. Israel denied Egyptian right to the area and was willing merely to concede *de facto* occupation by Egypt. In November, 1956, Israel declared that this occupation had ended.[36]

Since the Arab-Israel War, the Gaza Strip had been the scene of considerable conflict and concern. Hundreds of thousands of Palestine refugees, impoverished and embittered, remained unsettled in United Nations camps in the area; constant commando or guerrilla raids were executed from Gaza into Israel; retaliatory actions, sometimes in considerable force, were the Israeli Army's answer to the harassing incursions. After 1955, Israel complained more and more frequently of attacks from Gaza by *fedayeen* units (organized military formations of the Egyptian Army whose members were recruited from destitute elements of the Gaza population and the refugee camps).

They ambushed road traffic, killed men, women and children, blew up wells and water installations, mined roads at night, and demolished houses in which farmers and their families were peacefully asleep. These outrages culminated in major outbreaks during August and September 1955, April 1956 and October 1956.[37]

Elimination of these *fedayeen* groups was one of the major objectives sought by Israel in the Sinai Campaign.

In the course of her successful march into Egypt, Israel occupied the Gaza Strip, assumed civic and administrative responsibility in the area, and generally established law and order. Thereafter, she maintained the position that withdrawal of her forces from the Gaza territory should not be undertaken without assurances from Egypt that belligerent acts against Israel would cease.

It is inconceivable to my Government that the nightmare of the previous eight years should be re-established in Gaza with international sanction. Shall Egypt be allowed once more to organize murder and sabotage in this strip? Shall Egypt be allowed to condemn the local population to permanent impoverishment and to block any solution of the refugee problem? [38]

The Arabs, on the other hand, viewed the situation in an entirely different light:

The conduct of Israel was, of course, not so surprising to us, as the very existence of that State came about by aggression. Nothing can conceal or alter the fact that this State stands to this very day on land which belongs to another people. Nothing can conceal or alter the fact that over 90 per cent of the land under the control of Israel belongs to the Arabs of Palestine, ironically labeled . . . as "the Arab refugees." [39]

On January 24, Israel formulated a proposal in an *aide-memoire:* she would withdraw her military forces from Gaza but continue to supply administrative services in the Strip, maintain law and order by means of her police, make available and develop the public utilities of Gaza, develop local administration in towns and villages, and support the development of a means of livelihood for the local population.[40] Since Israel was of the opinion that an international military force would not be able effectively to undertake the police duties necessary to prevent a recrudescence of *fedayeen* activity or to fulfill measures of administration and of economic development, the entry of UNEF into Gaza was not envisaged under the plan. Indeed, the Israeli delegate to the Assembly had stated earlier that UNEF could not solve the problem of the Gaza Strip or freedom of navigation in the Gulf of Aqaba "until or unless greater precision and clarity are given to the functions of the United Nations force and the terms and conditions for its tenure." [41] Without an express understanding that UNEF's functions would include the prevention of belligerency and that the Force would remain in Egypt as long as necessary to discharge these functions, Israel would put no further faith in the Emergency Force.

This Israeli scheme was, in effect, roundly rejected by the Secretary-General in his report to the Assembly on January 24, 1957.

The Israeli demand for guarantees before withdrawing troops from Gaza and Sharm el Sheikh was also considered inadmissible. Recalling that United Nations action "must be governed by principle and must be in accordance with international law and valid international agreements," Hammarskjold thought it was "generally recognized as non-controversial" that "the United Nations cannot condone a change of the *status juris* resulting from military action contrary to the provisions of the Charter," and that "the use of military force by the United Nations other than that under Chapter VII of the Charter requires the consent of the States in which the force is to operate." Such a use of force must always respect legal rights and must be impartial "in the sense that it does not serve as a means to force settlement, in the interest of one party, of political conflicts or legal issues recognized as controversial." [42] Referring specifically to the situation in Gaza, the Secretary-General recalled the provisions of the general Armistice Agreement between Egypt and Israel of February 24, 1949, which delineated the line beyond which the armed forces of the respective parties were not to move and which left control of Gaza in Egyptian hands. He emphasized that the United Nations was not permitted to lend assistance to the maintenance of a *de facto* situation contrary to the one created by the Armistice Agreement. Hammarskjold thereby excluded the possibility of administrative control by Israel over the Gaza area. [43]

Upon withdrawal of Israeli forces, the Secretary-General envisaged deployment of UNEF in Gaza at the dividing line between the forces of Israel and Egypt, exactly as the Emergency Force had functioned in the Sinai Peninsula.

Any broader function for it in that area, in view of the terms of the Armistice Agreement and a recognized principle of international law, would require the consent of Egypt. A widening of the United Nations administrative responsibilities in the area, beyond its responsibilities for the refugees, would likewise, have to be based on agreement with Egypt. [44]

In regard to the situation near the Gulf of Aqaba (discussed later in this chapter), the Secretary-General contemplated UNEF action as in other parts of Sinai, but declared that should the need for such an arrangement exist, the Force would also assist in maintaining quiet in the region beyond what followed from its duties in respect of the cease-fire and withdrawal.

Commenting upon UNEF's functions in terms of the Armistice system, Hammarskjold asserted that whatever "the state of non-compliance with the Armistice Agreement in general before the crisis, it would seem apparent that a by-passing of that Agreement now would seriously impede efforts to lay the foundation for progress toward solutions of pending problems." Several articles of the Agreement seemed especially important in this respect. Article I, which provides that no aggressive action by the armed forces of either party shall be undertaken, planned or threatened against the people or armed forces of the other, assimilated the Agreement to a nonaggression pact. Restoration of more stable relations than those prevailing between the parties could therefore be based on a re-affirmation of this article. Observance of Articles VII and VIII, which provide for restriction on the deployment of military forces of the parties along both sides of the armistice demarcation line, likewise "would be a valuable step toward reduction of tension and the establishment of peaceful conditions in the region." With de-militarization of the El-Auja Zone already prescribed by these articles, the Secretary-General felt that UNEF should have units stationed on the Israel side of the armistice demarcation line as well as on the Egyptian side.[45] This "would have the advantage of the Force being in a position to assume the supervisory duties of the Truce Supervision Organization in all the territory where that Organization now functions under the Armistice Agreement between Egypt and Israel." If these new arrangements were not made, the functions of the Truce Supervision Organization and UNEF would overlap in certain respects at both Gaza and El-Auja. Working together, the two groups might be of special help in preventing incursions and raids across the demarcation lines. Deployment of the Force in this manner, however, would require not only a new decision of the General Assembly but the explicit consent of the Israeli government.

The discussion in the Assembly on the Secretary-General's report of January 24 and the issues involved was long and divided. Each viewpoint differed somewhat from the next and it was difficult to see clearly what the Assembly, as a group, envisaged next for the Emergency Force. A number of delegates, including those from Australia, Canada, and New Zealand expressed considerable sympathy with the Israeli demand for guarantees, urged the Assembly to seek a lasting settlement of the problem, and maintained that the basis for Israeli compliance might well be UNEF's indefinite deployment in the Gaza Strip and elsewhere. "If this is followed, the role of the United Nations Emergency Force would be to hold the scales between the parties and to prevent any recurrence of trouble." [46] New Zealand proposed assurances to Israel which, although never spelled out in the form of a resolution, appeared, later, to be acceptable to the Assembly. Sir Leslie Munro, delegate of New Zealand, said the questions of the Gaza Strip and the Gulf of Aqaba should be taken up by the Assembly after the Israeli withdrawal:

Alternatively, or additionally, leading delegations might make declarations to the effect, *inter alia:*

(a) That the decision that the tasks of the United Nations Emergency Force have been completed should be a matter for the United Nations, not for Egypt or any other country;

(b) That the decision to withdraw the Force should therefore also be a matter for the United Nations, not Egypt or any other country;

(c) That the Force, in the performance of its function of securing and supervising the cessation of hostilities, should remain in the area at least until the Suez or Aqaba issues are settled, and some progress is made towards an overall settlement;

(d) That consideration should be given to the creation of a demilitarized zone between Israel and Egypt, and . . . to the possibility of transferring to UNEF responsibilities so far carried by the Truce Supervision Organization;

(e) That the Assembly has an obligation to ensure against the future use of the Gaza Strip for attacks on Israel, and should give consideration to ways and means of bringing the area under some form of United Nations supervision;

(f) That freedom of passage must be secured for shipping of all nationalities, including Israel;

(g) That the Assembly must proceed at an early stage to frame recommendations designed to bring about a general settlement of the Palestine question.[47]

Elaborating upon UNEF's role in regard to the armistice, Norway was convinced that it was clearly within the competence of the Force to prevent a breach of the 1956 cease-fire and, accordingly, of the 1948 cease-fire.[48] In more masked form, the above views seemed also to be those of the United States government.[49] India, on the contrary, was more cautious. Although approving deployment of the Force on the armistice line in support of mutual restraint of the parties, she was concerned above all that UNEF should not be used as an army of occupation.[50] Indonesia also stressed the temporary nature of the Emergency Force and stated that "if the functions of the Force should be broadened or enlarged beyond its original purpose, such as linking it indefinitely with the Truce Supervision Organization, then my Government certainly would have to reserve its right to reconsider its continued participation."[51] And some of the countries of Latin America, skeptical of assumption by the UN of an administrative role, concurred with the words of Francisco Urrutia, the delegate from Colombia:

The United Nations is not an administering Power. We have on some occasions agreed that the United Nations should appoint committees or advisory councils, but the Organization has never been entrusted with the administration of a territory. Perhaps a solution could be found if the United Nations troops were asked to throw a kind of safety belt around Gaza by stationing troops along the frontier. But that is an entirely different matter.[52]

Finally, the Soviet Union and associated states were totally opposed to all suggestions concerning UNEF's deployment in Gaza, in Sharm el Sheikh or on the armistice lines. Any such action would be highly objectionable as it would "turn the United Nations Emergency Force into what would in effect be a permanent occupation force" and create "a dangerous precedent of interference in the domestic affairs of a sovereign State." [53] Upon the withdrawal of Israel from Egypt, the operation of the Emergency Force should cease.

A group of Asian and African countries contemplated a proposal which would demand complete withdrawal of Israel's troops from Egypt within five days upon penalty of imposition of sanctions in the event of noncompliance. These nations insisted that there should be no discussion of larger issues prior to withdrawal. Ambassador Lodge, however, reaffirmed the American view that long-range issues required solution, that prevention of those conditions existing before the outbreak of hostilities was in order, and that the United Nations Emergency Force could be utilized to act "as a restraint against any attempt to exercise belligerent rights or to engage in hostile actions contrary to the Armistice Agreement, the decisions of the Security Council and the resolutions of the General Assembly." [54] The Secretary-General declared that his efforts to obtain Israeli withdrawal had been "frustrated," but suggested that sanctions against Israel might introduce "new elements of conflict." And a majority of states seemed to come closest to the Indian view which did not favor sanctions but held that UNEF should not adopt administrative duties that would make of it an army of occupation or a means of supporting one side in a political negotiation.

The two resolutions adopted by the Assembly on February 2 called upon Israel to complete its withdrawal of forces "without delay," called upon the governments of Egypt and Israel to observe scrupulously the provisions of the Armistice Agreement, and considered that,

after full withdrawal of Israel from the Sharm el-Sheikh and Gaza areas, the scrupulous maintenance of the Armistice Agreement requires the placing of the United Nations Emergency Force on the Egyptian-Israel armistice demarcation line and the implementation of other measures as proposed in the Secretary-General's report, with due regard to the considerations set out therein with a view to assist in achieving situations conducive to the maintenance of peaceful conditions in the area.[55]

This resolution, however, left unanswered a number of vital questions: What precisely were the "other measures" mentioned by the Secretary-General in his report of January 24 and authorized in the February 2 resolution? What was the exact nature of the "considerations" governing the implementation of these "other measures?" What area did the Assembly have in mind when authorizing UNEF's deployment "on" the Egyptian-Israeli armistice demarcation line? What were UNEF's functions on that line to be and how long would the Force remain there? As Hamilton Fish Armstrong remarks, "the Secretary-General was left to interpret what had been the General Assembly's intent and to do his best to give it coherent execution." [56]

In effect, a stalemate existed: on the one hand, the Israeli point of view had many adherents, and the Assembly was conscious of the deep-seated problems underlying the Israeli demands for security which the UN had failed to settle; on the other hand, the United Nations was bound to uphold its resolution calling for complete withdrawal, presumably without conditions, of foreign forces from Egypt. It was bound to honor the Armistice Agreements, which had been approved by the Security Council, and bound to reject any action which might constitute acquisition of territory by conquest and war. The scene shifted to Washington: Secretary of State Dulles and Mrs. Golda Meir, the Israeli Foreign Minister, undertook discussions aimed at a peaceful *de facto* situation in Gaza and Sharm el Sheikh, while leaving a final settlement of the problems involved in these regions to future negotiation.[57]

During this time, despite extreme caution on the part of the Secretary-General, the impression gained momentum that the United Nations had in view some form of interim UN administration in Gaza, thus in fact aiming not merely to restore the *de jure* situation there but to assume positive international responsibility, pending conclusive Arab-Israeli arrangements in that area. On February 22,

Dag Hammarskjold, after declaring that the Washington conversations were "deserving of warm appreciation," told the Assembly of Egypt's "willingness and readiness to make special and helpful arrangements" in Gaza "with the United Nations and some of its auxiliary bodies, such as United Nations Relief and Works Agency for Palestine Refugees and UNEF. For example, the arrangement for the use of UNEF in the area should ensure its deployment on the armistice line at the Gaza Strip and the effective interposition of the Force between the armed forces of Egypt and Israel." [58] This statement implied that Egypt had agreed to United Nations presence in the Strip. Lester Pearson specifically urged that the United Nations should "accept responsibility to the maximum possible extent for establishing and maintaining effective civil administration in the Gaza Strip; for fostering economic development and social welfare; for maintaining law and order." [59] He proposed appointment of a United Nations Commissioner for Gaza to coordinate and make effective the necessary arrangements and assume responsibility for UNEF activities inside the Strip.

Influenced, no doubt, by these impressions which envisaged future United Nations control of Gaza, and strongly pressured by the United States and other governments,[60] Mrs. Meir on March 1 announced Israel's plans for full and prompt withdrawal from the Gaza Strip and the Sharm el Sheikh area in compliance with the first resolution of February 2.* In outlining Israel policy Mrs. Meir listed, presumably on the basis of discussion and negotiation, a number of "assumptions" and expectations on her government's part regarding future policy in the Strip: Israel assumed that immediately upon withdrawal of her forces, United Nations troops would be deployed in Gaza and that UNEF alone would take over the military and civilian control of Gaza from the withdrawing Israelis. It was Israel's clear "expectation" that such arrangements would be made with the United Nations as will contribute toward "safeguarding life and

---

* For basis upon which Israeli evacuation of Sharm el Sheikh was under-taken, see pp. 93–97.

property in the area by providing efficient and effective police protection," which in turn would "guarantee good civilian administration; . . . assure maximum assistance to the United Nations refugee program; and . . . protect and foster the economic development of the territory and its people." Furthermore, Mrs. Meir's government was confident "that the aforementioned responsibility of the United Nations in the administration of Gaza will be maintained for a transitory period from the take-over until there is a peace settlement, to be sought as rapidly as possible, or a definitive agreement on the future of the Gaza Strip." [61] Israel, then, made its decision to withdraw upon the "assumption" that the United Nations would control Gaza until a permanent solution for the area was found by Egypt and Israel.[62]

The American delegate, Ambassador Lodge, quickly commended this decision and, taking note of Mrs. Meir's declarations, stated that they did not have the character of making Israel's withdrawal conditional, for they "constitute, as we understand it, restatements of what has already been said by the Assembly or by the Secretary-General in his reports, or hopes and expectations which seem to us not unreasonable in the light of the prior actions of the Assembly." [63] Since it was understood that the Israeli assumptions had been discussed in detail with American authorities, this cautious support by the United States, deeming the Israeli position merely "not unreasonable," surely was heard with some surprise by the government of Israel; indeed, a flurry of excitement ensued in Tel Aviv, withdrawal was postponed for a day, and it was not until President Eisenhower strongly reassured Premier Ben-Gurion that Israel's hopes and expectations were "reasonable" that withdrawal of Israeli troops was finally effected.[64] By March 7, UNEF was fully deployed in the Gaza Strip and Israel had evacuated the entire area.

Functioning in the Gaza Strip in order to maintain quiet during and after the withdrawal of the Israel defense forces, UNEF assumed duties of a police and an administrative nature. The Force entered at the same time as the Israeli contingents withdrew, took up positions in all centers of population and camps in the area, controlled all entry into and exit from the Strip, and exercised (with the assistance of UNRWA *) internal security functions of guard, check post duty, and patrol. Temporary control of the prisons was undertaken by UNEF, key installations were guarded, and border territory was patrolled to prevent infiltrations and crossings of the demarcation line for any purpose.[65] Execution of these measures was predicated upon orders from the Secretary-General that the reception of both military and civil control from Israel would be "exclusively" by the United Nations Emergency Force "in the first instance." [66] The "first instance," however, was never defined by Hammarskjold. Presumably, UN control was to last a short time. Actually, no express authority had been given Hammarskjold by the Assembly regarding United Nations control of the Strip. Was this omission, this lack of definition and precision to doom United Nations efforts in administering Gaza?

An account of the actual course of events in Gaza during the days immediately following UNEF's arrival provides interesting information, not only on the variable tasks of the Emergency Force in the Middle East, but on the limitations under which it operated. Hamilton Fish Armstrong reports that the military take-over of the Strip by the UN forces on March 7, 1957, was efficiently and expertly executed.[67] In the course of early planning for the operation, Secretariat officials had contemplated a procedure whereby several hours would elapse between Israel's withdrawal from and UNEF's entry into the area; or, alternatively, the mere entry of United Nations observers to displace the Israeli forces in the first instance was envisaged. These ideas were, however, abandoned, and through the night of March 6 Israel's soldiers quietly left the Strip while the international troops entered. Military authority over Gaza was transferred without ceremony by General Moshe Dayan, Israeli Chief of Staff, to Colonel Carl Engholm of Denmark who acted as

* United Nations Relief and Work Agency for Palestine Refugees in the Near East.

Burns's deputy. "There was no vacuum of authority and hence no murdering or looting. The rioting came later." [68]

On the same day, a group of experts who had been assembled from the ranks of UNEF personnel and United Nations technical assistance missions in the Middle East, together with a group of officials from UNRWA, reported to UN headquarters in the Sinai Peninsula and in Gaza. The civilian experts were skilled in operating a civil government, but had not been briefed on local problems, nor had they been given specific instructions as to their duties or tasks. Since UNEF officials in Sinai and Gaza, with whom they were to serve, likewise lacked clear instructions as to the United Nations role in the Strip, decisive action in regard to administration was not taken. Indeed, the local population of Gaza, prompted by Egyptian demonstrators, soon displayed evidence of independent action. Before the civilian experts "could get their bearings, while they were still searching for beds and desks, Egypt had stepped in again." [69] The UN civil administrators remained unnoticed by the inhabitants of Gaza.

United Nations officials in New York and in the field hardly expected an immediate move by Egypt to resume control of Gaza. Nasser's step in this direction may have been prompted by Israel's insistence upon UN presence in the Strip. In any case, Nasser began his campaign for renewed Egyptian rule by sending agents to the territory. They organized demonstrations against UNEF and stimulated favorable feeling toward Egypt: "UNEF, which had counted on being welcomed to Gaza as friends, found that the population was being organized against them."

Difficult questions haunted United Nations officials on the scene. The international police force was equipped with arms, yet no instructions had been issued from headquarters regarding their use. When faced with the possibility of losing his weapon to Arab rioters, was the UNEF soldier entitled to resist forcibly? The UN troops had entered Gaza with the understanding that their mere presence would be sufficient to maintain order and prevent any eruption of violence. Presented with actual trouble, however, were the soldiers merely to fire into the air and allow incidents to happen as they would? On March 9, without precise instructions from the UN, Colonel Engholm finally gave orders that all unauthorized arms would be outlawed. But enforcement of this measure could only be negligible; for, UNEF did not possess the authority to imprison violators, and UN administrative machinery did not exist in regard to legal processes.

The ambiguity of UNEF's functions in Gaza proved increasingly troublesome: by March 10, shortly after General Burns had changed his Sinai headquarters for the old Police Station in Gaza, and after Colonel Engholm had been appointed Military Governor of the city, a group of rioters surrounded United Nations headquarters and attempted to raise the Egyptian flag.

UNEF soldiers used tear gas to disperse them and also fired over their heads: a bullet ricochetted and killed one of the demonstrators. What would have happened if the mob persisted is hard to say. . . .

March 10 marked the turning point. The mob was not in control of Gaza but it knew that the United Nations was not in control either. The U.N. civil administrators had been trickling in and had begun by now to get their bearings. It was too late.[70]

On March 12, Egypt accused the Emergency Force of exceeding its authority in Gaza and announced that Egyptian authorities would henceforth assume complete control of the Strip.[71] In this way, President Gamal Abdel Nasser made clear his intention of reducing the role of the United Nations Force in Gaza to mere supervision of the demarcation line between Egypt and Israel. He named General Hassan Abdel Latif as Gaza's new Egyptian Governor.[72] At a meeting of Hammarskjold's Advisory Committee on March 18, six members insisted that the United Nations retain control of internal security in the territory to prevent resumption of Arab raids upon Israeli border settlements. Exclusive and effective international control was, however, never again attempted.[73]

In the course of consultations with the Secretary-General, Egyptian Foreign Minister Fawzi indicated that his government was unwilling to make definite commitments regarding the continued presence of UNEF in Gaza and at the Gulf of Aqaba unless Israel also agreed to deployment of the Force on the Israeli side of the 1949 demarcation line.[74] Israel refused consent to such deployment. An "interim arrangement pending full implementation by Egypt and Israel of the general armistice agreement" was, however, made on March 30 when it was announced that a Palestine Arab police force would patrol jointly with UN troops along the borders of Gaza. By the terms of this "gentleman's agreement," the Egyptian government agreed to withhold its own military forces from the area during the interim period.[75] After the spring of 1957, UN troops were assigned almost exclusively to the task of patrolling the demarcation lines.

The objective of UN administration in Gaza was thus never fulfilled. Negotiations for the evacuation of Israeli troops at the time had been so intense that UN officials had considered it unwise to formulate detailed plans for United Nations administration of Gaza. They feared that Arab and Soviet opposition to such plans would be strong. UN officials, moreover, expected to control Gaza for a longer period of time than they were actually given.

Had the entire enterprise proved more successful, however, and had its scope been somewhat greater, the importance of UNEF and its usefulness in preserving world order would have been considerably enlarged; an important precedent would have been set for future police actions by the world organization; thereafter, the conception of an emergency international military force for limited purposes might have widened to include in its functions the important possibility of international administration.

Moreover, in every respect, "the problem clamored for an international solution." [76] The Gaza Strip was the main center for the organization of *fedayeen* raids against Israel, and the main target for Israeli reprisals. It was a territory under the sovereign control of neither Egypt nor Israel, a land whose people had not voiced their wishes as to their future status, a terrain filled to overflow with refugees. Most of the people in the region, particularly the refugees, were unfriendly to Israel, but they might still have accepted an interim period of *international* administration. Possibly, they might even have favored the eventual conversion of the Gaza Strip into a small Palestinian state, supported by international guarantees—a buffer between the two squabbling nations.[77] Administration and occupation of the Gaza Strip by the United Nations would have given the United Nations Relief and Works Agency an excellent opportunity to find a permanent solution to the refugee problem.[78] Furthermore, international administration of the territory might well have made it a focus of international strength while the search for a final solution of the Arab-Israeli problem continued. But the experiment was never made.

Hamilton Fish Armstrong declares that this

denouement can be traced to many errors of commission and of omission, but to the latter more than the former. The first and probably decisive omission, we see in retrospect, was the General Assembly's failure to relate the measures taken to force the withdrawal of Israeli troops from Egyptian territory with measures to deal with the circumstances out of which the attack had arisen.[79]

Also, lack of speed, coordination, and authority on the part of the organizers of the UN administration of Gaza doomed their efforts to failure even before definitive arrangements were instituted. Faced with resolute UN action,* Nasser might well have permitted international control of the Gaza area. Lacking this, he was determinedly swift in his reoccupation of the Strip and UNEF was not empowered to balk his moves.

THE PROBLEM OF THE GULF OF AQABA

The small piece of land which comprises the Sharm el Sheikh area commands, through the Straits of Tiran, the entrance to the Gulf of Aqaba. This Gulf leads to the Red Sea and is bounded

* See below, pp. 110–15.

by the territories of Israel, Jordan, Saudi Arabia, and Egypt. For Israel, free and unimpeded use of the waterway is of singular importance: development of the southern part of the country, expansion of commerce with African and Asian nations, improved communication between Israel and the rest of the world, growth of port facilities at Elath, all depend upon maintenance of free navigation in the Aqaba Gulf. In 1950, however, Egypt set up gun emplacements in the Sharm el Sheikh area to prevent ships from freely sailing in the Gulf of Aqaba to and from the Israeli port of Elath.

Upon strong protest by the government of Israel, the Egyptian blockade was discussed several times in the Security Council, but no further action was taken upon the matter.[80] Therefore, in the course of Israeli penetration of Egyptian territory in October 1956, Israel occupied Sharm el Sheikh for the purpose of destroying the Egyptian blockade and opening the waterway to free navigation. Thereafter, she staunchly upheld her right to this action, refused withdrawal without satisfactory guarantees that the blockade would not be restored, and demanded of the UN "effective arrangements" and "special measures" to that end. "Effective arrangements" for Israel, however, did not comprise solely the take-over of the territory in the first instance by United Nations soldiers. As Mrs. Meir stated before the General Assembly,

The mere entry into this area of the United Nations Emergency Force, even with the specific aim of preventing belligerency, would not in itself be a solution. For there is as yet no clarity about the functions of the United Nations Emergency Force or about the duration of its tenure. No temporary measure for preventing belligerency and securing free navigation would be effective unless it were ensured in advance that it would operate until a peace settlement had been . . . established by international guarantees for ensuring permanent freedom of navigation. Such guarantees could, perhaps, be furnished either by the principal maritime Powers or by an agreement among the four coastal states, or by some combination of the two forms of guarantee. But, if the United Nations

Emergency Force were to be regarded as a key to the solution of this problem, greater clarity and precision would be needed in defining its functions and the conditions and duration of its tenure.[81]

Israel, accordingly, would have liked not "mere entry" into the Sharm el Sheikh territory of United Nations troops, but the following arrangements: occupation by UNEF of the positions which would be evacuated by Israel's soldiers along the western coast of the Gulf of Aqaba; maintenance of free navigation and prevention by the Emergency Force of belligerent acts in the Gulf and Straits; guarantees that UNEF would remain in the area "so long as it has its function to prevent any renewal of hostilities"; maintenance of UNEF's position along the western shore of the Aqaba Gulf "until another effective means" was agreed upon between the parties concerned for ensuring permanent freedom of navigation and the absence of belligerent acts in the Straits of Tiran and the Gulf of Aqaba. By "another effective means" was meant a final peace settlement or another international instrument securing these ends.

Secretary-General Hammarskjold was not adverse to the Israeli position: certainly, he upheld the view that "the international significance of the Gulf of Aqaba may be considered to justify the right of innocent passage through the Straits of Tiran and the Gulf in accordance with recognized rules of international law." [82] However, he was adamant in his view that, because of principles guiding the UN, the Israeli military action and its consequences should not be allowed to influence the matter. Moreover, the Secretary-General pointed out that the legal questions involved were still controversial:

in its commentary to article 17 of the articles of the law of the sea (A/3519, page 20), the International Law Commission reserved consideration of the question "what would be the legal position of straits forming part of the territorial sea of one or more States and constituting the sole means of access to the port of another State?" This description applies to the Gulf of Aqaba and the Straits of Tiran.[83]

Although the legal position of the Straits remained undetermined, it was clear to the Secretary-General that any claim to belligerent rights, including, of course, such rights in the Gulf of Aqaba and the Straits of Tiran, was strictly forbidden by the Armistice Agreement. Hammarskjold sought assurances that they would no longer be asserted. As for UNEF's role in the situation,

Israel troops, on their withdrawal from the Sharm el-Sheikh area, would be followed by the United Nations Emergency Force in the same way as in other parts of Sinai. The duties of the Force in respect of the cease-fire and the withdrawal will determine its movements. However, if it is recognized that there is a need for such an arrangement, it may be agreed that units of the Force (or special representatives in the nature of observers) would assist in maintaining quiet in the area beyond what follows from this general principle.[84]

"Maintaining quiet in the area" could encompass much or encompass little: it was an ambiguous phrase. In the Assembly, some delegates had forwarded the view that UNEF's deployment should be such as to assure freedom of passage through the Straits until a final settlement between the parties was reached.[85] Others had objected to this position by maintaining that such deployment must not be made to signify occupation of any sort and that UNEF's tasks in Sharm el Sheikh must be made to conform strictly to the wishes of all the parties concerned.[86] The delegate from Colombia had expressed another view, to wit, that the problem embodied such complexities as to be incapable of any solution by the Emergency Force.[87] And, the Arab States had declared that the Suez and Aqaba issues were part and parcel of the entire Palestine question and could not be resolved until Israel recognized "Arab rights to their own homes." [88]

The Assembly, then, seemed entirely agreed on two points only: the total withdrawal of Israeli forces from the Sharm el Sheikh area was to be effected forthwith; and, in

accordance with the general legal principles recognized as decisive for the deployment of the United Nations Emergency Force, the Force should not be used so as to prejudge the solution of the controversial questions involved. The Force, thus, is not to be deployed in such a way as to protect any special position on these questions, although, at least transitionally, it may function in support of mutual restraint in accordance with the foregoing.[89]

Again the *status juris* was to be reaffirmed.

The United States finally took a firmer line, thus in effect hastening Israel's withdrawal. Henry Cabot Lodge told the Assembly that it was essential for UNEF to be stationed at Sharm el Sheikh until it was clear that Israel's right to use the Gulf of Aqaba had been established in practice. The United States assured Israel that the U.S. would "exercise the right of free and innocent passage [through the Gulf] and [would] join with others to secure general recognition of this right." [90]

Discussions were also held between Abba Eban and the Secretary-General outside United Nations meetings. In a memorandum issued on February 26, Hammarskjold gave assurances, in response to questions raised by Israel, that following the withdrawal of Israeli forces from Sharm el Sheikh, the functions of the Emergency Force would be "the prevention of possible acts of belligerency." Once more he asserted "that UNEF is never to be used in such a way as to force a solution of any controversial political or legal problem." Asked whether the Secretary-General would give notice to the Assembly before the withdrawal of UNEF from the area (with or without Egypt's insistence), Hammarskjold reserved his position. He pointed out, however, that an indicated procedure would be for the Secretary-General to inform the Advisory Committee on the United Nations Emergency Force, which would in turn determine whether the matter should be brought to the Assembly's attention.[91] Israel's suggestion of adding a naval unit to UNEF for purposes of instituting a United Nations patrol in the Gulf of Aqaba and the Straits of Tiran to ensure free and innocent passage was rejected by the Secretary-General. Such action, he declared, would be beyond the competence of the Secretary-General, for it would go beyond the prevention of belligerent acts as envisaged in the basic Assembly resolutions.

Following upon the Israeli government's decision to withdraw, the Commander of UNEF met the Israeli Commander-in-Chief at Lydda airport on March 4 and agreed upon technical arrangements for the Israeli withdrawal and the take-over of the Sharm el Sheikh area by the Emergency Force.[92] Finnish infantrymen were ordered to garrison Sharm el Sheikh, patrol the surrounding land, and man observation posts along the shipping channel. Contact was made with all vessels passing through the Straits. These tasks are still being performed successfully by UNEF soldiers. Indeed, Elath has grown into a thriving and expanding port-city to and from which trading vessels freely go.

THE PROBLEM OF THE ARMISTICE LINES

Since the time of complete British, French, and Israeli troop-withdrawal from Egypt, UNEF's functions devolve essentially from the Assembly's resolution of February 2, 1957, and concern "the scrupulous maintenance of the Armistice Agreement [between Egypt and Israel]," in addition to the patrolling of the Sharm el Sheikh area.

The Armistice Agreement provides that "no aggressive action by the armed forces—land, sea, or air—of either Party shall be undertaken, planned or threatened against the people or the armed forces of the other" and that "the right of each Party to its security and freedom from fear of attack by the armed forces of the other shall be fully respected." [93] Assisting the parties in ensuring that these provisions are carried out and in preventing any renewal of general hostilities in the period of transition from armistice to formal peace, is the United Nations Truce Supervision Organization. Originally formed in 1948 by the United Nations Mediator in Palestine to regulate the work of the observers assisting him in supervising the truce, UNTSO has existed ever since.[94] Its Chief of Staff is chairman of the four Mixed Armistice Commissions (MACs), which are invested with duties of investigation and observation. Each MAC also takes action with a view to a just and mutually acceptable settlement on all claims or complaints.[95] The chairman of the pertinent MAC is notified by the complainant party, meetings are held and decisions, whenever possible, are made with unanimous approval. Failing unanimity, the MAC comes to agreement "by a majority of the members present and voting, 'which for all practical purposes means that the chairman votes for one or the other side.' " [96] Although a useful institution for observation and a practical mechanism for the airing of complaints, the Egypt-Israel armistice machinery—comprising UNTSO and the MAC—has been unable to prevent skirmishes, theft, and smuggling along the border, or guerrilla raids across the demarcation lines. Therefore, in February 1957, the prevention of these incidents was designated as UNEF's task.

While members of the Truce Supervision Organization and the MAC, unarmed and small in number, were mainly authorized to engage in activities of observation and investigation,[97] UNEF soldiers were, in addition, competent to establish observation posts, patrol the demarcation lines, and actively prevent movement across the frontiers. To prevent duplication in their tasks, however, arrangements were made for the Egypt-Israel Mixed Armistice Commission to be placed under the operational control of UNEF's commander.[98] The legal status of both organs remained unchanged. In March 1958, at the time of the appointment of a new Chief of Staff for UNTSO, these arrangements were confirmed by the Secretary-General: the Commander of the Force, said Hammarskjold, "would continue to exercise his functions as Chief of Staff in respect of the Egypt-Israel General Armistice Agreement, i.e. as Chairman *ex officio* of the MAC, in accordance with Article X of that Agreement." [99]

These measures were instituted despite the fact that the Israeli government has denied the validity of the Armistice Agreement between Israel and Egypt:

Israel's view is . . . that the General Armistice Agreement has been consistently violated by Egypt both in letter and in spirit ever since it was signed on 24 February 1949. Its central purpose of non-belligerency and its character as a transition to a peaceful settlement have been constantly repudiated by Egypt. Egypt has even held, most incongruously, that the Agreement could co-exist with a "state of war" against Israel. This policy of Egypt and the actions flowing therefrom have brought the Agreement to naught, with the result that a new system of relationships must now be constructed.[100]

The absence of an Armistice Agreement, declared the Prime Minister of Israel, does not signify the existence of a state of war with Egypt. To confirm this position, the Israeli government is at all times prepared to sign an agreement of nonbelligerency and mutual nonaggression. But, "the Armistice Agreement, violated and broken, is beyond repair." [101]

Israel's position on this matter has not been accepted by the United Nations or by Egypt. "United Nations actions," declared the Secretary-General, "must respect fully the rights of Member States recognized in the Charter, and international agreements not contrary to the aims of the Charter, which are concluded in exercise of these rights." [102] International agreements may not be broken unilaterally.[103]

The Armistice Agreement was signed by both parties and, according to article XII, remains in force until a peace settlement between them is achieved. It was approved by the Security Council. Whatever arrangements the United Nations may now wish to make in order to further progress toward peaceful conditions, the Agreement must be fully respected by it.[104]

On its side, the government of Egypt reaffirmed its intent to observe fully the provisions of the Armistice Agreement, as indicated in the acceptance of resolution 997 (ES-I) of November 2, 1956, provided of course that observance would be reciprocal.[105]

Despite this reaffirmation, Israel chose to maintain its formal position denying the Armistice Agreement and, as a result, preferred to lodge any complaints against Egypt with the United Nations Emergency Force, rather than with the Egypt-Israel Mixed Armistice Commission, although UNEF representatives "consistently maintained that official investigations of incidents can be carried out only through the Mixed Armistice Commission." [106] But Israel's position has not hampered the Emergency Force in its quotidian operation.

The bulk of the Force is still deployed on the western side of the armistice demarcation line, along that part of the line which separates Egypt from Israel, and along the international frontier south of the Gaza Strip. This area extends for 273 kilometers. UNEF also surveys the coast of the Sinai Peninsula from the northern extremity of the Gulf of Aqaba to the Straits of Tiran, an area of about 187 kilometers. Each part of the line is divided into sectors where a different national battalion is stationed (see Chapter V).

What, then, are the daily tasks of the Force in regard to the armistice demarcation lines and the international frontier? A system of observation posts, guard and sentinel posts, patrol groups, and mobile motorized surveillance teams has been set up by UNEF for the purpose of checking infiltration across the armistice lines, preventing commando raids or marauding, and forestalling any trouble between Egypt and Israel in sensitive border zones.[107] During the day, every observation post along the armistice lines is manned by two men, who stand guard for a period of six hours each. The series of observation posts are inter-visible, making possible complete surveillance of all movement on the demarcation line.[108] At times when the observation post is in need of additional support, a mobile group is dispatched from the headquarters of the company or section in charge of the sector to the post in question. Such support would be necessary, for example, during haying or harvesting season, when local inhabitants might try to cross the lines in massive numbers, or when suspected infiltrators, heavily armed, might attempt to evade a sentry. Each reserve unit is so organized as to appear at a danger spot ten to fifteen minutes after the call for aid. Telephone lines connect neighboring posts with one another and with the headquarters of the company. It is thus fairly easy to oversee and stop all infiltrators.

At night, the men of the observation post are withdrawn and patrols are organized, varying in strength from five to seven men. These patrols are numerous in all sectors and each group operates on foot along its section of the line on an average of three times each night. Reserve groups are also stationed to the rear of the observation post during the night hours, ready to respond to signal lights in the event of need. Furthermore, the head of each sector or company is advised of the activity of the patrols by radio.

They [U.N. soldiers] move quietly, sometimes wearing sneakers, and if they hear anything, they drop to the ground and wait, and then shine searchlights. Sometimes they set up an ambush at a spot where people are likely to try to cross. If they catch anyone on the A.D.L., he is automatically in the wrong, because the local people are not supposed to go near it at night. They may, and do, work the land right next to the line by daylight—Egyptians and Israelis almost within reach of each other—but before dark they must drop back 500 yards.[109]

Along the international frontier experience has shown that only especially troublesome areas necessitate constant patrol and observation, for broken terrain and other factors (scattered uncleared minefields) limit the possibilities of infiltration in certain regions. The Force sends daily patrols into vulnerable spots, where vehicles find it possible to pass without undue difficulty.[110] In other sensitive sectors, aerial reconnaissance has been organized and land patrol undertaken only two or three times a week. Otherwise, camps and observation posts were established along the frontier with functions similar to those of the posts on the demarcation lines. The Canadian reconnaissance squadron and the Yugoslav reconnaissance battalion keep in constant touch by radio with the aerial reconnaissance groups as well as with the Brazilian battalion, which oversees the armistice demarcation line at the approaches to the international frontier. This system ensures rapid and immediate transmission of messages concerning suspect movements and permits the reserve patrols to move quickly into trouble-zones.

Following upon UNEF's deployment on the Gaza line and to the south of it, the number and severity of incidents in these areas diminished considerably. Serious incidents have been very few and no raids from either side have been reported. Moreover, Egyptian and Israeli troops have been kept apart effectively and the Straits of Tiran kept under constant observation. In his progress reports on UNEF, the Secretary-General again and again rendered homage to the efficacity of the Force.[111] He did not doubt that, were UNEF not stationed along the armistice line from the Mediterranean to the Red Sea, the risks of trouble in this area would have been far greater. Quiet reigns where UNEF operates.

United Nations soldiers possess the right to fire in self-defense— a right which, on occasion, has been used—but the question whether they have authority to fire during darkness at infiltrators approaching the line from either direction is still undetermined. Effective prevention of infiltration across the frontiers would seem to necessitate the right to shoot at marauders, and indeed General Burns requested this right. But only authority to shoot in self-defense was granted by the Secretary-General and the Advisory Committee, though it was understood that "self-defense" would be broadly interpreted. According to William Frye,

> Some countries contributing troops did not want their men shooting at Egyptians (or Israelis) without the consent of the Egyptian and Israeli Governments, and Hammarskjold did not press them to do so. Instead, he sought the necessary permission from Cairo and Jerusalem. These capitals haggled interminably, through him, over the terms and conditions and places where UNEF would shoot. The negotiations finally broke down because Israel would not let Burns' men operate on its side of the armistice line, and Egypt would not let them operate effectively on the Egyptian side alone.

UNEF's success in quieting the Egyptian-Israeli armistice line therefore was something of a miracle, no doubt reflecting in large part the fact that . . . both Cairo and Jerusalem considered it to be in their national interest to have a quiet border.[112]

Almost all the incidents that have occurred on the border are of a minor nature,[113] involving mines, crossings of the armistice demarcation line, firing across the armistice demarcation line, crossings of the line involving firing, theft or, occasionally, kidnapping.[114] Most of these incidents are reported upon by UNEF, others are brought to the attention of the Force by Egypt (after the Israel-Egypt Mixed Armistice Commission has looked into the matter), and still others are brought up by Egypt or Israel without UN confirmation. Violations of air space on the part of both Egypt and Israel, as well as violations of territorial waters (mainly by fishing vessels) have also occurred. But "in both the latter cases UNEF cannot exercise any control other than that of observing and informing the parties concerned." [115]

In his summary study on UNEF, the Secretary-General revealed his views on the right of self-defense. This right, for the most part, must be exercised under strictly defined conditions only, for too wide an interpretation of it "might well blur the distinction between operations of the character discussed in this report * and combat operations, which would require a decision under Chapter VII of the Charter and an explicit, more far-reaching delegation of authority to the Secretary-General. . . ." He counseled caution:

A reasonable definition seems to have been established in the case of UNEF, where the rule is applied that men engaged in the operation may never take the initiative in the use of armed force, but are entitled to respond with force to an attack with arms, including attempts to use force to make them withdraw from positions which they occupy under orders from the Commander acting under the authority of the Assembly and within the scope of its resolutions. . . . This definition of the limit

* That is, operations of a para-military nature, which are not to be used as part of enforcement action under Chapter VII.

between self-defense, as permissible for United Nations elements of the kind discussed, and offensive action, which is beyond the competence of such elements, should be approved for future guidance.[116]

UNEF's limitation in regard to combat initiative represents one of the distinguishing marks of the Force and establishes it definitely as a police and patrol operation. Without this restriction, support for UNEF's creation and for its functioning would probably have been withheld not only by the contributing states and the parties concerned in the conflict, but by the Assembly itself.

In the course of United Nations action in the Congo, however, it became necessary to reconsider the issue of prerogative on the part of UN soldiers in their use of arms and, eventually, wider powers in this respect were granted to ONUC contingents than were ever delegated to UNEF. The issue is a highly important one: UNEF operated and still functions very clearly as a *para*-military force—the first such force ever utilized for an international purpose. ONUC expanded upon this concept to become an entity with greater strength and authority in the military realm. Just how far the idea of an international military force for the United Nations will continue to grow and expand depends, of course, upon the Organization's Members. Some look forward to a permanent international military institution with effective military power, which the United Nations could call upon in the event of a limited war or breach of the peace or situation requiring pacific settlement. Others feel that such an organ is undesirable, although they would, perhaps, as in the case of UNEF, support a small, temporary, para-military group.

During August 1960, two divergent concepts of what an international security force should do were brought into focus by an exchange between Major General H. T. Alexander, Chief of the Defense Staff of Ghana,[117] and Ralph J. Bunche, Special Representative of the Secretary-General in the Republic of the Congo.[118] The officer of the Ghana contingent serving with ONUC had declared that orders to his men were unclear and inconcise, that these orders did not "give United Nations troops any liberty of action even to the use of minimum force," and that United Nations personnel could not be protected if orders were only to the effect that passive resistance and noninterference with the Congo Army had to be used. Major General Alexander was convinced "that if the United Nations troops were put in a position, as they have been, of losing the initiative, their task was hopeless." [119] In effect, the operation in the Congo could be a success only if ONUC were given power to use initiative, especially in the retraining and disciplining of the Congo *Force Publique.*

But, Bunche replied, the force in the Congo is a "peace force, not a fighting force."

I have stressed always that the arms carried by the members of this international army are to be used only in self-defense, and that the force is in the Congo to do harm to no one, if it can be avoided.[120]

Orders issued to troops, Bunche declared, were very clear indeed: "*On no account,* are weapons to be used unless in cases of great and sudden emergency and for the purpose of self-defence." Firing, even in self-defense, was to be "resorted to only in extreme instances," although efforts to disarm UN soldiers were to be regarded as a legitimate cause for using fire-arms. Altogether, profound care and caution was to be taken, for ONUC's functions in the Congo were based on a policy of restraint and cooperation.

Obviously, if the UN Force began to use its arms to wound and kill Congolese its doom would be quickly sealed, for it cannot long survive amidst a hostile public. Indeed, this would defeat its very purpose. I think it not the least exaggeration to say that the UN Force gained very much in the way of prestige and moral superiority by the remarkable restraint it displayed, under severe provocation. . . .[121]

This policy, then, was the one which had been applied to UNEF. Subsequent troublesome events in the Congo, however, were to persuade Hammarskjold to ask the Security Council for increased powers for ONUC, which would permit the United Nations Com-

mand to bring the Congo Army under its control, disarm soldiers of
any faction, and prevent all military forces from intervening in
the political conflicts of the area. Consequently, the Council adopted
a resolution on February 21, 1961, urging "that the United Nations
take immediately all appropriate measures to prevent the occur-
rence of civil war in the Congo, including arrangements for cease-
fires, the halting of all military operations, the prevention of clashes,
and the use of force, if necessary, in the last resort." Whether this
power to use force would also have been granted to United Nations
soldiers in the Middle East if serious difficulties had arisen between
Britain, France, Israel, or Egypt on the one hand, and UNEF soldiers on the other, remains speculative. The Force in the Middle
East is under the jurisdiction of the General Assembly, while ONUC
operates by way of a decision of the Security Council: perhaps here
lies one crucial difference between the two organs. The Security
Council is, after all, empowered to act *decisively* under Chapter
VII of the United Nations Charter.

During the years of its existence, UNEF has been effective in
the fulfillment of its tasks.[122] This conclusion has been reached by
many observers as well as by the UN Secretary-General:

Looking back to November of last year, it may be recalled that UNEF
was, in the first place, a pre-condition set by France, Israel and the United
Kingdom for the cease-fire. Subsequently, it was a pre-condition for the
withdrawals from Egypt of the Anglo-French and Israel forces. Upon
completion of the withdrawals, it became, and undoubtedly continues to
be today, one of the pre-conditions for the preservation of quiet along
the line between Egypt and Israel. Such quiet, in turn, is indispensable to
fruitful effort towards the removal of the major obstacles to peace in the
Near East.[123]

In his annual reports on the Organization, the Secretary-General has repeatedly stated that the continuing quiet along the
armistice lines between Israel and Egypt was a condition attributable to the presence of UNEF. Indeed, "its absence would, in the

judgment of all concerned, be likely to result in a recurrence of dangerous border disturbances and violations." [124] Therefore, it was difficult to foresee when the Force might be withdrawn without inviting risk of dangerous circumstances.

Looking at representative opinions on the Force, we find that it is often praised. Denmark characterized UNEF as "the instrument which helped to make the efforts of the United Nations effective," and as "a seed from which something greater might grow."

It was not UNEF's military might which by force brought about an end to the fighting. But the very fact that UNEF came to that part of the world was a decisive contribution in relieving tension. The UNEF soldiers in their blue caps did not have their strength in their light weapons but in the moral power with which the United Nations backed them.[125]

The representative from Brazil, when discussing UNEF, spoke of "a miracle in the sense of the peace it brought to a disturbed zone." [126] Japan spoke of the "outstanding contribution made by UNEF to the maintenance of peace and order in the Middle East," a sentiment echoed by delegates from Indonesia, Liberia, Cuba, El Salvador, Ecuador, and Sweden.[127] And, Lester Pearson, "father" of the Force, felt deep gratification in the organization he had sired:

Since the dark days of November 1956, a great deal has been said and written about the role of UNEF in the Middle East. Members of this Assembly may not have been wholly in agreement on the principles which should govern the presence and functioning of that Force. But what we are now agreed on, I believe, is that UNEF has made a valuable contribution to the maintenance of quiet and order in the area of deployment. This, in turn, has done much to allay the anxiety, the fear and the frustration which had produced international tension there.

Pearson described November 1956 as a time which provided a decisive test of the vitality of the United Nations and congratulated Member States for meeting this test, for providing "evidence that the United Nations ideal can be given practical expression." The creation of UNEF, he declared, "has been a practical application of the foremost among the purposes and principles enunciated in Article I of the Charter." In establishing the Force, an effective and collective step was taken by the world organization toward the prevention and removal of a threat to the peace.[128] In a similar manner, the delegate from Pakistan underlined UNEF's peace-making role. It was the establishment of the Emergency Force that brought a halt to the armed conflict in the Middle East.[129] The Indian spokesman, although reluctant to draw "general conclusions from that one experience," found the usefulness of the Force to be indisputable and also desired UNEF's continued operation.[130]

From the very beginning, the United States government has viewed UNEF in a favorable light. One year after its inception, the American delegate was able to say in the Assembly that creation of this para-military group "is one of the outstanding achievements of the Organization and one of which we can all be proud."

It has demonstrated the ability of the United Nations to act concretely in a very difficult and complex situation. It has demonstrated the capacity of this Organization to create new instruments to deal with new problems. . . . That the Emergency Force has been successful is evidenced by the fact that we are today discussing this question in a period when quiet reigns in the area to which UNEF is assigned.[131]

As a result of UNEF's creation, benefits accrued to all concerned, declares C. Chaumont; for not only did Egypt profit from the Force, but Britain, France, Israel and every Member of the Assembly gained thereby. By accepting the UN Force, Egypt found a way to end hostilities gracefully and assure the withdrawal of troops which had won a decided victory. Egypt thus gained a political victory—the complete fulfillment of her claim to the Suez Canal. The three other parties to the conflict saw a way of extracting themselves from a situation which, politically, would have led nowhere. And, by means of UNEF, the ensemble of UN Members found a way of putting an end to dangerous tensions capable of menacing world peace.[132]

Maxwell Cohen calls creation of UNEF a "brilliantly tactical stroke," which resolved in part at least the "almost classically tragic dislocation of friendships and alliances caused by the Suez-Sinai actions, and the implied threat to the existence of the United Nations order by the military efforts of three states otherwise known to be supporters of the Charter and its system." [133] Cohen believes that the development of the Force has caused the boundaries of control by the international community to widen and that we may look forward to still greater advance toward this end in the future.

But all these points in UNEF's favor have disturbed the Soviet Union. Supported by Albania, Bulgaria, Czechoslovakia, and Rumania in the Special Political Committee in 1958, the USSR delegate was reluctant to view UNEF as anything other than an emergency measure whose purpose had been fulfilled. In expressing his conviction, the Soviet representative spoke in "cold-war" terms:

Recently, certain circles had made a great deal of fuss about the valuable experience which it has alleged the United Nations Emergency Force had acquired after two years of operation and had even gone so far as to represent the Force as the only safeguard of peace and security in the Middle East. However, it was well known that the purpose of those fine words was to check the real designs of the Western Powers, which wanted to prove the need to set up a United Nations international police force on a permanent basis, in order to use it for aggressive purposes which had nothing in common with the Purposes and Principles of the Charter.[134]

Yet the Soviet bloc really stands alone in minimizing UNEF's value. Most of the UN's Members speak justifiably in its favor.

Undoubtedly, UNEF provided the United Kingdom and France with a measure of face-saving, for it represented a "peace force" not unlike the one they had requested. It was consequently possible to effect a cease-fire within a relatively short time after the outbreak of hostilities. Anglo-French troop withdrawals also occurred at a fast pace and the supervision of these withdrawals by UNEF insured quiet at a delicate time, a time when awkward incidents might well have erupted once more into harsh combat between the opposing sides.

UNEF is the sort of procedural guarantee which has in previous cases led belligerents to accept a cease-fire. States unwilling to lose face by obeying purely and simply a UN call because they do not want to appear to give in to their enemy in the field have often proved more ready to bow to an international mechanism.[135]

While the functions attributed to UNEF were fulfilled and while the Force unquestionably served a highly useful purpose, it is regrettable that in defining UNEF's role in the crisis, the Secretary-General and the Assembly continually affirmed a return to the "*status juris*" and an elimination of illegally obtained advantages instead of settlement of long-range issues.[136] Hammarskjold stated that UNEF's functions would be to prevent acts of belligerency, "subject to the qualification that UNEF is never to be used in such a way as to force a solution of any controversial or legal problem." Likewise, the Force "is not to be deployed in such a way as to protect any special position or (controversial) questions, although at least transitionally, it may function in support of mutual restraint in accordance with the foregoing." These statements indicate a rather narrow concept of the functions of the United Nations in fulfilling its goals.

Hammarskjold was limited in his actions and interpretations by the views of Member governments, particularly those which were contributing contingents to the Force. He was limited, as well, by the General Assembly's resolutions on UNEF. Yet, these resolutions gave the Secretary-General wide latitude. In the early days of the crisis, he might well have *led* the Assembly and guided it by his own interpretations.

When looking upon the situation in the Middle East during the autumn of 1956, what must be stressed is that mounting tension between Israel and the Arab States had developed into a full-scale local war, followed almost immediately by serious border incidents, to be succeeded again by a local conflict containing, this time, the seeds of a full world war. Would not the United Nations, then, dedicated as it is to establishing conditions of peace and security, have been fully justified in seeking to end forever this state of strain and hostility?[137] What must also be stressed is that, although UN resolutions had resolved that Britain, France, and Israel must leave Egyptian territory, the UN was not bound to establish the exact situation as it had existed before the conflict. Rather, it was committed to uphold the dictums of the Armistice Agreement which it had itself approved and which had been flouted—dictums demanding respect for the cease-fire and the armistice frontiers. The Organization had responsibility to attempt again the *final* adjustment or settlement of those disputes troubling Israel and the Arab States which might again lead to a breach of the peace—the question of refugees, final border delimitation, passage of Israeli ships through the Suez Canal and the Gulf of Aqaba, the status of Jerusalem, economic boycott, rights of belligerency, and many other problems.

Hammarskjold's interest that UNEF should not be used to force a settlement of political conflicts or controversial legal issues *in the interest of one party* remains unchallenged. The United Nations Force unquestionably must represent a neutral, objective instrument of an impartial world community. "But," as Armstrong remarks, "did this preclude the use of UNEF to maintain an open situation in areas about which both parties entered claims and complaints and regarding which the United Nations had a function to perform in attempting to induce both of them to accept an impartial settlement in the interest of peace?" [138] The world assembly was divided and reluctant to adopt a firm policy of its own in this regard, and the Secretary-General formulated a narrow interpretation which held sway. In Armstrong's words,

The major interested party was the community of nations which had been putting tremendous efforts into extricating Egypt from the consequences of her military defeat, and was now about to succeed in forcing Israel's withdrawal. Was it to be foreclosed from any gain except the highly important but nevertheless abstract victory of having frustrated aggression? Was no use to be made of that victory to exact a negotiation of the underlying disputes which had menaced the world with war? [139]

In effect, Members of the United Nations failed to seize a number of opportunities. During the early days of the emergency, one delegate after another remarked upon the need to change those conditions prevailing in the Middle East prior to the outbreak of conflict. In November 1956, John Foster Dulles told the Assembly:

All of us, I think, would hope that out of this tragedy there should come something better than merely a restoration of the conditions out of which this tragedy arose. There must be something better than that. . . . There needs to be something better than the uneasy armistices which have existed now for these eight years between Israel and its Arab neighbors. There needs to be a greater sense of confidence and security in the free and equal operation of the Canal than has existed since three months ago, when President Nasser seized the Universal Suez Canal Company.[140]

The Canadian Foreign Minister and the delegate from Italy spoke in similar terms: Lester Pearson asked,

Are we to return to the *status quo*? Such a return would not be to a position of security, or even a tolerable position, but would be a return to terror, bloodshed, strife, incidents, charges and counter-charges, and ultimately another explosion. . . .[141]

And the representative from Italy declared,

We consider that negotiations must be started as soon as possible to obtain a peaceful solution, not only to the present controversy, but also to all the questions which have for too long a time been disturbing peace in . . . [the Middle East].[142]

Sentiment for solution of the wider issues involved in the situation was widespread in November. Later, persistence toward this goal of change dimmed; later, by emphasizing withdrawal of the invaders and relinquishment of advantages gained by force, rather than stressing solution of larger political problems in the area, the Assembly and the Secretary-General pushed the important substantive issues into the background.

Gradually the essential questions underlying the crisis were separated from the problem of cease-fire and withdrawal; the latter issue emerged more and more prominently, while the question of the Canal and the tension-producing questions between Israel and the Arab States were postponed for future consideration. Anxious to relieve the primary tensions, the United States on November 3, 1956, had submitted a draft resolution to the Assembly urging the creation of a special committee of five states to consult with the parties to the Armistice Agreements "regarding a settlement of the major problems outstanding between the Arab States and Israel, with a view to establishing conditions of permanent peace and stability in the area" and to submit recommendations to the parties, to the Assembly, or to the Security Council as seemed appropriate.[143] Another resolution was also introduced which called for the establishment of a three-member committee to take measures for the immediate reopening of the Suez Canal and for the preparation of a plan dealing with its operation and maintenance.[144] Both proposals were again brought to the Assembly's attention on November 10. But Ambassador Lodge did not press for a vote on his draft resolutions in view of the urgency of obtaining a complete cessation of hostilities, and, in the days ahead, anti-Israel feeling among certain delegations—the Arab, Soviet, and Indian—was allowed to coalesce so strongly that hope of compromise solutions, for a time, seemed dim. Indeed, " 'Let Dag do it' supplanted 'Do it yourself.' "[145] The United States draft resolutions were shelved, never to be considered again.

Thereafter, in January 1957, another opportunity was missed when the Secretary-General and the Assembly insisted upon Israel's withdrawal without stressing simultaneous resolution of "intermediate" issues (issues "half way between the return to the *status quo* and a general political negotiation"):[146] the *fedayeen* and

Gaza; the blockade and the Gulf of Aqaba; the passage of Israeli ships through the Suez Canal. A return to the *status quo* or the *status juris* certainly did not go far enough: the entire Suez crisis testified to that. Indeed, was not the Israeli invasion itself the direct result of a precarious *status quo* that had never been intended to continue as long as it actually did? [147]

Had the Assembly and its chief executive officer been able to define more firmly their policies regarding the "intermediate" issues, a great deal of uncertainty surrounding these troublesome questions would have been removed and their explosive nature tempered. With UNEF in operation, the Gaza area has been tranquil, border raids have ceased, and violence along the Egypt-Israel demarcation line has been ended. The Gulf of Aqaba and the territory surrounding it are no longer sites of hostile incidents. But the Emergency Force is a *temporary* mechanism, not a final solution to Arab-Israeli problems. An "unresolved peace" exists today; most particularly it is the vital issue of belligerency and of passage of Israeli ships through the Suez Canal that remains indeterminate and liable to produce another armed outbreak.

Certainly, the Assembly was cautious in its vague formulation of policy directives to the Emergency Force. The last resolution dealing with the functions of UNEF merely endorsed Hammarskjold's report of January 24, 1957, requested deployment of UNEF "on" the armistice demarcation line, and called for "the implementation of other measures as proposed in the Secretary-General's report. . . ." The term "on" the demarcation line was left undefined; "implementation of other measures" was also left obscure; no direct reference was made to stationing the Force at the entrance to the Gulf of Aqaba; nor was there mention of the length of time UNEF would serve in the Middle East.

Of course it may be said that the General Assembly's failure to clarify the role of UNEF and to insist on the settlement of certain issues simply reflects the facts of international life: the Assembly's directives to the Force represent the maximum area of agreement between Members. Indeed the Great Powers were themselves divided and in some instances of two minds. Hammarskjold was therefore compelled to move cautiously in attempting to interpret Assembly opinion. And, apparently, he did not feel free, despite the high degree of initiative left to him by the Assembly, to solicit for the Force that larger role which might have made UNEF a factor in promoting a general settlement.[148]

In sum, the mission of the United Nations Emergency Force was not completely clarified and the Assembly's resolutions left UNEF somewhat at the mercy of time and circumstance and daily events. The Emergency Force has not played a role in the *definitive* settlement of longstanding problems in the Middle East. Nonetheless, it has by its actions and its presence helped to avert further hostilities—possibly even an extended war—and to achieve an atmosphere of calm and quiet along the Egypt-Israel frontier. A series of sensitive questions have been settled *de facto,* if not *de jure: fedayeen* activity and border raids between Israel and Egypt have visibly diminished; the regular Egyptian Army has been kept from Gaza; the Straits of Tiran are open and the area near Sharm el Sheikh remains devoid of conflict. And UNEF remains, after all, of "great value as a background for efforts toward resolving . . . pending problems, although it is not in itself a means to that end."

Chapter Five

COMPOSITION, ORGANIZATION, CONTROL

The organization and structure of an international military force have long interested students and observers of world affairs, many of whom, at one time or another, have proposed schemes for the construction of a multinational army. Blueprints for such an organization have, in fact, often been elaborate and detailed. When the Secretary-General, however, was asked on November 4, 1956, to prepare a plan for an *emergency* international United Nations Force, it was necessary for him to consider carefully not only what means were available to him for this purpose, but also which principles of organization would be most efficient in practice and most acceptable to the world community at the time of immediate crisis.

AN INTERNATIONAL FORCE

In choosing the concept on the basis of which the Emergency Force would be developed, the Secretary-General had three courses before him.[1] It was possible for the United Nations to charge one country or a group of countries with the task of organizing a command, as the Organization had done during the Korean invasion in 1950.[2] At that time, the Security Council was anxious for assistance to *repel* the North Korean armed attack; as a result, there was need for considerable resources and a full-scale military organization. But the majority of states in the Assembly had no intention during the days of the Suez crisis of actually repelling by military means the Anglo-French-Israeli thrust into Egypt. There was no need for a powerful force. Furthermore, while in 1950 the United States had assumed the initiative in military action against North Korea by "neutralizing" Formosa and by sending the Seventh Fleet to the area of conflict, no comparable measures were undertaken in 1956; nor, indeed, would they have been possible as no ready forces were available anywhere for immediate action in the Middle East.

As a second possibility, the Emergency Force could have been established on the basis of agreement among a group of nations, later to be brought into an appropriate relationship with the United Nations. Britain and France had, in effect, proposed such an organization,[3] thus making the concept wholly unpalatable to the majority of United Nations Members. This possible form of organization had also been open to the criticism that it might hamper the Force from achieving real independence from the policies of any one group of nations.

The third possibility—the one actually proposed by the Secretary-General (in his report of November 6, 1956) and adopted by the Assembly—was to place the Force entirely under United Nations direction and control, to appoint a Commander who would be solely responsible to the Secretary-General and, through him, to the Assembly, and to adopt policies which would have a truly international nature and would leave the Commander independent of the authority of any one state. In making his proposal, the Secretary-General indicated that he based his view on the legal considerations created by the Assembly's decision of November 5, 1956, which established a United Nations Command and Chief of Command. This decision implied that the Assembly desired a force which would be created, recruited, and led by the United Nations alone.

Major General E. L. M. Burns of Canada, Chief of Staff of the United Nations Truce Supervision Organization, was appointed Chief of Command of the new emergency international force by the Assembly's resolution of November 5.[4] Having served with UNTSO for more than two years, Burns was familiar with the problems of the Middle East; and, as alternate delegate for Canada to the fourth session of the General Assembly, he had acquired considerable experience in dealing with United Nations affairs.[5] By the resolution of November 5, Burns was directed to recruit a limited number of officers from the observer corps of the United Nations Truce Supervision Organization or directly from various Member States other than Britain, France, the United States, the Soviet Union, or China.

This recruitment procedure affords an important indication of the character of the Force. . . . On the one hand, the independence of the Chief of Command in recruiting officers is recognized. On the other hand, the principle is established that the Force should be recruited from Member States other than the permanent members of the Security Council.[6]

There were many reasons, all political, for excluding the Great Powers from participation in the Force with respect to both officers and contingents. Britain and France, as invaders, were not to be associated with the enterprise nor deputized as United Nations policemen. Most of the Assembly delegates agreed on this point and Egypt, if pressed, would have insisted upon it. Moreover, "cold-war" antagonisms were to be kept free of this international operation: "few diplomats—even from the Arab States—wanted Soviet foot soldiers in the Middle East." [7] This was part of the United Nations policy of "preventive diplomacy"—an attempt at safeguarding neutral areas from the strife and dissension between the Russians and the West.

The "cold war" had, indeed, changed the earlier conception of United Nations military action which had relied primarily on great-power forces. In the days of the Charter's inception, all Member States agreed that the permanent members of the Council possessed leading responsibility for peace and security and, therefore, for collective action to achieve its goals. In 1956 these states were painfully at odds with one another; the clash of differences between them had their reverberations everywhere and influenced each event on the world scene. No "neutral" country would welcome embroilment in a cold-war issue; no "uncommitted" nation would receive with cordiality soldiers from the super-powers on its terrain. And thus the small or "middle-powers" themselves came to the rescue.

UNEF'S COMPONENTS

Anxious to establish the Force as soon as possible, the Secretary-General had proposed in his second report that self-contained national contingents "drawn from countries or groups of countries which can provide such troops without delay," be utilized for the Force. Considerable time and effort would be expended in joining together small groups of different nationalities if recruitment was to be on an individual basis; should some Member States provide sufficiently large units, however—units of battalion strength—organization of the Force would be rapid and efficient. In his approaches to governments for contributions, Hammarskjold endeavored "to build up a panel sufficiently broad to permit such a choice of units as would provide for a balanced composition in the Force." Additional planning and decisions on organization would "to a large extent have to depend on the judgment of the Chief of Command and his Staff." [8]

Twenty-four Members, on their own initiative, offered to contribute military forces to UNEF: Afghanistan, Brazil, Burma, Canada, Ceylon, Chile, Colombia, Czechoslovakia, Denmark, Ecuador, Ethiopia, Finland, India, Indonesia, Iran, Laos, New Zealand, Norway, Pakistan, Peru, Philippines, Rumania, Sweden, and Yugoslavia.[9] Ten of these offers—those of Brazil, Canada, Colombia, Denmark, Finland, India, Indonesia, Norway, Sweden, and Yugoslavia—were accepted to form a force of about 6,000 men. In selecting contingents, the Secretary-General excluded troop contributions from countries of the Middle East or from states which for whatever reason might be thought to have a special interest in the conflict situation.[10] He placed weight on such factors as the suitability of the contingents for the needs of the Force, their size and availability, the extent to which they would be self-contained, the undesirability of too great a variation in ordnance and basic equipment, and the goal of balanced composition. It was desirable to obtain as wide a geographical representation as possible and to take account of the sensitivities of the parties directly concerned, particularly Egypt, on whose territory the Force would operate.[11]

A difference of opinion existed, however, as to what constituted a "balanced composition" and as to Egypt's right to veto a choice of contingents for UNEF. In the Assembly, the delegate from the Philippines declared that except "for those who are actually in the controversy, countries who are not may contribute or *may insist on contributing* a part of their forces to this international police force." And, in determining the Force, he advised:

the need should be emphasized for avoiding any preponderance of any group—not only of any particular country—which may make the international police force suspect before the eyes of the world. It is therefore important that the balanced composition should not relate only to the size of the forces contributed by a country, but to the relative balance of the groups, taking into account the overt alignment of sympathies.[12]

As we have seen (Chapter III), comments on Egypt's role in choosing contingents for the Force have been numerous. Observers point out that Egypt was successful in rejecting the participation of Pakistan in the Emergency Force, in restricting Canadian participation to certain types of personnel, and in acquiring a Force consisting of nations sympathetic to her cause.[13] These assumptions are debatable. The Secretary-General readily accepted the offer of supporting units from Canada, but asked the Canadian government to hold in reserve the infantry battalion which it had proposed to contribute to UNEF. Apparently during the early days of the Force's operation, General Burns required reconnaissance, air, transport, administration, signal, engineering, and medical units as well as foot soldiers; furthermore, the similarity in dress of the Canadian battalion (the Queen's Own) to that of the British armed forces gave the government of Egypt cause for concern that there might be cases of mistaken identity and resulting incidents. In any case, a Canadian reconnaissance squadron with sixteen armored cars, after waiting at the UNEF staging area near Naples for several weeks, was admitted to Egypt in late March 1957; and, by September 15, the total Canadian personnel serving with UNEF were 1,172 in number, constituting one of the largest single national groups participating in the Force.[14]

In regard to the offer of assistance by Pakistan, it was apparently thought wise to reject that government's participation in UNEF in view of the critical utterances against the Egyptian government which had been made at the time by the government of Pakistan.

While the attitude of the Egyptian Government in these two cases was, undoubtedly, a factor influencing the Secretary-General's decision, his position would appear to have been that with many more offers made than were needed, it was unwise to accept an offer which might jeopardize the success of the whole operation unless it was the only way of meeting a particular need.[15]

Whatever the attitude of the host state, it is well to remember that UNEF soldiers, although integrated under United Nations command, are in practice—though not always in a legal sense—subject to the will of their own national governments. Consequently, any number of conceivable factors—Egyptian disapprobation, uneasy political developments on the world scene, adverse internal circumstances, an order to UNEF to take up arms against one or another state—might cause a contributing state to withdraw its armed forces from Egypt.[16] The United Nations Emergency Force does not, as a matter of policy, directly recruit individuals for service in its units. In the last analysis, the composition of UNEF is dependent upon the will of United Nations Members.

The size of the Force, however, was determined by the commander-in-chief's assessments of need, which were reviewed from time to time. Manpower needs of UNEF to perform the tasks assigned by the Assembly were estimated at approximately 6,000 men, and this goal was reached in early February 1957 by the arrival, in

Egypt, of the Brazilian contingent. Estimates were formed by weighing the following considerations: UNEF's needs on the basis of its functions and responsibilities (at first in the Suez Canal region and, later, in the Sinai Peninsula, the Gaza Strip and the Sharm el Sheikh areas); the desirability of balancing the Force in both geographical distribution and military organization; the comparative utility and efficiency, in the light of assessed needs, of the forces offered; and the relative availability and economy of transport for these troops, together with their equipment and vehicles.[17]

On September 15, 1957, the manpower size of each national contingent in the United Nations Emergency Force was as follows: [18]

Contingent	Officers	Other Ranks	Total
Brazil	44	501	545
Canada	113	1,059	1,172
Colombia	31	491	522
Denmark	25	399	424
Finland	15	240	255
India	27	930	957
Indonesia	37	545	582
Norway	71	427	498
Sweden	27	322	349
Yugoslavia	55	618	673
Total	445	5,532	5,977

The Indonesian contingent withdrew on September 12, 1957, and although the Commander emphasized in his reports that, for the task it was called upon to perform, UNEF's ground deployment was "very thin," the Finnish unit withdrew on December 5, 1957, and other contingents were reduced in strength. In August 1958, only 68 platoons (2,500 officers and men out of a total of 5,400) were available for patrolling and guard duties, the strength of each platoon varying from 20 to 40, all ranks. Since, necessarily, a substantial part of the Force (2,900 officers and men) was engaged in vital support functions, such as administration, signals, engineering, supply and transport, workshop, ordnance, medical, dental, postal, pay,

provost, and movement control, the Commander felt "that any reduction of the Force below its present numerical strength would
result in loss of effectiveness through inability to cover adequately
the long lines involved and lack of the necessary reserves." [19]

When the Colombian battalion withdrew on October 28, 1958, the
remaining contingents were increased in size, but after dispatch of
two companies from the Swedish battalion to the Congo in April
1961, the Force in its absence has had to operate at reduced strength,
and dispositions have had to be adjusted on a long-term basis. Again,
at the end of August 1961, the Secretary-General, the Commander
of the Force, and many delegations voiced the opinion that UNEF
could not effectively discharge its responsibilities with any less
strength then it had at that time.

The consolidated strength of the Force on August 22, 1962, was
5,133 men: [20]

Contingent	Officers	Other Ranks	Total
Brazil	40	590	630
Canada	82	863	945
Denmark	45	517	562
India	80	1,169	1,249
Norway	84	529	613
Sweden	33	391	424
Yugoslavia	68	642	710
Total	432	4,701	5,133

PRACTICAL ARRANGEMENTS AND ORGANIZATION

The military organization of the Emergency Force, later modified
to respond to further clarification of the functions of the Force, was
built around regimental combat teams. It was estimated that an
independent signals company (expanded to provide all necessary
communications facilities for UNEF headquarters and in the field),
headquarters, engineer, transport, shop repair, and medical personnel would be needed. Normal regimental weapons were issued to
the infantry, and a transport company, equipped to lift one infantry

battalion, was supplied to the Force. Each battalion was to be administratively self-contained. Furthermore, in view of the nature of the terrain and the tasks of the Force, an armored car squadron for reconnaissance work was considered desirable by the Commander, and a light air unit was thought essential for operations inside the UNEF operations area.[21]

Supporting facilities and personnel for the Force were voluntarily furnished by many nations. In addition to providing the staging area for the troops (Capodichino, near Naples), the Italian government supplied accommodations, "mountains of spaghetti and cooperation of a sort that is rare even in wartime."[22] Brazil, Canada, Italy, Switzerland, the United States, and Yugoslavia donated airlift and other transport. At the Secretary-General's request, normal flight services were curtailed by Swissair during the early days of recruitment and were made available for UNEF transport. After November 15, 1956, Swissair flew a regular service to Abu Suweir—the airfield near Ismailia which had been chosen by General Burns, in agreement with Egypt, for the preliminary landing of forces. Engineers, signal and medical units, and army services were volunteered by the Canadian government. The United States established a supply line to the forces in the field and Army "C" rations were flown to Naples and later to Egypt. A postage plan for the Force was devised and negotiated with the governments concerned. Questions of post-exchange supplies and recreation were answered. Dozens of problems, often requiring the aid of national governments, were in need of solution.

The practical arrangements involved in UNEF's creation and organization were intricate, and the actual details of assemblage had to be worked out step by step. The primary aim was to constitute the Force and land it in Egypt as quickly as possible. Pending final arrangements with the Egyptian government regarding UNEF's arrival, it was decided, with the consent of Italy, to use Capodichino airport as a staging area. This arrangement expedited the flow of UNEF soldiers and matériel to the Middle East. United Nations

Headquarters in New York made the arrangements for the initial movement of troops from their home countries to Italy. The United States provided the transport. Information regarding size of forces and equipment was sent by the contributing states to headquarters, which relayed it to United States Air Force authorities, who, in turn, transmitted final details to the military representatives of the governments concerned. Throughout, speed was a propelling factor in planning the United Nations Emergency Force.

Secretary-General Hammarskjold's own staff worked round the clock on these numberless arrangements.

Almost at once there came into being on the thirty-eighth floor of the United Nations a sort of informal military council that met daily. It was an exercise in pure goodwill. The military attachés of the accepted nations telephoned to ask how they could help, and were at once roped in. . . . Military phraseology, the talk of "second echelons" and "third-line maintenance," proved at first a little mystifying to ears attuned to diplomatic language. But the soldiers understood each other, even if one was a mustachioed Indian brigadier raised at Sandhurst, another a Colombian major of Scottish descent, a third a Yugoslav general of the partisans, and a fourth a . . . [general] from the forests of Finland.[23]

What were the initial problems? Forests of mild to frigid temperature were the natural habitat of soldiers from Finland. How were they to face the desert in Sinai with their customary clothing and equipment? Conversely, the troops from Colombia were seasoned to tropical temperature. Would not winter clothing be needed in Egypt during the nights of desert winds? UNEF required a distinguishing mark: American-style helmets would be sprayed light blue in color and issued to the troops. The turbaned Sikhs of the Indian group—would they wear the blue helmet or beret? Only wood is burnt in Swedish Army stoves. From where would fuel be brought?[24]

Swiftly and determinedly, these issues were tackled and troops were put on the way. Having started preparations while still in Jerusalem, a selected group of military observers—temporarily on

leave from the United Nations Truce Supervision Organization—
rapidly formed the nucleus of a UNEF headquarters staff, entered
Cairo on November 12, 1956, and, together with Secretariat personnel, made provision for receiving and billeting the first group of
United Nations soldiers. The early procurement, storage, and issue
of necessary supplies and equipment were also arranged as was the
use of Abu Suweir for the purpose of an arrival depot. Officers of
the national contingents, upon arrival, undertook the duties shouldered by the group of UNTSO personnel and the latter returned to
their former posts.

Movement by air seemed the most efficient means of transporting
contingents to Egypt, but some difficulties were encountered regarding restrictions on the arrival and departure of flights and regarding the nationalities of the aircraft carrying the soldiers. During
the early days of the troop airlift to Abu Suweir, Swissair executed
the flights; later, the Royal Canadian Air Force, with some aid from
the Italian Air Force, undertook this task. The Yugoslav reconnaissance battalion and the Canadian and Brazilian contingents, however, traveled to Egypt by ship, and all heavy equipment for UNEF
was, likewise, transported by sea.

Upon arrival in Egypt, UNEF was faced with a shortage of vehicles; this difficulty was, at first, alleviated by the purchase and
rental of these supplies from UNRWA. Later, shortages mounted
and, although some further purchases were made from the British
forces, UNEF's transportation problems did not completely end until
the arrival, in January 1957, of vehicles ordered from the United
States. This seems to have been the major shortage suffered by
UNEF; other problems, which inevitably came up, were handled as
they arose.[25]

The periodic movement of soldiers to and from their national
homes has created constant demand for air and ship service and required considerable planning. Some communication services exist
within the area of operations and are handled by UNEF military
personnel. Arrangements for traffic to and from New York, Geneva

and other points is in the hands of United Nations Field Service personnel. A number of problems involving different standards of performance and types of equipment have created some difficulty. Indeed, an effective and cohesive communications pattern for the Force was hard to achieve.

A good part of the supplies and equipment needed by UNEF is furnished by the participating governments directly to their own contingents. Otherwise, United Nations Headquarters in New York arranges for those supplies that can be economically obtained through its own procurement channels, or the UNEF supply office in Italy arranges shipment from military sources in Europe with which the United Nations has standing arrangements. A fourth source of supply is local purchase.

Experience soon indicated the desirability of limiting the number of countries providing support matériel, "in view of the difficulties in coordinating and controlling a number of relatively small units having different arms and equipment, requiring varying diets and speaking different languages." [26] To further efficiency and to simplify organization, the Supply Depot and the Service Institute were made the responsibility of the Indian contingent; Canada and India supplied units for transport, the Provost Marshal, and Signals; medical needs were provided by the Norwegian and Canadian governments; and members of the group from Canada were given charge of the Ordnance Depot and Workshop, the Base Post Office, Engineering, the Dental Unit, Movement Control and Air Support.

Position and assignment of units were changed from time to time. Characteristic of the deployment of the Force were the positions held on September 15, 1957, when the Danish-Norwegian,* Brazilian, Indian, and Colombian battalions, and a Swedish company were to be found along the armistice demarcation, Gaza Strip line; one Canadian reconnaissance squadron and one Yugoslav reconnaissance battalion were placed along the international frontier, East

* By voluntary agreement, the Danish and Norwegian contingents constitute a single battalion, commanded in rotation by officers of the two countries.

Central Sinai Line; the Finnish company patrolled the Sharm el Sheikh and Ras Nasrani area; the UNEF headquarters staff was stationed in Gaza town, as was the Swedish battalion (minus one company) and the Norwegian medical company; at Rafah, Canadian and Indian administrative and other support units went about their tasks in the UNEF maintenance area together with a Finnish guard detachment; a Royal Canadian Air Force communication flight, consisting of 33 officers and 150 other ranks, was located at Naples, where a UNEF liaison staff and a movement control detachment also operated; [27] El Arish was the location of another Canadian communication flight (made up of 13 officers and 45 other ranks), a small detachment of the Brazilian battalion for guard duty, and a group of 21 officers and men for movement control; a security guard of one platoon, on monthly rotation among contingents, as well as a permanent movement control and post detachment (required for post clearance and storage) were deployed at Port Said; and at Beirut (Lebanon) 19 officers and men of UNEF made up a leave center detachment.[28] The entire area patrolled by the Emergency Force, consisting of the perimeter of the Gaza Strip (from the Mediterranean in the north to the international frontier in the south), the international frontier (extending from the sea southwards to the Gulf of Aqaba), and the distance from the northern end of the Gulf to Sharm el Sheikh, measures 460 kilometres. The Assembly asked that the Force be stationed "on the Egyptian-Israel armistice demarcation line," [29] but to date Israel has not given her consent to deployment of UNEF on Israeli territory.

UNEF's swift and efficient operation was facilitated by the presence in the Middle East of the United Nations Truce Supervision Organization and the United Nations Relief and Works Agency for Palestine Refugees. Not only was valuable assistance rendered by these groups through their personnel, facilities, and extensive experience in the area, but the chief officers of the Emergency Force were recruited from the ranks of UNTSO, and the tasks of the Force in the

Gaza Strip were facilitated by UNRWA's substantial assistance through aid to both the refugee and nonrefugee population.[30]

It might be mentioned again that the personnel and facilities of the United Nations Secretariat were utilized to the maximum:

The Secretariat, as a result of long and well-tested experience, could provide UNEF with efficient services and personnel in such necessary fields as administration, financial procedures, personnel recruitment, legal and political advice, public information, procurement and supply and communications. High-level responsibility for the organization and direction of the operation was facilitated by the principle of flexibility in the use of senior staff.[31]

One of the Under-Secretaries for Special Political Affairs was placed in charge of direct supervision of UNEF's organization and operation and was asked to handle all administrative actions relating to it.[32] In one way or another, every major unit of the Secretariat participated in the total task. Experience which had been gained by international civil servants in administration of missions abroad was particularly valuable here, for well-tried procedures could be put to good use in serving UNEF. But countless smaller matters essential to the success of the operation—the arrangements for identity cards, visas, passports, and inoculations, the clearances needed to fly over the territory of a number of countries—were also efficiently and expertly handled by Secretariat personnel.[33]

CONTROL AND LEADERSHIP

Ultimate responsibility for all arrangements rested, however, with the Secretary-General and, indeed, his role in the creation and functioning of the UN Emergency Force was extremely significant. Resolution upon resolution of the Assembly enlisted Hammarskjold's aid in reporting on compliance, in arranging with the parties concerned for the implementation of the cease-fire, and in halting shipment of forces and arms to the area. With the assistance of Major General Burns and the military observers of UNTSO, the Secretary-

General was requested to obtain withdrawal of all forces behind the armistice lines and later was asked to continue securing the complete withdrawal of all Israeli forces from Egypt.

But it was especially in regard to the United Nations Emergency Force itself that the Secretary-General had such remarkable importance. Before the birth of the Force, Hammarskjold canvassed its feasibility and potentiality in discussions with Lester Pearson and other representatives (see Chapter II). Pearson, at first, did not envisage a United Nations force such as ultimately evolved; rather, he favored a UN police force composed essentially of British and French troops in order that the Anglo-French military action would be placed under United Nations control and be made to serve different ends than those initially pursued. This idea was soon dropped and the idea of the force as it came to be established emerged from further talks. At a luncheon in the Secretary-General's thirty-eighth-floor apartment, attended by Lester Pearson, Andrew Cordier, and the Secretary-General, it was agreed that Pearson should present the idea of the Force to the Assembly, along with a number of guidelines that had also been agreed upon. Dag Hammarskjold, however, was decisively one of the coauthors of the Force. Moreover, in complying with the Assembly's request on November 4, 1956, to submit to it a plan within forty-eight hours for the setting up of a United Nations Force, Hammarskjold's plan became the basis upon which UNEF was built.

In its resolutions pertaining to UNEF, the General Assembly delegated a remarkable degree of power to its chief executive officer. Consultations with Member delegations were extensive prior to the drafting of his reports, but Hammarskjold, nevertheless, remained the chief architect. His mandates endowed him with considerable freedom and, indeed, the Secretary-General's power, throughout the Middle East crisis, to interpret as he saw fit the vague resolutions of the Assembly and its 81 delegates was very wide. Most of the Assembly's resolutions on the United Nations Emergency Force were broad and undefined; this was not because the situation was so obscure that Members wished to give Hammarskjold wide latitude in their interpretation, but because each resolution represented the highest common factor of Member policy at the time in question. Hammarskjold was well aware of the situation, noted that Assembly decisions on the Force were "in more general terms than is customary," and asked that "a margin of confidence . . . be left to those who will carry the responsibility for putting the decisions of the General Assembly into effect." [34] It seemed from the beginning that the "tactical diplomacy" President Eisenhower had called for to resolve the conflict would devolve mainly upon the Secretary-General's shoulders.[35] Thus, it is interesting to note in this connection Ahmed S. Bokhari's suggestion that "the more single-minded and determined the General Assembly, the more it will have to rely on the executive for the implementation of its decisions and even the finer interpretation of its intentions." [36]

Most of the principles basic to UNEF seem to reflect Hammarskjold's influence (see Chapter IV). His general attitude to the crisis was frank condemnation of the Anglo-French-Israeli invasion, which he considered contrary to the principles of the Charter. Although aware that "the Secretary-General has the duty to maintain his usefulness by avoiding public stands on conflicts between Member nations . . . ," Hammarskjold felt that he must also be a "servant of the principles of the Charter" and the aims of the Charter "must ultimately determine what for him is right and wrong." [37] An act of armed force, a military intervention by three Members of the world organization on the territory of another was a wrongful act not to be justified by the policies of any single nation or people.

Secretary-General Dag Hammarskjold, more than any single individual, was responsible for UNEF's success. Quick to embrace the entire scheme, diligent and firm in bringing about its implementation, sensitive to the various strains of opinion in the Assembly, Dag Hammarskjold harnessed all his admirable skills and aptitudes to the task at hand. His work during the crisis was of such distinction and integrity as to leave a marked impression on the pattern of organization and leadership in the General Assembly. At the same time, he increased the prestige of the Organization throughout the world. Hammarskjold very nearly approached the role of Foreign Minister of a nation state. In this role, he brought the United Nations to new heights of activity and achievement.

In effect, a series of difficult and responsible tasks were given into the Secretary-General's hands and admirably executed. By the terms of resolutions 1000 and 1001, the Secretary-General was asked to undertake, together with the Chief of Command, recruitment of contingents from various Member States for the projected police force; was invited to take all administrative measures necessary to the establishment of the Command; was requested to decide with Major General Burns questions of size, composition, and organization of the Force; was appointed Chairman of the Advisory Committee on UNEF; was authorized to issue all regulations and instructions essential to the effective functioning of the Emergency Force, following consultation with the Advisory Committee, and "to take all other administrative and executive action." Succeeding resolutions charged him with certain tasks in the realm of financial and budgetary arrangements for UNEF. Undoubtedly, then, the Secretary-General was the chief executive of the United Nations Emergency Force as well as its leader, pilot, and guide.

One authority declares, however, that the responsibilities assigned to Secretary-General Dag Hammarskjold by the General Assembly at the emergency session in 1956, and later at the eleventh regular session, not only reflected general confidence placed in him by United Nations Members, but also were the products of emergency and circumstance:

The temporary break-up of the traditional United States, British, and French close consultation and initiative in the Assembly, the interposition of a presidential election in the United States, the particular relationship of the countries of western Europe to the Middle Eastern crisis, and the substantial increase in UN membership during the preceding fifteen months with a shift in the balance of political power toward the Asian-

African group, all played their part in setting the stage for the initiative Mr. Hammarskjold was asked to assume. It is very clear that he could not have continued to carry the load placed upon him had he not worked in the closest consultation with Member states. In particular, he could not have carried it without the very active support of the United States.[38]

Since the United States was deeply anxious to settle the crisis without causing further rift between itself and its NATO allies and without producing direct Soviet interference in the Middle East, it may well have welcomed the opportunity to place responsibility for solution of the matter in neutral and international hands. Furthermore, the United States could not itself have taken the initiative in the planning and organization of the United Nations Force without incurring the suspicion of the Communist states and the Afro-Asian bloc. Early in the discussions concerning the Egyptian invasion, the principle was enunciated of excluding the permanent members of the Security Council from the Emergency Force operation. In the hands of one or more of the Great Powers, it may be questioned whether an international police force for the Middle East would ever have been possible.

Despite his extensive powers, the Secretary-General was, of course, ultimately subject to the authority of the Assembly and was required to act in consultation with an Advisory Committee, the establishment of which Mr. Hammarskjold had himself proposed. This Committee was made up of one representative from Brazil, Canada, Ceylon, Colombia, India, Norway, and Pakistan.[39] In addition to assisting him in his plans for the Force, the Committee was empowered to solicit reports from the Secretary-General and "to request, through the usual procedures, the convening of the General Assembly." [40] It could also give notice to the Assembly "whenever matters arise which, in its opinion, are of such urgency and importance as to require consideration by the General Assembly itself." This authority was, however, never invoked.

The Advisory Committee held meetings whenever matters requiring discussion arose or whenever advice was sought by the Secretary-

General or, occasionally, to keep members of the Committee informed on current events. More particularly, consultation was sought in those matters which the Assembly had indicated would be specifically within the Committee's realm, such as the Regulations of the Force, the policy of the Force with regard to self-defense, and the issue of medals. A free exchange of views took place in closed meetings "where advice can be sought and given." [41] Final decisions were made by the Secretary-General, who was Chairman of the Committee and chief executive of UNEF. Dissenting opinions were not registered by formal vote, but minutes of the proceedings were kept and held confidential.

Hammarskjold noted that this arrangement proved highly useful and that it might well provide a laudable precedent for the future:

Extensive operations with serious political implications, regarding which, for practical reasons, executive authority would need to be delegated to the Secretary-General, require close collaboration with authorized representatives of the General Assembly. However, it would be undesirable for the collaboration to be given such a form as to lead to divided responsibilities or to diminished efficiency in the operation. The method chosen by the General Assembly in the case of UNEF seems the most appropriate one if such risks are to be avoided.[42]

From his statement, we may assume that the Secretary-General did not favor endowing the Committee with greater power than it possessed, though a group of this nature—neutral, carefully selected, trusted by the Assembly—could conceivably be given greater authority in deciding some of the ambivalent questions concerning the Force. A committee similar to UNEF's was established for the UN Force in the Congo.

"Full command authority" in respect to the operation of the Force is vested in the Chief of Command.[43] Major General E. L. M. Burns, of Canada, held this post until early December 1959. Upon his resignation, Major General P. S. Gyani, of India, was named as his successor.[44] Appointed directly by the Assembly, the Commander remains at all times responsible to that body or the Security Council or both, but his instructions and guidance stem from the Secretary-General, since executive responsibility for UNEF's operation is entrusted to that office. From the beginning the Commander has acted, within the limits of his post, as the principal agent of the Secretary-General in the area of operation.[45]

Supervisor of all activities of the Emergency Force, director of operations, UNEF's commander-in-chief is operationally responsible for the performance of all functions assigned to UNEF by the United Nations, and for the deployment and assignment of troops placed at the disposal of the Force. Acting in consultation with the Secretary-General, he is empowered to arrange for the provision of facilities, supplies, and auxiliary services. It is he who established the Headquarters for the Force, recruited officers for the Command from Member governments, designated the chain of command, and, through the Command, assigned all members of the Force. The Commander, moreover, is entitled to issue orders "not inconsistent with resolutions of the General Assembly relating to the Force" or with the Regulations for the United Nations Emergency Force. He has general responsibility for the good order of the Force, for military police, for billeting and provision of food, for negotiation with governments and private suppliers concerning premises and supplies. Arrangements for providing transportation, equipment, supporting units, and public information, all fall within the Commander's functions.[46] "The position of Commander combines leadership of the Force with the role of representative of the United Nations." [47]

Assisting the Secretary-General, his staff, and the Chief of Command during the early stages of planning, was a UNEF Military Staff comprising the military representatives of those states whose offers of troops for the Emergency Force were initially accepted by the Secretary-General—Canada, Colombia, Denmark, Finland, India, Norway, Sweden, and Yugoslavia. With established headquarters in New York City, this group worked in close cooperation with members of the Secretariat. It provided, under the informal chairmanship of a Finnish Major General (who was temporarily selected as personal advisor to Hammarskjold on UNEF military matters), expert planning and advice on matters of military organization, transport, equipment and logistics, and helped to expedite dispatch of troops from their home countries. The Secretary-General declared that in future operations of the UNEF-type, similar assistance and cooperation by delegations and governments would be essential to success.[48]

The military staff organization of the United Nations Emergency Force comprises officers from each contingent and has a Chief of Staff at the head who acts in place of the Commander when the latter is absent. Personnel, Operations, and Logistics sections make up the Headquarters staff. In addition, a group of specialized officers render services to the Commander in particular fields and, in some cases, coordinate, supervise, or carry out functional activities. Advice and assistance is given to the Commander, who issues instructions and directions to the national contingents. These contingents are self-contained, each with its own national commander, who cannot be changed without consultation between the chief Commander of UNEF and the appropriate authorities of the contributing government. The commander of each unit is militarily subordinate to the commander-in-chief, but is permitted to communicate with his government on questions concerning the contingent.

Liaison representation is maintained by the Emergency Force in Cairo, Tel Aviv,[49] Beirut, and Pisa, with most of the officers detailed for this duty drawn from UNTSO. A number of participating governments have also assigned liaison officers to the task of representing their interests in the area of operation and serving as a point of contact for them, but these officers are not formally part of the Force.[50] The liaison activity is extremely useful in keeping those states with a direct interest in the operation not only closely informed as to developments, but also perpetually in contact with UNEF, so that United Nations presence in the Middle East is continually in evidence.

UNEF represents a fusion of military and civilian activities which the Commander, who is the only officer operating in both a military and civilian capacity, must direct and coordinate.[51] Requiring considerable knowledge and understanding, this task is a difficult one for the Commander as well as for senior military and civilian officers. In day-to-day practice, the Chief of Staff sets the tone for civil-military relationships; but the possibility of friction appears to be always present, for differences of background, training, and discipline are sources of constant difficulty. Some clearly defined areas, such as military and air operations, health services, military police, legal affairs, or public information, give cause for little military-civilian misunderstanding. Problems have, however, arisen in regard to logistics, finance and accounting, radio communications, transportation and travel, and the issuance of directives and instructions covering general administration. These are the areas where civilian-military responsibilities are not sharply differentiated. Future military operations would, in all probability, benefit greatly from knowledge obtained in grappling with these difficulties.

Indeed, many of the arrangements made for UNEF in regard to composition, organization, and leadership have established precedents which will, undoubtedly, be looked to in future situations involving use by the United Nations of a para-military task force. In his summary study on the Emergency Force, the Secretary-General selected certain points in this realm which he considered especially worthy of attention.

The principles which had been applied to UNEF's composition "should be considered as essential for any stand-by arrangements." [52] The prevailing rule was that units from the permanent members of the Security Council as well as from countries with a special interest in the situation which had called for international action, should be excluded from participation in the Force. Recruitment of personnel should be undertaken in consultation with the host state, but a serious difference of opinion between the United Nations and the country in which the Force was to function would be a matter for political negotiation.

Appointment by the Assembly of a Commander for the Force responsible directly to the Assembly, dependent upon instructions from the Secretary-General, and possessed of duties which are administratively integrated with the United Nations Organization has, in experience, proved to be highly practical and politically of decisive importance.

Thus, a United Nations operation should always be under a leadership established by the General Assembly or the Security Council, or on the basis of delegated authority by the Secretary-General, so as to make it directly responsible to one of the main organs of the United Nations, while integrated with the Secretariat in an appropriate form.[53]

UNEF's Advisory Committee, as we have noted, has proved useful and may be taken as model for succeeding endeavors. On the basis of these and other principles, it might prove possible to make arrangements with governments for prompt provision—on an emergency basis and in response to a special appeal from the Assembly or Council—of men and matériel to be used by the United Nations in para-military operations. Otherwise, Hammarskjold was somewhat reluctant in his summary study to set forth the UNEF experience as a future guide in matters of organization and administrative detail.

In view of the great diversity likely to characterize the experience in practice of using United Nations units within the scope of this report, it is impossible to enunciate any principles for organizational arrangements at Headquarters or in the host country that should be made in anticipation of each case.[54]

This caution seems, in truth, unjustified. Since the arrangements which were made for UNEF have proved valuable and efficient, why would not similar operations in the future rely upon tested experience?

Indeed, the organization and rapid convocation of the second international force in UN history were invaluably promoted by the experience of the United Nations Emergency Force. The Secretary-General's first step in constituting the UN force for the Congo in the summer of 1960 was to send ten military officers, drawn from the United Nations Truce Supervision Organization, to the troubled African state. On July 15, 1960—one day after the Security Council's decision—the first detachments of United Nations troops arrived in Léopoldville. Many of the experts and officials who had been concerned with the UNEF operation were mobilized to aid Hammarskjold in setting up ONUC. Ralph Bunche was foremost in this group and was on the spot at the time of the outbreak of hostilities; he had been sent by the UN to the area to survey the possibilities of international assistance to the Congo. Brigadier I. J. Rikhe of India, former Chief of Staff of the United Nations Emergency Force, was invited to serve as the Secretary-General's military adviser at UN Headquarters. Virgil deAngelis, administrative officer in charge of the staging area for UNEF in Naples during 1956, headed a group of advisers and officers sent to Kano, Nigeria, the staging area for the Congo airlift. And, Major General Carl Carlsson von Horn, Chief of Staff of the United Nations Truce Supervision Organization (and, as such, in close contact with the work of UNEF), was named commander-in-chief of the UN troops in Africa.

Again, as with UNEF, the permanent members of the Security Council were excluded from participation in the Force. The general preference was that the enterprise consist mainly of African soldiers (contingents from Ghana, Guinea, Tunisia, Morocco, Ethiopia, and the Federation of Mali were drawn into service). However, the principle of universality was again applied so that Swedish, Irish, and Canadian troops were also utilized in considerable numbers. By September 11, 1960, twenty-two countries had contributed troops, staff officers, and military technicians to bring the military strength of ONUC to 18,800 men.

Since the need for a para-military international force similar to UNEF and ONUC may arise again in the future, it would be useful

to establish a nucleus of military experts at United Nations Headquarters to keep under review such arrangements as may be made
by governments of Member States to meet possible appeals for UN
military or para-military aid. Such a group would not only extend
advice and help at a time when a new international military operation is being constituted, but, by continuous consultation and communication with governments regarding use of their forces by the
United Nations, would promote the cause of a permanent international army. Thus, as Lester Pearson has declared:

The first step would seem to be to create a permanent mechanism by
which units of the armed forces of member countries could be endowed
with the authority of the United Nations and made available at short
notice for supervisory police duties.[55]

One task of the standing group of military experts would be to help
create a permanent police force.

But the Secretary-General, sympathetic as he was to the idea of a
nucleus of experts, concluded after the Suez experience that creation
of such a standing group "at the present time" would probably be
premature. Henceforth,

Were a more far-reaching understanding than I have indicated to prove
possible, the matter obviously would have to be reconsidered and submitted again in appropriate form to the General Assembly, which then
might consider the organizational problem. Pending such a development
later, the present working rule, in my view, should be that the Secretariat,
while undertaking the soundings mentioned above and the necessary continuing contacts with the Governments, should not take any measures beyond keeping the situation under constant review, so as to be able to act
expeditiously, if a decision by the General Assembly or the Security Council should call for prompt action.[56]

The Secretary-General's views on UNEF and a future force have
come to exert a mighty influence and will not be easily disregarded.
Indeed, his role in the Middle East crisis helped to raise his office
to one of unprecedented stature and to inspire new confidence in the

United Nations Organization. In the light of subsequent criticism of Hammarskjold in regard to his Congo policy,[57] we may ask, however, whether the Secretary-General's success in the Middle East was ultimately influenced not only by the good will of the states concerned in the crisis, but by the good will of the "super-powers," as well. The Soviet Union's criticism of UNEF was always perfunctory and never expressed itself in attack upon the Secretary-General. Its tacit, though possibly reluctant, approval of the Force may, therefore, be assumed. Summarily, then, UNEF and its controlling officers may be said to be dependent for smooth operation and successful enterprise upon the feelings toward them of the Soviet Union and the United States.

Chapter Six

STATUS IN INTERNATIONAL LAW

The exceptional character and specific objectives of the United Nations Emergency Force have necessitated special regulation of the legal status of the Force. As a novel experiment in the international field, new legal questions arose with each phase of UNEF's deployment and were regulated mostly by means of bilateral agreements between the United Nations and the state in question. Other arrangements were devised through mutually acceptable working procedures.

Authorized by the Assembly to take all administrative and executive actions which might be essential to the effective functioning of UNEF, the Secretary-General, after consultation with the Advisory Committee, negotiated and concluded an agreement with the government of Egypt concerning the status of the Force in its territory.[1] He also made formal a number of arrangements between the UN and contributing states by an exchange of letters with each of these nations on June 21, 1957, in which he referred to the guiding principles and policies adopted on the status of the Force.[2] These documents together with the Convention on the Privileges and Immunities of the United Nations [3] and the Regulations for the United Nations Emergency Force [4] embody the essential rules, orders, instructions, and practices governing UNEF's legal order.

UNEF'S POSITION AND RIGHTS

As a subsidiary organ of the United Nations governed by Article 22 of the Charter, the United Nations Emergency Force is entitled, under Article 105, to all privileges and immunities necessary for the achievement of its purposes in the territories of Member States. Enumeration of these rights and prerogatives is set forth in the General Convention on the Privileges and Immunities of the United Nations to which Egypt acceded on September 17, 1948. Article II, Section 2, of this Convention, which stipulates that the "United Nations, its property and assets wherever located and by whomsoever held, shall enjoy immunity from every form of legal process except as in any particular case it has expressly waived its immunity," directly covers the Emergency Force. The Agreement with Egypt on the status of the Force unequivocally emphasizes this point. UNEF, therefore, possesses immunity from suit and cannot be made a respondent in a proceeding before a national court. Its independence in the exercise of its functions is assured.[5] Furthermore, provisions of Article II, Section 2, of the General Convention are declared to apply to "the property, funds and assets of Participating States used in Egypt in connection with the national contingents serving in the United Nations Emergency Force."[6] As a result, no contributing state may be sued or involved in legal suit in regard to any of its contingents or equipment. Still another privilege of the Force includes the right to import—free of duty—equipment, provisions, and supplies.

The immunities granted to UNEF as an international institution derive from the immunities of the United Nations itself. The legal status of the Emergency Force, like that of the Organization, seems to be based on the functional principle: complete independence from the local authority is necessary for UNEF to perform its international functions. In regard to arrangements concerning criminal and civil jurisdiction, the status agreement of February 8 states that they "are made having regard to the *special functions* of the Force and to the interests of the United Nations, and not for the personal benefit of the members of the Force."[7]

UNEF's presence was accepted by Egypt in the "area of operations," which includes the theater where the Force is deployed, its installations and premises, its communications and supply. Head-

quarters, camps, and other premises necessary for the accommodation of the Force and the performance of its functions were provided
by the Egyptian government in agreement with the Commander.
"Without prejudice to the fact that all such premises remain Egyptian territory, they shall be inviolable and subject to the exclusive
control and authority of the Commander, who alone may consent to
the entry of officials to perform duties on such premises."[8] The
freedom of movement of the Force was also agreed upon between
the government of Egypt and Major General Burns. UN soldiers are
exempt from passport and immigration regulations.[9] They enjoy
within their area of operation unrestricted freedom to communicate
by radio, telephone, telegraph, or other means, and the right to their
own postal services.[10] Members of the Force normally wear the
uniform prescribed by the Commander; their equipment, especially vehicles, vessels, and aircraft, carries distinctive United Nations
markings. The United Nations flag and emblem are displayed at
headquarters, camps, posts or other places designated by the Commander.[11] Use of roads, waterways, port facilities, air fields, and
railroads by the Force is allowed without the payment of dues, taxes,
or tolls.[12]

Extremely beneficial, indeed essential, to the operation of UNEF,
was Egyptian agreement to assist the Force, upon the request of the
Commander, in acquiring necessary provisions, supplies, services and
equipment from local sources. The government of Egypt was also
helpful in making available local currency at a favorable rate of exchange. Without such essential cooperation—cooperation which included such practical matters as obtaining water, electricity, and
other utilities [13]—an international military force would be substantially hampered, if not totally hindered, in discharging its duties.

PRIVILEGES AND IMMUNITIES

Since Articles 19 and 27 of the General Convention on the Privileges and Immunities of the United Nations were made applicable
to the Commander of UNEF, Major General Burns and his family
enjoyed "the privileges and immunities, exemptions and facilities ac-

corded to diplomatic envoys, in accordance with international law." [14] These prerogatives are the same as those enjoyed by the Secretary-General and all Under Secretaries-General and include those rights granted to all United Nations officials: immunity from legal process in respect of words spoken or written and all acts of an official nature; exemption from taxation on salaries and emoluments; right to import free of duty all furniture and effects.[15] Furthermore, the Commander's immunity from jurisdiction covers the acts of his private life, the inviolability for his person, effects, papers, and correspondence; [16] and when traveling on United Nations *laissez-passer* in pursuit of United Nations business, he is granted the same facilities as are accorded to diplomatic envoys.[17]

Officers serving with the United Nations Command are, on the other hand, entitled to coverage of Article VI of the Convention which applies to "experts performing missions for the United Nations." [18] To these officers are extended

such privileges and immunities as are necessary for the independent exercise of their functions during the period of their missions. . . . In particular they shall be accorded: (a) immunity from personal arrest or detention . . . (b) in respect of words spoken or written and acts done by them in the course of the performance of their mission, immunity from legal process of every kind . . . (c) inviolability for all papers and documents. . . .[19]

Members of the Secretariat serving with the Force are entitled to protection under Article V and VII which designate them as "officials of the United Nations" and grant them, *inter alia*, immunity from all legal process connected with their official work.[20] Right to immunity in respect of official acts provided in Section 18 (a) of the Convention on Privileges and Immunities extends to locally recruited personnel as well.

UNEF: AN INTERNATIONAL INSTITUTION

In the Regulations for the United Nations Emergency Force issued by the Secretary-General pursuant to the Assembly resolution of November 7, 1956, the international character of the Force is stressed. Although members of UNEF remain in their national service, they are, during the period of their assignment to the United Nations Command, international personnel under the authority of the Commander. Therefore, members of the UN Force are called upon to discharge their functions and regulate their conduct with the interest of the United Nations only in view.[21] This requires members of the Force to "exercise the utmost discretion in regard to all matters relating to their duties and functions" and to refrain from communicating "to any person any information known to them by reason of their position with the Force which has not been made public, except in the course of their duties or by authorization of their commander." [22] It also entails the duty "to respect the law and regulations of a Host State and to refrain from any activities of a political character in a Host State." [23] UNEF personnel may receive instructions *only* from the Commander and the chain of command designated by him. They are still subject, however, to the military rules and regulations of their respective national states, a fact which does not derogate from their responsibilities as components of the Force. Acceptance by a UNEF soldier of any honor, decoration, favor, gift, or remuneration incompatible with the individual's status and functions as a member of the Force is not permissible. Finally, UNEF is required to observe the principles and spirit of the general international conventions applicable to the conduct of military personnel.

The commander-in-chief has general responsibility for the good order of the Force, but the commanders of the national contingents exercise disciplinary authority within their own units. While members of UNEF have thus to perform their duties and regulate their conduct with care and caution, they are entitled to legal protection from the United Nations "and shall be regarded as agents of the United Nations for the purpose of such protection." [24]

As part of a body exclusively international in its responsibilities, personnel of the Emergency Force assume obligations similar to those of the "international civil servants" of the Secretariat. UNEF's

Staff Regulations actually contain stipulations for the police force similar in spirit to Article 100 of the Charter which applies to the United Nations Secretariat:

1. In the performance of their duties the Secretary-General and the staff shall not seek or receive instructions from any government or from any other authority external to the Organization. They shall refrain from any action which might reflect on their position as international officials responsible to the Organization.

2. Each Member of the United Nations undertakes to respect the exclusively international character of the responsibilities of the Secretary-General and the staff and not to seek to influence them in the discharge of their responsibilities.

Likewise, Article 1 (4) of the Secretariat's Staff Regulations contains provisions which, in their fundamental resemblance to those embodied in UNEF's rules, might well apply to the Emergency Force as well:

Members of the Secretariat shall conduct themselves at all times in a manner befitting their status as international civil servants. They shall not engage in any activity that is incompatible with the proper discharge of their duties with the United Nations. They shall avoid any action and in particular any kind of public pronouncement which may adversely reflect on their status, or on the integrity, independence and impartiality which are required by that status. While they are not expected to give up their national sentiments or their political and religious convictions, they shall at all times bear in mind the reserve and tact incumbent upon them by reason of their international status.[25]

Like the staff of the Secretariat, members of UNEF, also international personnel, owe their entire responsibility with respect to official duties to the United Nations; their international responsibility takes precedence over national obligations. Ideally they are to adopt a spirit of international loyalty and outlook:

The international outlook required of the international civil servant is an awareness made instinctive by habit of the needs, emotions and prejudices of the people of differently-circumstanced countries, as they are felt and expressed by the peoples concerned, accompanied by a capacity for weighing those frequently imponderable elements in a judicial manner before reaching any decision to which they are relevant.[26]

Following upon this international loyalty, flowing from the integrity of an international organ, is the confidence in which the organ is held by the majority of states. UNEF seems to have gained that confidence. And yet its essential independence or international character is not quite complete: for UNEF soldiers, since they constitute self-contained units of national contingents, are subject to withdrawal upon the order of their own government; [27] and the operation of the entire Force is, in all probability, dependent upon the will of the host state.

CRIMINAL AND CIVIL JURISDICTION

Differing from the Secretariat Staff, however, members of UNEF are subject to the exclusive jurisdiction of their respective national states in respect of any criminal offenses which may be committed by them in Egypt.[28] This provision differs substantially from the provisions of many postwar arrangements, like Article VII of the NATO Status of Forces Agreement, which establish rules of concurrent jurisdiction: thus, the military authorities of the sending state, in the NATO Agreement, shall have the right to exercise all criminal and disciplinary jurisdiction conferred by the sending state's laws, and the authorities of the receiving state shall have jurisdiction over offenses, committed by members of the visiting force, punishable under the law of the receiving state.[29] However, the UNEF arrangement, whereby *exclusive* criminal jurisdiction is granted to the *visiting state* with the consent of the receiving state, is not unique.[30] A series of arrangements concluded with France during the First World War gave exclusive criminal jurisdiction to visiting armed forces. During the Second World War, an agreement between the United States and Egypt provided similar immunity for American forces in Egyptian territory.[31] These grants of immunity were, no doubt, necessitated by the special circumstances of wartime [32] and, in the case of UNEF, by its extraordinary character.

In effect, the principle of international law applicable to the jurisdictional status of a visiting military force on a sovereign state has been much disputed and no clear and unambiguous rule exists. Indeed, circumstances and special conditions seem to govern the various approaches to the problem. For example, the pattern of concurrent jurisdiction which has evolved in many postwar arrangements, the most significant of which has been the Agreement between the Parties to the North Atlantic Treaty Regarding the Status of their Forces, has almost always been the result of adaptation to circumstances and function, rather than application of a determinate principle of law.

The pattern of concurrent jurisdiction resulted from a compromise designed to strengthen the system of collective security. The NATO Status of Forces Agreement is an integral part of the NATO scheme and the desires of no single nation were paramount in its conception. In hearings before a Congressional committee Deputy Under Secretary of State Murphy described it as the best agreement that could then be obtained by the United States and as representing considerable concessions to the United States. The agreement reflects the unwillingness of nations to permit extensive immunity of large military forces permanently stationed within their boundaries from the impact of local law. The rationale of concurrent jurisdiction arrangements in other parts of the world is additionally supported by the unpopularity of extraterritorial rights and the reaction against anything tainted with colonialism.[33]

The Secretary-General's explanations of UNEF's singular regulations, which grant criminal jurisdiction exclusively to the sending states, also pointed to the importance of circumstance and function in their formulation; he stressed the need for preserving the independent exercise of the Force's functions. Furthermore, he stated that

Such a policy, obviously, makes easier the decision of States to contribute troops from their armed forces. At the same time, it was important that this waiving of jurisdiction by the host state should not result in a juris-dictional vacuum, in which a given offense might be subject to prosecu-tion by neither the host state nor the participating state.[34]

To avoid a vacuum of this type, Hammarskjold sought assurances from the contributing states that they would, indeed, exercise their privilege of jurisdiction in any crime or offense committed by one of their soldiers serving with the Force. In each agreement between the United Nations and the participating state, it is explicitly recog-nized that this "immunity from the jurisdiction of Egypt is based on the understanding that the authorities of the participating states would exercise such jurisdiction as might be necessary with respect to crimes or offenses committed in Egypt by any member of the Force provided from their own military services." [35]

Provision that no member of the United Nations Emergency Force is subject to the civil jurisdiction of the Egyptian courts or to other legal process in any matter relating to his official duties was also set forth in the Agreement of February 8.[36] "In those cases where civil jurisdiction is exercised by Egyptian courts with respect to members of the Force, the Egyptian courts and authorities shall grant members of the Force sufficient opportunity to safeguard their rights." [37]

However, a number of ambiguities exist in regard to the exclusive criminal jurisdiction of the national states. Some of the problems involved were highlighted in the Assembly by the delegate from the Philippines, but received no clarification.[38] This representative imagined the hypothetical case wherein a member of UNEF com-mits an act on Egyptian territory which under the law of Egypt is an indictable and punishable offense, but which under the laws of the state to which the member belongs is not an indictable offense. Would the phrase "exclusive jurisdiction" then mean that the laws of the national state to which the member belongs shall prevail? Sec-ond, he postulated a case wherein an act committed by a member of the Emergency Force might be subject to a very low penalty under Egyptian law and to a very heavy penalty under the laws of the member's national country. Which laws, asked Felixberto Serrano, should apply insofar as the phrase "exclusive jurisdiction" is concerned?

The third case is perhaps the most important. In our examination of criminal law in all civilized countries, we have found that there are cases of offences—and a great many of them—which carry civil liability. In certain jurisdictions, the civil liability cannot be prosecuted independently of the criminal offence. Note that under sub-paragraph (b) of paragraph 12,* on civil jurisdiction, the members of the Force may in certain cases be subject to the civil jurisdiction of the Egyptian courts. Suppose an act is committed on Egyptian territory by a member of the Force which is admittedly a criminal offence but which carries with it civil liability: may the Egyptian courts insist on subjecting him separately to civil process, while the criminal offence committed by him is subject to the jurisdiction of his own courts?

Again, there may be cases where, under the so-called exclusive jurisdiction of the State to which the member belongs, a certain aspect of the offence is different in the State to which he belongs from that of Egypt. For example, it will be noted that, under certain jurisdictions of civilized States, the rule of confrontation of witnesses is a constitutional right of the accused. These difficulties will arise because, if the case has to be prosecuted in the courts of the State to which the member belongs, the right of confrontation of witnesses against him may be invoked by the accused. How shall these difficulties be resolved? [39]

These questions were never answered in debate.

Since all troops and personnel of the police force are entitled to the legal protection of the United Nations and are regarded as its agents for the purpose of such protection,[40] the United Nations itself is responsible for providing the appropriate modes of settlement of disputes or claims of a private law character.[41] The agreement between the United Nations and Egypt provided that any claim made by "(i) an Egyptian citizen in respect of any damages alleged to result from an act or omission of a member of the Force relating to his official duties; (ii) the Government of Egypt against a member

---

* Reference is made to the Status Agreement of February 8.

of the Force; or (iii) the Force or the Government of Egypt against one another . . ." (excluding those claims dealing with the Convention on the Privileges and Immunities of the United Nations or with the interpretation of the February 8th Agreement) shall be settled by a Claims Commission established for that purpose.[42] Two members of this Commission were to be appointed by the Secretary-General and the government of Egypt respectively; the chairman was to be jointly chosen by them and, in the event of disagreement, by the President of the International Court of Justice. In practice, all settlements to date have been effected by informal negotiation between the parties directly or between the Force and the Egyptian Liaison Office subject to the ratification of the claimant.[43]

COMPENSATION FOR DEATH OR INJURY

One type of claim which has been the subject of much discussion, however, has been that concerning compensation for death, injury, or illness of UNEF troops attributable to service with the Force. In his first report on administrative and financial arrangements for the United Nations Emergency Force, the Secretary-General "assumed" that in case of death, injury, or illness incurred while serving with UNEF, soldiers and their dependents would qualify for benefits under their own national service pension or compensation regulations.[44] Benefits would not be received directly from the United Nations. Since it was expected, however, that contributing governments might present claims to UNEF for reimbursement of pensions and compensation paid by them, the United Nations had protected itself by commercial insurance covering death and dismemberment of soldiers of the Force.[45] The Secretary-General asked the Assembly to consider whether this commercial coverage should be continued or whether the United Nations would assume the risks on an uninsured basis.

The question was then submitted to the Fifth Committee and, in turn, to the Advisory Committee on Administrative and Budgetary Questions.[46] The assumptions outlined earlier by the Secretary-

General were approved and considered consistent with the existing practice regarding military officers seconded as military observers to United Nations missions, such as the Truce Supervision Organization. The question of basic policy was not decided—whether the United Nations should actually accept liability in respect of claims from governments for the reimbursement of pensions and compensation paid by them—although it was recognized that acceptance of such a liability appeared implicit in Hammarskjold's earlier report. It was announced, however, that both Advisory Committee and Secretary-General believed that the cost of commercial insurance, even on a limited "excess risk" basis, was too high in relation to the potential risk.[47] The United Nations, it was believed, should carry the related risks without commercial insurance, subject to a decision on the basic question of policy. This recommendation was later approved by the Fifth Committee.

Consultations between the Secretary-General and participating states regarding the entire question of compensation were numerous. The latter were informed that, pending establishment of a compensation system, the United Nations would reimburse idemnities paid by them according to their national regulations.[48] But no claims of this kind have, to date, been formally transmitted to the United Nations although more than fifty-six fatalities have occurred, resulting, for the most part, from accidental shootings, encounters with mines, and traffic accidents.[49]

In further comments on the subject of compensation, Hammarskjold upheld his earlier view that pension and death benefits should be paid in the first instance by the national governments participating in UNEF; and that, subsequently, these states could lodge their claims for reimbursement with the United Nations. This plan "is likely to prove the most feasible administratively, and the most equitable for all parties."[50] Certainly it seems just and equitable that the United Nations should, indeed, compensate Member States for damages caused to the property and to the soldiers which they have contributed to UNEF. Perhaps it would even be desirable if UNEF members were given compensation *directly* by the United Nations in the event of illness, accident, or death attributable to the performance of official duties, as is the procedure with members of the Secretariat. The international character of the Force and its independence from national policies would be justly served thereby. In any case, it seems clear that since the Organization has the capacity and right to bring a claim against one of its Member States for damage to its property and assets, and to the interests of which it is a guardian,[51] so, too, is the reverse procedure true. As a subject of international law and as a legal person, the United Nations has duties as well as rights.[52]

Further recommendations by the Secretary-General in regard to compensation policy seem sound; these were, in principle, first suggested by the Advisory Committee on Administrative and Budgetary Questions: [53]

(i) Claims of participating Governments should normally be restricted to cases of death or serious disability involving a material cost to the Government for medical costs and/or pension benefits;

(ii) No formal rules should be established at this time; but, until some experience is gained of problems likely to arise, such claims should be dealt with as presented, based on the circumstances of each case;

(iii) So far as possible, administration of monthly or other periodic payments should rest with the participating Government; consideration would be given, as and when appropriate, to the working out between the United Nations and the Government concerned of an arrangement whereby the United Nations liability would be commuted to a lump sum payment.[54]

Various other claims can, of course, be expected to arise as a result of the varied activities of the Emergency Force. No precedent exists, however, to indicate whether the United Nations would be expected to assume legal responsibility for acts of UNEF injurious to others. A member of the Force, while on patrol duty, might carelessly wound an Egyptian bystander. If there were proved negligence on the part of the UNEF soldier, would the Egyptian government be able to interpose a claim on behalf of its national? If a person serving with the Force were to acquire improperly information which could be utilized to the disadvantage of Egypt, would that country be justified in making a claim against the United Nations? If the continued presence in Egypt of the Emergency Force were to effect adversely the economy of that country, would the United Nations be liable to compensate this injury? Possible claims by participating states for equipment destroyed in the service of the United Nations Emergency Force are also conceivable.

In principle, the answers to these questions probably depend upon the answer to a further question: How far is the law of responsibility as developed for states to be applied to international organizations acting as legal persons? [55] In practice, should occasion arise, these questions would probably be settled informally by negotiation.[56] If the diplomatic procedure did not succeed, however, and a Claims Commission was established, a number of questions of international law would, no doubt, require settlement.

The field of international law dealing with the responsibility of the United Nations is still very new and undeveloped. In the past the United Nations has attempted—as in cases dealing with UNEF—to solve some of its legal problems informally. As a going concern interested in the effective operation of its organs and the achievement of its essential aims, the United Nations has not been unduly concerned with doctrine regarding its legal personality in the international community.

ARBITRAL SETTLEMENT OF DISPUTES

Consistent with United Nations preference and practice in settling legal arguments, the agreement of February 8 between Egypt and the United Nations concerning the status of the Emergency Force and the agreements between Member States and the Secretary-General, contain identical provisions for arbitral settlements. In case of a dispute between the United Nations and the state concerned regarding the interpretation or application of the agreements—a dis-

pute which is not settled by negotiation or other means agreeable
to both parties—the controversy is to be brought before a tribunal
of three arbitrators.[57] Each party is to choose one arbitrator, while
the umpire is to be jointly selected by the Secretary-General and
the government in question. Failure to agree upon the umpire within
one month of the proposal of arbitration will leave either party free
to ask the President of the International Court of Justice to make
the selection. In the event of a vacancy in the tribunal, it would be
filled within thirty days by the method laid down for the original
appointment.

The tribunal shall come into existence upon the appointment of the
umpire and at least one of the other members of the tribunal. Two
members of the tribunal shall constitute a quorum for the performance
of its functions, and for all deliberations and decisions of the tribunal
a favorable vote of two members shall be sufficient.[58]

The agreement with Egypt was deemed to have taken effect
from the date of the arrival of the first element of the Emergency
Force in Egypt and is to remain in force until the departure of
UNEF from that country.[59] The date when this departure will be
considered effective is to be defined by the Egyptian government
and the Secretary-General. In respect to the agreements with contributing states, they were to take effect from the date that the
national contingent provided by the government in question de-
parted from its home country to assume duties with the Force.
Each agreement, therefore, had a purely functional purpose; it was
to facilitate the effective operation of the Force and to expire when
no longer needed.

In his summary study on UNEF, the Secretary-General commended the legal arrangements for the Emergency Force. The status
agreement, he declared, has in its entirety stood up well to the test
of experience. "Its basic principles should be embodied in similar
agreements in the future, and their recognition, therefore, would

seem necessarily to form part of any stand-by arrangements for a force." [60] Especially noteworthy is the principle which ensures that UNEF personnel, when involved in criminal actions, come under the jurisdiction of the criminal courts of their home states.

The establishment of this principle for UNEF, in relation to Egypt, has set a most valuable precedent. Experience shows that this principle is essential to the successful recruitment by the United Nations of military personnel not otherwise under immunity rules, from its Member countries. The position established for UNEF should be maintained in future arrangements.[61]

Also valuable is the principle which furnished United Nations activity freedom of movement within its area of operations and all such facilities necessary for access and communications, including rights of overflight for aircraft connected with the international operation.

Although not designated as such by the Secretary-General, the rules governing the international status of UNEF's members may be considered the most significant of all the legal regulations for future developments in this realm. Military personnel employed by the United Nations in para-military operations are not under the same formal obligations in relation to the Organization as staff members of the Secretariat. Nevertheless, the basic United Nations rules for international service are applicable to them, in particular those regarding full loyalty to the aims of the Organization and regarding abstention from acts in relation to their home country or other countries which might be detrimental to the international character of the operation in which they participate. The observance of such precepts ensures good relations with the host state. Above all, however, it fosters a spirit of internationalism in the personnel and helps to promote the idea of loyalty to an international rather than a national cause. Without further development of this spirit, rules to govern the use of lawful force by the world community will remain forever limited in scope and application.

Chapter Seven

FINANCING THE FORCE

In making financial arrangements for the Force, the Assembly was faced with a series of important decisions: methods of financing such an unprecedented operation, means of apportioning expenses among Member States, and agreements with governments in regard to financial responsibilities and opportunities were all questions fraught with complexity and requiring answers. A number of these problems have actually remained unresolved, for the refusals of some states to pay contributions and the tardiness in payments have kept the Force in a permanently precarious financial position. A great number of states, even those which view UNEF with favor, are dissatisfied with the method adopted by the Assembly for apportioning UNEF's cost: indeed, there "has been much eagerness among many countries to let someone else—anyone else—pay it." [1]

The total expense incurred by the United Nations Emergency Force is not inconsequential. Subject to certain reimbursement procedures (discussed later in this chapter), salaries and equipment of individual soldiers are paid and supplied by their national governments, but UNEF, itself, is responsible for providing a substantial amount of gear, transport, fuel, currency, and food. A daily overseas allowance of eighty-six cents a day for all members of the Force is financed by the United Nations. Thus, each year the sum incurred for UNEF is almost equal to one-third the total of the regular annual budget of the entire Organization. Since its creation, the Emergency Force has cost over $100,000,000.

It is interesting to note, however, that despite vigorous controversy over many of the financial aspects of the UNEF operation, the Assembly has continually adopted the Secretary-General's proposals regarding cost almost without change. Debates in the Assembly, in the Fifth Committee, and in the Special Political Committee have been long and divided, but resolutions, based upon suggestions of the Secretary-General, have always been forthcoming with heavy support. Dissension, therefore, is mainly felt in the practical realm of actual payment and, at present, in the most important realm, for without requisite funds, UNEF, of course, is doomed to extinction. In fact, this dearth of payment of the expenses of the Emergency Force, together with similar defaults in regard to the payment of assessments for the United Nations Force in the Congo, have resulted in a major financial crisis for the entire Organization.

INITIAL ARRANGEMENTS

In his report of November 21, 1956, on administrative and financial arrangements for UNEF,[2] the Secretary-General recommended that the finances of the Force be handled under a Special Account outside the normal budget and "that the expenses of the Force be allocated to Member States on the basis of the scale of assessments to be adopted for the United Nations budget for 1957." Hammarskjold also suggested that the Assembly, as an initial assessment, appropriate an amount of $10 million to the Special Account. In order to meet the immediate cash needs of the Force, the Secretary-General requested approval "to advance monies from the United Nations Working Capital Fund to the Special Account and, should the necessity arise, to seek other means of providing for cash needs."

Why did the Secretary-General choose this method of financing the United Nations Emergency Force rather than include the costs of the Force in the ordinary budget of the Organization? To have followed the latter course, to have included UNEF, for example, within Part II of the regular budget concerning special missions and related activities, certain difficulties, it seems, would have ensued. The Secretary-General viewed the expenses of the Force as extraordinary and separate. Integration of UNEF's finances into the ordinary budget might well have presupposed the permanency of UNEF, which was undesirable. Likewise, Hammarskjold rejected the possibility of financing UNEF by using the annual Assembly resolution [3] which covers unforeseen and extraordinary expenses arising in the future, including expenses considered necessary by the Secretary-General for the maintenance of peace and security. This resolution usually authorizes expenditure of $2 million, but this sum might have been enlarged by the Secretary-General, with the consent of the Advisory Committee on Administrative and Budgetary Questions, to cover UNEF's costs.

Hammarskjold preferred a Special Account mainly because of the various uncertainties connected with the Force: uncertainty of its mission and duration of assignment; uncertainty of the exact expenses which would be incurred; uncertainty of the assistance which would be rendered without charge and of the sums which would be voluntarily contributed.[4] Moreover, he gave the following reasons for wishing to finance UNEF's initial expenses on an *ad hoc* and separate basis:

the initial basic rule for the sharing of costs, which was accepted by the General Assembly on 7 November 1956 [resolution 1001 (ES-I), par. 5], whereby a participating State would be responsible for all costs for the equipment and salaries of its contingent, had been submitted by the Secretary-General as provisional and subject to further study; . . . available balances in the Working Capital Fund were not sufficiently large to underwrite the expenses of even a relatively small Force for any appreciable time, in addition to financing other unavoidable United Nations requirements; . . . the procedure adopted would avoid the virtually certain delay that would otherwise have resulted from deep differences of opinion about who should be responsible for meeting the costs.[5]

At the time when the Special Account was proposed, there was no indication that difficulties would ensue in regard to payment of UNEF's costs. This method of budgeting expenses was not intended to have special legal significance.

In any case, the Assembly approved the Secretary-General's plan, established the Special Account in the initial amount of $10 million on November 26, 1956, and requested the Secretary-General to establish such rules and procedures to govern it as he deemed necessary.[6] Members of the Assembly disagreed, however, on the manner of assessment of these funds and the Assembly, therefore, requested the Fifth Committee and, as appropriate, the Advisory Committee on Administrative and Budgetary Questions to consider the matter further and to report to the Assembly as soon as possible.

The Fifth Committee met immediately, but upon the suggestion of the Secretary-General, deferred consideration of the main question—the method to be adopted for allocating the costs to be borne by the United Nations between Member States—since Hammarskjold wished to submit a proposal in due course.[7] As a matter of urgency, a number of other questions were referred to the Advisory Committee on Administrative and Budgetary Questions. In its report of November 30, 1956,[8] this Committee made various suggestions regarding administrative and financial aspects of the provisional arrangements concerning UNEF, recommending that contributing states be given necessary foreign exchange reimbursable in their own currencies and that members of the Force be paid a daily overseas allowance. To assure the cash requirements immediately needed to organize UNEF, the Committee advised that the Secretary-General should arrange for loans to the Special Account from appropriate sources, including governments and international agencies.[9] The Advisory Committee also upheld the Secretary-General's intention of following "to a maximum degree the regular financial rules and regulations of the Organization, as well as the machinery and processes that have been laid down by the General Assembly for the purpose of financial review and control." [10]

The question of the daily overseas allotment for UNEF troops raised some controversy. The Advisory Committee considered that the

. . . basic justification for the proposed allowance is that members of the Force are placed, by reason of the circumstances of their posting to the United Nations Emergency Force—which in the majority of cases was not a matter of individual decision—at a disadvantage by comparison with their situation if they had remained at a regular military establishment. For example, such an establishment would include, as an integral feature, various facilities and services which, in the circumstances attending the operations of the Emergency Force, cannot be made available. The "hardship" allowance which certain of these States grant to their troops varies widely in amount and also, because of differences in exchange rates, in its purchasing power in local currencies. In other cases, no such allowance is paid.

Although there are marked differences in the rates of pay of the members of the Force, the purpose of the proposed service allowance is not to attempt to compensate for such differences, but rather to provide in the area, on a common basis, a reasonable opportunity of meeting personal and recreational needs.[11]

No specific sum was mentioned by the Advisory Committee, but note was taken of the $1-a-day allowance suggested by the Secretary-General and his Military Advisory Group. Members of the Fifth Committee questioned the allowance: the United States felt that nothing could be done to remedy the disparity in pay, but the United Nations could place all troops on the same footing in regard to the purchase of incidentals by means of the proposed allowance; yet, $1 a day seemed a rather high rate. The delegate from Pakistan wondered whether the allowance was at all necessary or desirable and whether amenities could be provided instead of cash. Serious reservations about the allowance, particularly the rate proposed, were also made by the governments of Italy, France, and Cambodia: mention was made of the temporary nature of the Force, of the inability to gauge the length of its stay in Egypt, of the overwhelming burden even $1 a day might impose upon the United Nations. Most of the representatives believed, however, that the overseas allotment of $1 a day to UNEF soldiers should be paid not only to provide personal and recreational needs, but to alleviate hardships arising from national divergencies in pay.[12] Later, a compromise was effected and 86 cents was fixed upon as a daily allowance to each member.

ALLOCATION OF COSTS

It was the question of method of allocating UNEF costs which raised real debate in the Fifth Committee and which has split the Assembly ever since. The Comptroller of the United Nations indicated on December 3, 1956, that the Secretary-General, after further reflection, had come to the conclusion that the only practicable and equitable procedure was that which he had already proposed and which provided for UNEF costs to be shared by Member States in accordance with the scale of assessments adopted for the regular 1957 budget. Since the General Assembly had established the Force for the accomplishment of certain stated purposes, it was only logical that the UN itself assume the full and final responsibility for the financial and other obligations involved. UNEF was an international force, set up on the basis of Charter principles, with a Commander who was appointed by the world organization, responsible to the General Assembly, and independent of any one country. Thus UNEF's expenses, from a strictly budgetary and accounting viewpoint, might be treated as distinct from those in the regular budget. They "nevertheless remained United Nations expenditures within the general scope and intent of Article 17 of the Charter." [13] (Article 17 states, *inter alia*, that "the expenses of the Organization shall be borne by the Members as apportioned by the General Assembly.")

Many delegates in the Committee agreed with this thesis. The representative of Canada reminded the Committee that according to General Assembly resolution 1001 (ES-I), adopted by 64 votes in favor and only 12 abstentions, Member States were required to afford the United Nations Command the necessary assistance in the performance of its functions.[14] The Organization would not progress, declared the delegate from New Zealand, until the Member nations acknowledged the responsibilities as well as privileges which mem-

bership incurred; such responsibilities "must be borne not by a fifth
or a quarter of the Members or by one or two countries, but by
all." [15] He pointed to analogous situations in the past when special
commissions, often entailing much expense, had been established to
investigate conditions in a particular country. Never, in the past, had
the suggestion been forwarded (as several delegations now proposed
in regard to UNEF) that the financial obligations incurred by these
United Nations organs should be shouldered by the state with whose
conduct they were concerned. Even in the case of Korea, although
the Assembly had specifically named the aggressor, it had never been
considered that the aggressor country should be held financially
responsible. [16] The United States delegate declared that the decision
which the Committee would take was one of the most important, if
not the most important, with which it had ever been confronted. The
entire future of the United Nations as an instrument of collective
security was at stake. Stressing that the United States had made,
and would continue to make, substantial voluntary contributions to
the Special Account, the United States delegate regretted that unless
the $10 million already appropriated were apportioned among all
Member States, his government "would find it most difficult to
justify its voluntary contribution." [17]

Other representatives, notably the Danish and Brazilian, concurred with the views outlined above, but also felt that the position
of those countries which had contributed troops to the Emergency
Force should be taken into consideration and their financial obligations reduced accordingly. The financial burden involved for other
Members, however, was small compared to the huge damages that
would have been suffered by all countries throughout the world in
a major conflict. It would be of importance in the future if the
United Nations assumed entire responsibility for the expenses of the
Emergency Force. [18]

The delegates of the Soviet bloc insisted that the collective sharing of the costs of the UN Emergency Force was neither right nor

proper and, therefore, reference to Article 17 of the Charter was irrelevant to the point at issue. They maintained that all the material costs of the operation should be borne by those governments which had precipitated the crisis; they would thus not consider themselves bound by any resolution which provided that UNEF costs should be defrayed by the United Nations. The delegate from Rumania maintained:

The Committee was faced with a very clear situation: aggression had been committed and the aggressors were known. The aggression had had very unfortunate results for the Egyptian people and had adversely affected the economies of many countries, where production difficulties were being experienced owing to the shortage of raw materials resulting from the obstruction of the Canal. It would be very difficult for many delegations to explain to their Governments and Parliaments that they had to pay for the results of aggression. The only solution was that the aggressors should pay.[19]

The Arab States seconded this position. It was unfair that all Member States should be asked to bear the cost of aggression; it was even worse that Egypt, victim of aggression, should be required to contribute. Such a request was morally and logically unfounded.[20]

Some of the smaller nations apparently were concerned that the burden of financing the Force would be too heavy for their economies to support. The representative of Guatemala suggested that the Fifth Committee invite the Secretary-General to study other formulas for the apportionment of expenses which might reconcile the points of view expressed by the various delegates.[21] This opinion was shared by the Spanish delegate, who proposed that a new formula might be evolved whereby a part of the costs would be borne by the five permanent members of the Security Council, and the other part, by all Members of the Organization, including the five permanent members.[22] Such a formula would be just, it was believed, because the Great Powers undoubtedly had a greater responsibility for the maintenance of international peace and security than did other

Members; yet UNEF was serving the interests of all states, large and small alike. Still other proposals forwarded in the Fifth Committee entailed financing on the basis of voluntary contributions.

The Latin American countries, in a joint statement, rejected the proposition that UNEF expenses should be treated on the same footing as expenses referred to in Article 17 of the Charter. Although the expenditure covered by that Article was not precisely defined, it could not logically be taken to mean anything other than the normal operating costs of the United Nations. Furthermore, Article 19 was usually discussed in conjunction with Article 17 and it would certainly be regrettable if some Member States found themselves in the situation envisaged in that article. (Article 19 provides that a Member State "which is in arrears in the payment of its financial contributions to the Organization shall have no vote in the General Assembly if the amount of its arrears equals or exceeds the amount of the contributions due from it for the preceding two full years.") *
The Latin American countries, therefore, suggested: first, immediate fixing of a ceiling, which would not exceed, for example, 10 percent of the annual United Nations budget, or about $5 million. This sum would be supplied by all the Member States according to the scale applicable to the administrative and general expenses of the Organization; and, second, payment of additional expenses in 1957 by means of voluntary contributions, which would be handled by the Secretary-General or a special negotiating committee.[23]

The draft resolution which was finally recommended by the Committee, voting 57 in favor, 8 against, and 9 abstentions,[24] and adopted by the Assembly on December 21, 1956 (Resolution 1089 [XI]) provided

that the expenses of the United Nations Emergency Force, other than for such pay, equipment, supplies and services as may be furnished without charge by Governments of Member States, shall be borne by the United Nations and shall be apportioned among the Member States, to the extent of $10 million, in accordance with the scale of assessments

* For further discussion of this aspect of the question, see pp. 177, 179–82.

adopted by the General Assembly for contributions to the annual budget of the Organization for the financial year 1957 . . . that this decision shall be without prejudice to the subsequent apportionment of any expenses in excess of $10 million which may be incurred in connection with the Force.

A Committee composed of Canada, Ceylon, Chile, El Salvador, India, Liberia, Sweden, the USSR, and the United States was established to examine the question of the apportionment of UNEF expenses in excess of $10 million. The Committee was to take into consideration General Assembly opinion and divergent viewpoints and was to study the question in all its aspects, including the possibility of voluntary contributions, the fixing of maximum amounts, and the determination of different scales of contributions.

This resolution represented a fiscal milestone in the life of international organization. For the first time in history, the principle of collective responsibility was established in regard to meeting the costs of an international security force. It was to have important repercussions.

The new Committee met in due course and considered a statement by the Secretary-General in which he predicted that his obligational authority and the estimated cash available would be exhausted by the end of April 1957; he asked for authorization to enter into commitments for an additional $6.5 million.

This authorization was approved by the Special Committee in its report to the Fifth Committee, in addition to a recommendation that expenses above the $10 million already appropriated be financed by voluntary contributions.[25] During the debate in the Fifth Committee, many delegates again voiced their belief that costs of UNEF should be apportioned among Members in the same manner as other United Nations expenditures.[26] But, as the United States representative remarked, the initial decision of the Assembly had imposed financial sacrifice on many states. "Since the principle of collective responsibility had been established, the United States was prepared to agree that the additional expenses for the Emergency Force . . . should be met as far as possible by voluntary contributions." [27] The United States also made known its intention of contributing up to half the amount necessary, provided other governments contributed the other half.

Mindful of these opinions and of a recommendation to this end by the Fifth Committee,[28] the General Assembly, on February 27, 1957, adopted Resolution 1090 (XI) authorizing Hammarskjold to incur expenses for UNEF up to a total of $16.5 million for the period to December 31, 1957; inviting Member governments to contribute voluntarily to the Special Account; authorizing the Secretary-General to advance necessary funds from the Working Capital Fund, and to arrange for loans to the Special Account from appropriate sources; [29] deciding that the Assembly should consider at its Twelfth Session the basis for financing any costs in excess of $10 million not covered by voluntary contributions. This was an optimistic resolution, although adopted, no doubt, with some resignation on the part of several delegations: optimistic in the expectancy that several states would, indeed, willingly arise to the occasion and meet UNEF's costs; occasioning resignation in the fact that the Assembly, despite its moral influence and the popularity of the cause in question, was not able to muster greater acceptance of financial responsibility for UNEF.

EARLY REQUIREMENTS: FIRST FINANCIAL PERIOD

Operational expenditure borne by the United Nations for the cost of the Force during November 1956 to December 31, 1957 (or, "the first financial period"), amounted to $23,920,000. However, total expenditures and obligations for this period totaled $30,000,000.

This sum did not include reimbursements to governments of special allowances paid to their contingents as a direct result of their service in the area.[30] The figures below also exclude contributions in the form of military personnel and equipment which the ten contributing states had made available. Furthermore, facilities and equipment for transportation purposes were furnished voluntarily

TABLE 1. ESTIMATED OPERATIONAL COSTS OF UNEF FOR THE FIRST FINANCIAL PERIOD[31]

(*November 1956–December 31, 1957*)

I. Salaries and wages [32]	$1,621,200
II. Welfare and recreation [33]	683,000
III. Transportation of military personnel [34]	2,073,000
IV. Overseas allowance to military personnel [35]	1,924,000
V. Travel and subsistence of nonmilitary personnel	480,300
VI. Rental, reconditioning, and maintenance of premises and equipment	1,374,000
VII. Transportation and operational equipment	2,314,000
VIII. Operation and maintenance of motor transport and operational equipment (including petroleum, oil and lubrication)	2,840,000
IX. Rental of aircraft (including petroleum, oil and lubrication)	946,000
X. Miscellaneous equipment [36]	202,000
XI. Stationery and office supplies	80,000
XII. Operational supplies [37]	2,012,000
XIII. Food supplies for military personnel [38]	4,410,000
XIV. Communications services (telephone, telegraph, wireless, teletype, communications, and postage)	150,000
XV. Freight, cartage, express and air freight [39]	1,023,000
XVI. Miscellaneous supplies and services [40]	609,000
XVII. Insurance [41]	175,000
XVIII. External audit costs	4,000
XIX. Contingencies and unforeseen expenditures [42]	1,000,000
Total	$23,920,500

by some Member governments: airlifts arranged by the United States to transport troops from their home countries to Naples or Beirut approximated $2,250,000; Canadian aircraft carried Canadian troops and equipment from Canada to Egypt at a cost of $333,312, and by airlift, at a cost of $438,819; the government of Switzerland accepted charges of about $390,000 for commercial air transportation of soldiers and equipment from Italy to Egypt in the early stages of the UNEF operation; troop and supply movements from Naples to Egypt were provided by Italian airlift and supply movements; the Scandinavian governments arranged airlifts for regular transport service to and from Naples.

Other supplies, services and facilities were also provided to UNEF without charge. Italy contributed labor for loading planes and ships, crating and carting services, billeting facilities, airport and hangar facilities, and service personnel. The government of Egypt furnished office and other accommodations, transport facilities, and general supplies. A number of governments made available additional communications facilities and mailing privileges, or welfare and recreational facilities, or both.[43] Because of these contributions, the cost of the United Nations Emergency Force to the Organization has, of course, been substantially reduced.

Nevertheless, the burden of expense on Member States seems to have been considerable: by October 7, 1957, the United Nations had received only $5,743,644 from thirty-two states for the initial amount of $10 million which was apportioned in terms of resolution 1089 (XI) among Member States in accordance with the scale of assessments for the annual 1957 budget.[44] A number of states, whose percentage assessments amounted to approximately 20 percent, formally notified the Secretary-General of their decision not to participate in financing the Force. Immediately following upon the resolution of February 27, 1957, inviting voluntary contributions, six states pledged a total of $3,800,350:

TABLE 2. MEMBER STATE VOLUNTARY PLEDGES
AS OF OCTOBER 1957

State	Paid or Pledged U.S. Dollars
Dominican Republic	3,250
Greece	6,500
New Zealand	27,950
Pakistan	5,000
United Kingdom [45]	507,650
United States of America [46]	3,250,000

But actual cash receipts of these contributions in early October 1957 amounted to only $586,550.

This wide disparity between UNEF's financial needs and the cash resources which were available prompted the Secretary-General to urge the Assembly again to undertake review of the basic considerations involved in the entire problem. Above all, he asked for authorization to incur expenses for the period ending December 31, 1957, up to a total of $23,920,500. (Resolution 1090 [XI], it will be remembered, had envisaged the expenditure of $16.5 million only); and for the 1958 period, Hammarskjold wished appropriate obligational authority to incur up to a total of $20 million for UNEF.[47] In the light of the weak response which had been made to the request for voluntary contributions, and of the complexity and scope of UNEF operations, the Secretary-General was constrained to question whether this means of obtaining funds by contribution was either feasible or prudent in the future:

The Secretary-General is bound to stress the grave risks inherent in the present inadequate and insecure basis of UNEF financing. Unless, indeed, the possibility of UNEF successfully completing its mission is to be seriously jeopardized, it is essential that this vital United Nations undertaking be assured of the same degree and certainty of financial support as afforded to other United Nations activities which have as their purpose the maintenance of security and peace.[48]

Even the authorization requested for 1957, the Secretary-General reported, would be insufficient to meet the requirements of the situation unless it was broadly construed to permit loans from Member States. Once more Hammarskjold desired authority to advance sums from the United Nations Working Capital Fund, but warned that unless such advances were reduced in the future there would remain an insufficient balance of funds to cover the costs of the normal activities of the Organization.

Again there was sustained debate in the Assembly; [49] again the viewpoints voiced earlier were explored. The United States and the United Kingdom, "although considering that the expenses of the Force are a United Nations obligation which should be met by assessment against the Members in the proportions of the regular scale of assessment," made known offers of $12 million and $1 million respectively, as "special assistance" to be applied toward reducing those expenses of the Force outstanding for the period ending December 31, 1957.[50] Perhaps these offers were encouragement to the Assembly. Certainly, it was clear that the majority of delegates were gratified with the role which the Force had played in the Middle East and were anxious to continue its mandate. By a vote of 51 to 11 with 19 abstentions, resolution 1151 (XII) was passed on November 22, 1957, which authorized expenditure, for the period ending December 31, 1957, of an additional amount for the Force up to a maximum of $13.5 million.[51] For the continuing operation of the Force beyond that date, a maximum of $25 million was approved. It was decided that expenses would be borne by Members according to the scale of assessment adopted by the Assembly for the financial years 1957 and 1958 respectively.

TABLE 3. UNITED NATIONS SCALE OF
ASSESSMENTS FOR 1957[52]

Country	Percent	Country	Percent	Country	Percent
Afghanistan	0.06	Ethiopia	0.11	Nicaragua	0.04
Albania	0.04	Finland	0.37	Norway	0.49
Argentina	1.17	France	5.70	Pakistan	0.55
Australia	1.65	Greece	0.20	Panama	0.05
Austria	0.36	Guatemala	0.07	Paraguay	0.04
Belgium	1.27	Haiti	0.04	Peru	0.15
Bolivia	0.05	Honduras	0.04	Philippines	0.41
Brazil	1.09	Hungary	0.46	Poland	1.56
Bulgaria	0.14	Iceland	0.04	Portugal	0.25
Burma	0.10	India	2.97	Rumania	0.50
Byelorussia	0.48	Indonesia	0.51	Saudi Arabia	0.07
Cambodia	0.04	Iran	0.27	Spain	1.14
Canada	3.15	Iraq	0.12	Sweden	1.46
Ceylon	0.11	Ireland	0.19	Syria	0.08
Chile	0.30	Israel	0.16	Thailand	0.16
China	5.14	Italy	2.08	Turkey	0.63
Colombia	0.37	Jordan	0.04	Ukraine	1.85
Costa Rica	0.04	Laos	0.04	Union of South	
Cuba	0.27	Lebanon	0.05	Africa	0.71
Czechoslovakia	0.84	Liberia	0.04	USSR	13.96
Denmark	0.66	Libya	0.04	United Kingdom	7.81
Dominican		Luxembourg	0.06	United States	33.33
Republic	0.05	Mexico	0.70	Uruguay	0.16
Ecuador	0.05	Nepal	0.04	Venezuela	0.43
Egypt	0.36	Netherlands	1.15	Yemen	0.04
El Salvador	0.06	New Zealand	0.43	Yugoslavia	0.36

In summary: the first Assembly authorization, voted on November 26, 1956, was for an amount of $10 million. This was increased on

February 27, 1957 to $16.5 million in respect of the period ending December 31, 1957. Then, on November 22, 1957, it was increased to $30 million for the same period. The total sum was arranged in the following manner:

(a) To the extent of $1,841,700, by voluntary contributions made by Member States in response to the invitation to them extended in Resolution 1090 (XI);

(b) To an additional extent of $13,129,312, by grants of special assistance made by a number of Governments in order to reduce the total of the amount to be assessed on all Members, on the basis of Resolution 1151 (XII);

(c) The balance ($15,028,988), by assessments on Members in accordance with the approved scale of assessments for 1957.[53]

REIMBURSEMENT OF EXTRA AND EXTRAORDINARY COSTS

Several other important financial questions were considered by the Secretary-General and the Assembly. A number of contributing states had made known to Hammarskjold their desire for reimbursement of the "extra costs" which they were obliged to incur in making troops available for service with UNEF. Some governments considered that resolution 1089 had altered the earlier rule that a nation providing a unit would be responsible for all costs of equipment and salaries; they believed that these costs should now be shouldered by the United Nations.

The latter thesis was outspokenly rejected by the Secretary-General.[54] Debates in the Assembly and Fifth Committee, he said, reflected the view that contributing states should continue to pay such expenses as they would normally have incurred in any event, and that any reimbursement obligation to be assumed by the United Nations should be limited to the *additional* expenditure which these countries incur as a direct result of their having made contingents available for service with UNEF. He suggested that for the first six months of service of a national contingent, the United Nations should reimburse participating governments for any special allowances, as distinct from basic salaries, paid to members of their units as a direct result of their service with the Emergency Force. Contingents which had served beyond the initial six-month period should be reimbursed by the United Nations for all extra and extraordinary costs which a government was obliged to incur because of the UNEF operation.

In commending this general principle to the General Assembly, the Secretary-General is conscious of the fact that those Member States which have been maintaining UNEF contingents for more than ten months are finding it increasingly difficult to prolong the period of service of their troops, or to make replacements available in the absence of any firm assurance that identifiable direct expenses thereby incurred will be borne by the United Nations. It would seem to the Secretary-General, moreover, that beyond a limited emergency period, any arrangement under which a few Member States carry a disproportionately heavy financial burden does not represent a sound or equitable basis on which to discharge a collective United Nations responsibility.[55]

Hammarskjold estimated that reimbursement of special allowances for the first six months would amount to $2 million and that extra and extraordinary costs relating to pay and allowances until December 31, 1957, would require $6.5 million. In "the interests of an equitable sharing of costs," it was also proposed that the United Nations assume appropriate financial responsibility for the replacement of equipment.[56] These principles and proposals were approved by the Assembly, although they added another large sum to the estimated expense of the Force.[57]

The Secretary-General pointed out, however, that in practice the application of these principles is not easy. For example,

it has been extremely difficult, in view of widely differing national practices, to define what may be reasonably regarded as a "special allowance." Furthermore, although it has been assumed that national contingents would be composed of regular army personnel who would, in any event, have been in the service of their country, certain Governments organized special volunteer units to serve with UNEF. This was done because national laws precluded the assignment of members of the regular armed forces to service overseas other than in defense of the homeland. In other cases, new units had to be organized within the contributing States to replace regular units dispatched for UNEF duty. In these circumstances, some Governments from the outset assumed additional financial liabilities which they believed should be compensated for by the United Nations.[58]

But Hammarskjold was also convinced that experience "indicates the validity of the view that the most equitable collective arrangement is one which distributes among the membership as a whole those costs which a participating government would not otherwise have incurred."

LATER EXPENDITURES AND ASSESSMENTS

As in the first financial period of the Emergency Force, budget estimates were subsequently prepared by the Secretary-General for Assembly approval.[59] The appropriations of the General Assembly were often below the estimates submitted.[60]

TABLE 4. BUDGET FOR THE UNITED NATIONS EMERGENCY FORCE

Year	Operational Expenses	Reimbursement *	Total
Jan. 1–Dec. 31, 1958 [61]	$14,200,000	$6,000,000	$20,200,000
Jan. 1–Dec. 31, 1959 [62]	12,500,000	6,500,000	19,000,000
Jan. 1–Dec. 31, 1960 [63]	12,500,000	7,500,000	20,000,000
Jan. 1–Dec. 31, 1961	11,484,800	7,900,000	19,384,000
Jan. 1–Dec. 31, 1962 [64]	10,911,800	8,925,000	19,836,800

* Reimbursement to governments of costs incurred in providing contingents. See above discussion.

The sums assessed were on the basis of the regular scale of assessments. In December 1959, however, the Assembly

considered it desirable to reduce the financial burden on these Governments having the least capacity to contribute and decided accordingly that voluntary contributions pledged prior to 31 December 1959 should be applied as a credit to reduce by 50 per cent the contributions of as many Governments as possible, commencing with those Governments assessed at the minimum percentage of 0.04 per cent.[65]

This move by the Assembly was made in an attempt to improve the financial situation of the Force and decrease the burden upon the less-developed states. In 1960, voluntary contributions were used to reduce up to 50 percent the assessment of states receiving assistance during 1960 under the Expanded Programme of Technical Assistance, starting with those states assessed at .04 percent and then including, in order, those states assessed at the next highest percentages until the total amount of the voluntary funds had been applied.[66]

In his report of August 30, 1961, the Secretary-General again asked the Assembly to consider the increasingly unsatisfactory financial status of the UNEF Special Account. Indeed, on July 31, 1961, the number of governments which owed assessments for UNEF in full or in part were as follows: [67]

Assessment for:	Owed in full	Owed in part
1957	21	8
1958	30	2
1959	35	3
1960	42 [68]	1
1961	80	3

Hammarskjold indicated that it was necessary, as a result of the steady increase in the arrears of contributions to the UNEF Special Account, to have recourse as had been done before to advances from the United Nations Working Capital Fund for current UNEF expenses during 1961 and 1962. This mode of meeting costs, however, was highly precarious and the Organization faced a fiscal crisis which was regarded by many as one of the greatest threats the United Nations had, as yet, encountered.[69]

The issue had become increasingly complicated with the rise of similar difficulties in regard to ONUC.[70] Expenses for the Congo Force, like those for UNEF, are treated as a special account and are assessed on the basis of the scale for regular expenses of the Organization, with reductions granted to states with a limited capacity to pay. Unlike the resolutions on UNEF's finances, however, the Assembly on December 20, 1960, explicitly stated that the 1960 costs of the Congo Force were to "constitute 'expenses of the Organization' within the meaning of Article 17" and that assessments for the *ad hoc* account were to create "binding legal obligations." The principle of obligation was thus definitely established and a sum of $48,500,000 to finance ONUC was authorized by the Assembly for 1960.[71]

Further debate on the best way to finance the UN force in Africa ensued. The Assembly's next financial resolution on ONUC, while apportioning $100 million as "expenses of the Organization," made no direct reference to Article 17, did not specify ONUC's cost as a "binding legal obligation," described the expenses in the Congo as "extraordinary" and, finally, underlined the special responsibility of the Security Council's permanent members for the financing of peace and security operations.[72] The Assembly was back where it started in its first debate regarding UNEF's cost. Disgruntlement ran rampant in the Organization. Arrears in the financing of ONUC were substantial.

After much debate and disagreement, the Assembly during its sixteenth session took supplementary action. The 104-member body voted on December 21, 1961, to ask the International Court of Justice for an advisory opinion: "Do the expenditures authorized in General Assembly resolutions . . . relating to the United Nations operations in the Congo . . . and the expenditures authorized in General Assembly resolutions . . . relating to the operations of the United Nations Emergency Force . . . constitute expenses of the Organization within the meaning of Article 17, paragraph 2, of the Charter of the United Nations?"[73] Article 17 gives the Assembly authority to consider and approve the United Nations budget and declares that the expenses of the Organization shall be borne by the Member States as apportioned by the General Assembly. In submitting the question to the Court, many Members hoped, no doubt, for an affirmative answer which might encourage delinquent states to pay their UNEF and ONUC assessments. They desired a ruling that the expenses of the current peacekeeping operations were apportionable by the Assembly.

Acting with determination, the General Assembly decided to authorize U Thant, Acting Secretary-General, to issue up to $200 million in United Nations bonds in order to meet a deficit that was expected to reach $107.5 million by the end of 1961 and $170 million by the middle of 1962. These bonds, with a 25-year maturity and 2 percent interest, were to be sold to governments, national banking establishments, and approved nonprofit trusts and foundations. A sum of $50 million was appropriated to support the Congo operation until June 1962, and $9.75 million was authorized for UNEF's expenses for the same period.[74] These amounts were to be assessed upon Members in accordance with the 1962-assessment scale. The upper limit of reductions was raised to 80 percent for states paying 0.25 percent or less of the regular budget and 50 to 80 percent for those paying more than 0.25 percent but benefiting from the Expanded Programme of Technical Assistance. Voluntary contributions were again to be applied to offset the resulting deficits.

Actually, Member States have over the years been fairly generous in their voluntary donations to support UNEF.[75] Aside from those states which supplied troops to the Force, twenty-two governments during 1957 to 1962 made contributions totalling over $26 million and representing almost twenty-one percent of UNEF's entire cost. Some governments made direct cash contributions, while others waived the reductions allotted to them under the Assembly's resolutions. The United States, the United Kingdom, and France (the largest contributors) paid approximately $23 million, $2.5 million, and $400,000 respectively. The remaining nineteen donors contributed between $310,00 and $1,000: Canada, Australia, Netherlands, Sweden, Italy, Belgium, Japan, Denmark, Norway, New Zealand, Ireland, Mexico, Greece, Ceylon, Pakistan, Liberia, Burma, Dominican Republic, and Austria. A number of states, moreover, did not claim reimbursement for goods and services supplied to UNEF. The total of all these donations is impressive. But arrears in the payment of *assessments* for UNEF have remained considerable.

TABLE 5. CONTRIBUTIONS ASSESSED, RECEIVED, AND DUE AS OF JULY 31, 1962[76]

Year	Amount Assessed	Amount Received (Including Credits)	Balance Due
1957	$15,028,988	$11,040,057	$ 3,988,391
1958	25,000,000	17,739,582	7,260,417
1959	15,205,000	10,844,055	4,360,945
1960	20,000,000	15,260,678	4,739,321
1961	19,000,000	14,030,144	4,969,855
1962 *	8,360,526	3,797,944	4,562,582
Total	$102,594,514	$72,712,462	$29,822,051

* January–June.

On July 21, 1962, the World Court rendered its opinion. The expenses occasioned by the United Nations operations in the Middle East and in the Congo were "expenses of the Organization" within the meaning of Article 17, paragraph 2 of the Charter of the United Nations.[77] The Court rejected the idea that Article 17 referred only to "regular" or "administrative" budgetary items. Each year, from 1947 through 1959, "unforeseen and extraordinary expenses" arising in connection with the maintenance of peace and security had been included in the annual budget. This had been done without dissenting vote, except for the years 1952, 1953, and 1954, when controversial expenditures for United Nations Korean war decorations were included. Paragraph 2 of Article 17 used the term "expenses" to mean all expenses rather than such items as might be called "regular expenses."

The Court does not perceive any basis for challenging the legality of the settled practice of including such expenses as these in the budgetary amounts which the General Assembly apportions among the Members in accordance with the authority which is given to it by Article 17, paragraph 2.[78]

Rejecting the argument that the expenses of peacekeeping operations should not be assessed by the Assembly because such matters were within the purview of the Security Council, the International

Court of Justice said that under Article 24 of the Charter, the Council's responsibility for peace and security affairs was "primary" not exclusive. An argument that Article 43 placed with the Security Council the sole power for meeting the costs of peace agreements made by the Council with Member States was dismissed as inapplicable to the case at hand.[79] Also rejected was the contention that the budgetary authority of the General Assembly in regard to peace and security measures was limited by Article 11, paragraph 2. This paragraph, which declares that questions of peace and security on which action is required shall be submitted to the Security Council by the General Assembly "either before or after discussion," referred to *enforcement* action only.[80] The peacekeeping operations under discussion did not entail coercive, enforcement action.

Peace and security expenses, declared the Court, must be tested by their relation to the purposes of the world organization "in the sense that if an expenditure were made for a purpose which is not one of the purposes of the United Nations, it could not be considered an 'expense of the Organization.' " [81] However, if the United Nations did something in line with its proper purposes set forth in Article 1 of the Charter, "the presumption is that such action is not *ultra vires* the Organization." [82] The resulting financial obligations had to be honored even if the wrong organ of the world body had taken action. The operations of UNEF and ONUC were in conformity with the general purposes of the UN.

The fiscal situation is a complex one, and the attitudes of Member States toward UNEF's finances involve a number of intricate questions. To explain their conduct some states, although admitting their legal responsibility to respond to assessments, have voiced dissatisfaction with what they consider an inequitable system of financing.[83] Such an attitude poses a practical problem: the legal obligation to contribute is not denied, but the execution of the obligation may remain incomplete. Those states which reserve their rights [84] or, *a fortiori,* those which refuse to finance UNEF in principle, pose on the contrary the complex problem of legal obligation.[85] In the case of the governments which reserve their rights, contribution depends in their opinion not on the financial rules of the General Assembly, but on acceptance by the state in question of the *particular* Assembly resolution. They regard each distinct resolution solely as a recommendation and not as a legal obligation. Finally, those states which refuse in principle to contribute to UNEF's costs adopt the most radical attitude on the matter and bring into sharp focus the entire question of obligation. They declare firmly that this obligation is nonexistent and that they are not bound by the Assembly's resolutions on the matter.

As noted above, this latter doctrine is essentially the viewpoint of the Soviet Union and the Soviet-associated states.[86] Stressing always that the "aggressors" must pay and that the UN could only raise and use armed forces under Chapter VII, Article 11 (the end of paragraph 2), and Article 43 of the Charter (i.e., in accordance with a *decision* of the Council), the USSR stands directly opposed to the United States on this question. For the United States, Article 17 is clear: "The expenses of the Organization shall be borne by the Members as apportioned by the General Assembly." No distinction is made in this article, according to the American view, between the various categories of expenses, be they administrative or operational; expenses for peace and security operations, such as UNEF and ONUC, are "expenses of the Organization" and "shall be borne by the Members." [87] But, the Soviet countries reply, if this interpretation of Article 17 were accepted, there would be a contradiction between that Article and Article 10, which provides that "the General Assembly . . . may [only] make recommendations." If the General Assembly can in no event make decisions binding upon Member States, it might be asked how it can compel these states to bear the cost of applying a recommendation. Such a contradiction, the Soviets maintain, creates a difficulty which can be solved only by interpreting Article 17 in relation to *all* the Articles of the Charter and to its fundamental principles, in other words, by taking it to refer solely to the ordinary, or administrative, expenses of the Organization and to no others.[88]

It seems clear, however, that not only the World Court but the Secretary-General and many Member governments believe that *all* Member States are legally obligated to participate in the financing of the Emergency Force.[89] UNEF, they contend, is fundamentally the responsibility of the entire Organization and, as a result, the expenses of the Special Account must be considered as coming under Article 17 of the Charter. In the past, the creation of a number of other subsidiary bodies was also cause for protest by certain states; [90] yet no defaults on budgetary payments, no rejection of legal obligation to contribute, were ever made by these states because of their objection to the body in question.

The finances of all other United Nations organs have, however, been integrated into the *regular* budget of the Organization. We are brought, then, to wonder whether the procedure for financing UNEF recommended at the very beginning by the Secretary-General and, subsequently, adopted by the Assembly—the procedure of the Special Account, separate and exclusive of the regular United Nations budget—has not had an adverse influence. It permitted states to default in their contributions to UNEF, without, at the same time, defaulting in their assessments for the regular budget. It permitted nations, in essence, to veto an important activity of the UN. Psychologically, the system of separate accounting obstructed any immediate financial benefits which might have been gained at the very start, when UNEF was being given near-unanimous approval by Assembly Members. It opened the way to doubts concerning the application of Article 17 of the Charter. Finally, it made more difficult a possible conversion of the Force into a permanent organ, as had been done with other operations in the past.[91]

One may thus question whether there is not a certain contradiction between the Secretary-General's and the Assembly's concern "that this vital United Nations undertaking be assured of the *same degree* and certainty of financial support *as afforded to other United Nations activities* which have as their purpose the maintenance of security and peace," [92] and the adoption of a financial procedure which distinguishes UNEF from the other activities. Integration of UNEF's cost into the regular budget of the Organization would, perhaps, have been possible in the early days of the crisis when nearly all states were convinced of the *necessity* of the Emergency Force for the restoration of peace. Later, by bringing contradictions to the fore and provoking discussion on technical, legal, and political aspects of financing, the Special Account compromised the very existence of the Emergency Force.

Not only the future of UNEF, but the financial position of the United Nations itself has become critical as a result of the arrears in assessments for the Special Accounts of UNEF and the Congo Force. Hence, the Advisory Committee on Administrative and Budgetary Questions listed in its first report to the General Assembly at its fifteenth session, without indicating concurrence or approval at that stage, the following possible alternative measures for dealing with the situation which the Assembly might wish to consider:

(a) An Assembly decision to increase the Working Capital Fund sizeably. . . .

(b) An Assembly decision to finance UNEF, after taking account of voluntary contributions, from a section of the regular budget in order to clarify the liability of Governments to pay UNEF assessments;

(c) An Assembly decision to include annually in the regular budget, during the period UNEF continues in existence, an item of $5 million in lieu of the $2 million now provided in the annual resolution on unforeseen and extraordinary expenses, with a proviso that surpluses remaining under this item at the end of each year be accumulated in a reserve fund for peace and security. Cash could be borrowed from this fund to pay UNEF bills, and this would relieve some of the pressure on the Working Capital Fund;

(d) An Assembly decision to establish a Peace and Security Fund, to be maintained at a level of $20 to $25 million, which might be financed partly from the regular budget and partly by voluntary contributions. The present UNEF and similar operations in the future might be financed from this fund.[93]

These are only a few of the many proposals that have been made to alleviate the burden of United Nations deficits. With respect to the financing of peacekeeping operations, the discussions in the Fifth Committee concerning UNEF and ONUC had, by the end of December 1961, revealed majority consensus on two points only: first, that the contributions of Members should be in proportion to their ability to pay; and, second, that the scale of assessments for the apportionment of costs connected with the maintenance of peace and security should be different from the scale used for the apportionment of the expenses covered by the regular United Nations budget.

To some, the United Nations' financial difficulties would indicate that there exists no political consensus within the Organization in regard to its policy of "preventive diplomacy," especially when this involves the use of peacekeeping forces. Financial support, it might be argued, implies approval, and refusal of support may be taken as evidence of disapproval. Thus the suggestion is that the Organization not court financial disaster by undertaking activities that are not firmly supported by the bulk of the membership.

In reply to this approach, it might be pointed out that UNEF has indeed received a good measure of political support over the years, and support for the Force was almost unanimous during 1956 and 1957. This would suggest that there are other problems than the political involved in its financial troubles. A substantial number of states have contributed to the political consensus but are unwilling or unable to offer any significant financial contribution. The argument that the Great Powers should be required to shoulder a larger measure of the financial burden is thus not without appeal. Reflection might well be given to the construction of a scale of assessment for peace and security expenses, which would increase the percentages of the high and middle income countries above the present ones for the regular budget and start the minimum percentage of payment at a much lower point for the states with frail economies. The low percentages could be made to rise as gross national product and economic growth rates rise. The suggestion that the United Nations institute a system whereby it would acquire a limited amount of independent revenue to help pay for its major expenses is also sound.

Certainly, United Nations commitments must correspond to the degree of consensus in the Organization. However, even if only a minimum consensus exists, "in a changing world the consensus may also be changing and as a result the U.N. must be probing along the outskirts of the minimum consensus." [94] Throughout United Nations history, the world body has had to choose whether or not to move in the face of a stubborn minority-opposition. It has not failed to act. Nor must it give up the probing operation.

In view of the many divergent opinions on how to finance UNEF, any new measure adopted by the General Assembly to decrease the deficits will probably elicit some criticism and opposition. But in all events, it is the following principle which must be stressed in the future: *All* Members of the United Nations—large and small states alike, the parties to the conflict as well as the contributing states— are responsible for financing the organ which they have created and which they have considered a useful instrument to help achieve peaceful conditions in the Middle East.

Chapter Eight

UNEF: WEAPON FOR PEACE

UNEF is still on duty. There is reasonable calm along the Israel-Egypt border. The actions of the world community in 1956 remain evident in the Middle East.

In creating the United Nations Emergency Force to help effect peaceful conditions in Egypt and Israel, the General Assembly had indeed moved with vigor and imagination. A wave of constructive enterprise had stirred the international organization after a long period of placidity. The states of the United Nations were able, at a moment of acute danger, to establish a general consensus, to move along the "middle way"—the road of compromise—which has not failed to lead toward success.

First in accomplishment was the realization of peace. Fighting in Egypt was quickly checked, widespread hostilities were contained, cold-war antagonisms were not allowed to enter the fray. Immediate danger of world war was averted and the invasion retained its character of an incursion—a "Sinai campaign."

Although Soviet and American pressure no doubt exercised considerable influence upon the British, French, and Israeli governments to cease fire and to withdraw, the genesis of a neutral police force, designed for the purpose of supervision, control, and representation, was of cardinal importance. UNEF represented a "face-saving" mechanism for the parties to the conflict. It established a United Nations presence in zones of special sensitivity in the Middle East. It undertook grave tasks at times of keenest tension. The rift between the Allies had been great; with the help of UNEF as an instrument of pacific settlement, it did not become a gulf of unbridgeable proportions. The United Nations played well its role of preventive diplomat.

For the first time in history a completely international police and para-military force came into being. The idea was old. The achievement is new. UNEF itself, unique machinery for peacemaking, was a triumph for international organization. As such, the Force helped to raise the prestige of the world assembly and the authority of its Secretary-General. His office "has developed into field action of so extensive a character that wide diplomacy and security responsibilities seem 'naturally' to have gravitated to that office." [1]

On the Israel-Egypt border a heartening quiet prevails. Patrol by UNEF soldiers of the Egyptian side of the armistice demarcation line continues effectively. Certainly Gaza, with its impoverished and unsettled thousands of refugees, remains an area of potential unrest and discord. But the terrorizing *fedayeen* raids from Gaza, succeeded by violent reprisal measures from Israel, have been kept under control.

At the mouth of the Gulf of Aqaba, a UNEF unit oversees peaceful conditions in the area of the Straits. The legal status of the Gulf has not yet been determined, nor has UNEF's mission in regard to the waterway been totally clarified. Perhaps the quiet prevailing in the region is as much due to Israel's firm warning that Egyptian interference with free navigation will be construed to mean deliberate attack against Israel necessitating self-defensive action, as to UNEF activity in the area. United Nations presence in this trouble zone, however, accompanied as it is by the backing of world opinion, is no doubt an additional factor in forestalling bloodshed.

Indeed it is UNEF's *presence*, indicating active United Nations interest, which seems to have distinctly lessened tension between Egypt and Israel. Both countries, heavily dependent upon great-power aid and world opinion, are reluctant to risk global disapprobation.

It must, moreover, be mentioned that both Egypt and Israel have emerged from the crisis with noticeable gains and have received mutual satisfaction from the presence of the Emergency Force. Each side has lived for many years in daily fear of attack by the other. With United Nations soldiers as a shield between them, the danger of overt military maneuvers diminishes and both countries are left freer to tackle internal problems. In 1956–57, Egypt freed her soil of foreign invaders; she attained most of her demands regarding the Suez Canal by a *de facto* acceptance of a unilateral Egyptian declaration, unaccompanied by any United Nations pronouncement on the subject. Israel saw destroyed the great bulk of tanks and artillery and bombers which Nasser received from the Communist bloc over a fourteen-month period. And, she viewed with satisfaction the diminished prestige of the Egyptian leader, which the rapid Israeli victories in Sinai helped to effect. With the decrease in border incidents and the opening of the Aqaba Gulf to ships of all nationalities, Israel's citizens live a life of increased security and enhanced prosperity.

And yet critics of United Nations action in the Suez-Sinai question speak with some justification in bemoaning the failure of the Organization to settle the remaining substantive issues underlying the dispute between the Arab States and Israel. Egypt has not renounced its policy of belligerency vis-à-vis Israel. The Suez Canal remains closed to Israeli ships. The Arab League's boycott of Israel grows increasingly effective.[2] And, although there is little friction on the border between Egypt and Israel, tension and clashes along the Syrian frontier have erupted periodically. After one such incident, President Nasser declared that "the recent clashes in the demilitarized zone were no surprise at all. . . . Since we expect—every day —to receive reports of Israeli aggression on Arab borders we have prepared our plans on this basis."[3] Arab fears of Israeli expansion have not diminished. Particularly distressing to the Arab world, moreover, is the unsettled refugee problem.

We might, therefore, ask with Stanley Hoffmann "whether another 'middle road,' a different combination of coercion and conciliation, might not have been *tried*."[4] When the General Assembly condemns violations of the Charter, it would be well if, simultaneously, it provided means to remove the conditions which brought about these violations. "For it is one thing to condone violations of the Charter, but it is quite another to refuse to follow a course that makes new violations timely." [5] Indeed, the Assembly might have adopted Pearson's proposal for clear statements by the United Nations political organs on all substantive issues and on suggested methods for their peaceful solution.[6] Unfortunately, it required Hammarskjold to solve problems on a day-by-day basis, instead of proceeding by a master plan.

Lester Pearson had desired affirmation of free navigation in the Aqaba Gulf. He had stressed the Assembly's duty to prevent new raids from Gaza and to establish a transitional international regime in the Strip until final disposal of the territory by the parties.

We have at hand an agency of the United Nations, our own agency, which can be used effectively for these purposes if we so desire. If we do not use it—the United Nations Emergency Force—all our work of last autumn will have been wasted, and our failure will extend far beyond this particular situation . . . We must, therefore, in any draft resolution . . . be sure that we are giving the Secretary-General *clear and definite authority* so that, in the subsequent discussions and consultations which are required, he can make the United Nations and the United Nations Emergency Force effective for the purpose of *bringing about action, following withdrawal* of Israel forces.[7]

Denied a resolute mandate, denied diplomatic pressure upon the parties for the settlement of certain issues, the Secretary-General's approach was more pragmatic. For Hammarskjold, the cease-fire, withdrawal, and restoration of the *status juris* became primary aims. He felt that the November 2 resolution urging the parties to desist from raids across the demarcation lines and to observe scrupulously the armistice agreements would gain "added importance" *after* Israel's withdrawal from Egypt. Although withdrawal was also "first in order of priority" for Pearson, he stressed that a "middle course" could be found whereby the resolution of outstanding issues would *accompany* withdrawal. This would "take effect only *after* Israel has accepted . . . to withdraw" but would be decided upon *before* withdrawal. Lester Pearson's approach would still have endorsed the prescript which declares that advantages acquired by illegal war must not be kept.

It may be that the United Nations Emergency Force will have proved of highest value in the realm of precedent. Speaking of UNEF, the Secretary-General observed in 1957 that "this force, although modest in size and, for constitutional reasons, also modest in aim, broke new ground which inevitably will count in future efforts to preserve peace and promote justice." [8]

An international peace force serving primarily as a United Nations presence in a turbulent area represents a procedural guarantee which tends to discourage further hostilities between opponents. Antagonists unwilling to lose face by "giving in" to the enemy in the field, may prove more inclined to submit to a truce supervised by an international security force. Thus a force such as UNEF may become important at times when an international crisis is highly explosive and liable to extend itself; when the area where the force will operate is not definitively within the sphere of influence of only one "super-power"; and when the smaller and middle powers of the world community possess a positive interest in maintaining the peace.

A number of other principles—possible harbingers of further action—are also suggested by study of the UNEF experience. It is clear, for example, that the General Assembly deemed itself empowered, by virtue of Articles 10, 11, and 14 of the Charter, to bring into existence an international para-military organ. The Assembly thus established a framework within which Members desiring to carry out the resolutions of the General Assembly could act together. It created not an enforcement army, but an instrument for the pacific settlement of disputes. By excluding the Great Powers from the operation, it expressed the change which has occurred in the Organization over the years regarding peace and security. No longer was the United Nations relying primarily on the permanent members of the Security Council for contributions to international forces. Rather, the major powers were deliberately barred from participation in UNEF. Effective action in the Middle East, the Assembly decided, would result only if the Great Powers did not become directly involved in its para-military operation. This edict worked well.

UNEF also symbolizes a changed attitude in international organization toward the use of force. Statesmen and officials of the League had paid particular attention to the concept of collective security, had indeed tried—in vain—to institute a system for mobilizing the strength of the world community to prevent or suppress aggression by any member of the community against any other. The framers of the United Nations Charter also undertook to prohibit the aggressive use of force by states, but provided for the organization of collective force to frustrate aggression only when the Great Powers were in agreement and willing to support such action.[9] In 1956, however, the United Nations showed itself uninterested in and unwilling to participate in collective measures. Rather, it condemned the use of illegal force—even by great powers—and called upon the offenders to cease and desist. No longer was the emphasis placed upon collective military responses to violence. The use of enforcement action by the world community had become a less important means of keeping the peace than the authority of and respect for the Organization, symbolized in its peacekeeping organ—UNEF.

While the Assembly, then, considered itself legally entitled, by a two-thirds vote of its Member States, to create the Emergency Force, provide for its financing, and decide upon its organization and composition, deployment of such a force remained dependent upon the consent of the host state. Lacking a Council decision under Chapter VII of the Charter or explicit consent of the host government, the United Nations may not station a force in territory under a sovereign state's jurisdiction or control. Once consent has been obtained, however, it would seem consistent with Charter articles for the Assembly, in cooperation with its Members, to decide upon the composition of the force, its functions, organization, regulations, and terms of withdrawal.

Were another force, like UNEF, established in the future, Member States would do well to have it led by a commander-in-chief appointed directly by the Council or Assembly. The operation would thus be under the immediate control of one of the major UN organs, integrated with the Secretariat in appropriate form. UNEF's military organization and leadership might also be simulated: chief executive of the operation is the Secretary-General, aided by an Advisory Committee composed of the participating states. The commander-in-chief receives his orders directly from the Secretary-General, exercises full command authority, and directs all activities. A small military staff assisted the Secretary-General, his advisers, and the Chief of Command during the early planning stages of the Force.

The key regulations of the UNEF status agreement will no doubt stand up well to the test of time and will probably be reproduced in subsequent arrangements of this type. Likewise, the rules governing the international status of UNEF's members may prove significant for future developments. The only regrettable precedent of the UNEF experience is the establishment of the Special UNEF Account. Integration of the costs of the Emergency Force into the regular budget of the Organization at an early time might have prevented the difficulties and dilemmas which subsequently emerged in regard to the financing of UNEF's Special Account.

Many of the principles basic to the United Nations Emergency Force have already been embodied in a new military enterprise, the United Nations Operation in the Congo. The structure, organization, and legal arrangements of ONUC are not dissimilar to those of UNEF. Each is to be regarded as a temporary, security operation, functioning with the consent of the government on whose territory it is stationed. UNEF and ONUC are both distinctly international in character and under United Nations control.

This is in accordance with the principles generally applied by the Organization. The Force [ONUC] is thus not under the orders of the Government nor can it . . . be permitted to become a party to any internal conflict. A departure from this principle would seriously endanger the impartiality of the United Nations and of the operation.[10]

Real danger existed in 1960, as it did in 1956, that the "cold war" would impinge upon the situation and would result in extended conflict.[11]

Both military groups are required to keep law and order, although they are not to function as occupation forces or enforcement armies. ONUC has been given wider initiative in the use of armed force than was granted to the soldiers of the Emergency Force.[12] Yet, the Congo operation, essentially, is also a para-military endeavor with restricted powers and limited aims. Although ONUC was authorized by a Security Council decision rather than an Assembly recommendation, the legal regulations applied were identical to those of UNEF, namely,

that, while, on its side, the host Government, when exercising its sovereign right with regard to the presence of the Force, should be guided by good faith in the interpretation of the purpose of the Force, the United Nations, on its side, should be understood to be determined by similar good faith in the interpretation of the purpose when it considers the question of the maintenance of the Force in the host country.[13]

A basic agreement between Hammarskjold and the Congo Republic regularized this understanding. Following the UNEF example, freedom of movement, facilities, and communication were granted to ONUC within its field of operations.

Again, the universality concept was adopted in determining the composition of the Congo force,[14] and the permanent members of the Security Council were excluded from the operation. Again, strict neutrality in attitude and action became prerequisite to the effective functioning of ONUC.

More so than at any time during the Suez crisis, the United Nations in the Congo has confronted a host of delicate problems requiring unwavering impartiality.[15] The importance of impartiality had already been stressed by the Secretary-General during the Suez crisis. It was not until ONUC's experience, however, that the full significance of this concept to UN military operations came to the fore. Since the Congo Republic was hazardously split with internal dissension, since opposing groups within the new state were struggling for control of the government, the United Nations has at times been caught in between, leaving ONUC's future in doubt and raising the problem of UN involvement in an unruly civil war. Each side has charged the United Nations with aiding its opponent. A number of the contributing states, dissatisfied with UN policy, have made known their desire to withdraw from ONUC. Nikita Khrushchev sharply attacked Hammarskjold for "abuse" of his position in "pursuing the line of the colonialists," and called for elimination of the present post of Secretary-General, to be replaced by a three-man executive committee which would be representative of Western, Soviet, and neutralist blocs.

ONUC's experiences, then—perhaps even its very nature—differ in a number of significant ways from those of its predecessor. ONUC has encountered greater opposition by UN Members, which has expressed itself significantly in the financial as well as in the political realm. The definitive scope of ONUC, the exact mission it is to fulfill, remains in greater obscurity than that of the Emergency Force. ONUC has been forced to employ arms in carrying out its objectives. It is "far bigger and far more complicated," with many more nations involved, military units with very different traditions, and "a vast area to be covered." [16] The military phase alone is more problematic than has been that in Egypt. For, immense indeed are the logistical problems of getting thousands of United Nations soldiers into the area and deploying them in the roadless interior. Communications between units of a multi-lingual force scattered over a 1,500 mile distance is a feat fraught with hazards. Likewise Gargantuan in scope is the establishment of a supply line. But UNEF's experience with similar—if less intricate problems—were highly useful to the administrators and officers of the Congo operation.

The success of the Emergency Force has renewed enthusiasm for the establishment of a permanent United Nations force: a force to restore or maintain international peace. In the Assembly, the delegates of Canada, Chile, Greece, Iran, Ireland, Laos, New Zealand, and Norway have expressed the conviction that UNEF represents a first step in this direction.[17]

Lester Pearson has been quite forceful in propounding the need for a stand-by arrangement. Permanent machinery, he declared, by which units of the armed forces of member countries could be endowed with the authority of the United Nations and made available on short notice for supervisory police duties should be established as soon as possible. "The early arrival of a United Nations force of this kind at a scene of emergency would give assurance to the fearful and hope to the despairing. It would act as the United Nations policeman and his watchdog." [18]

Sir Leslie Munro of New Zealand is another enthusiastic advocate of a standing United Nations army:

The purpose of such a force would be to stand as a symbol of the United Nations and to act as a deterrent. It would assure the inviolability of frontiers: there are few aggressors who will flout public opinion in an area where an effective United Nations force is either functioning or is about to function.[19]

Answering the major objection to a permanent force—the severe expense involved—Sir Leslie declares: "This cost is a trifling insurance premium against the risk of war."

The United States government has supported the principle wholeheartedly. Upon the recommendation of their respective committees on foreign affairs, the U.S. Senate and House, in July 1958, voted in favor of the establishment of a permanent United Nations force similar in character to the United Nations Emergency Force in the Middle East. The House resolution stated merely that it is the sense of the Congress that consideration should immediately be given by the General Assembly of the United Nations to the development, within its permanent structure, of such organization and procedure as will enable the United Nations promptly to employ suitable United Nations forces for such purposes as observation and patrol in situations that threaten international peace and security.

However, much more detailed resolutions were considered, particularly resolution 109:

Whereas the United Nations emergency force . . . has made an important contribution to international peace and security in the Middle East; and

Whereas the need for such a force seems likely to continue; and

Whereas such a force could be an important instrument for the maintenance of international peace and security not only in the Middle East, but also in other areas of the world: therefore, be it

Resolved by the Senate (the House of Representatives concurring), that the Congress welcomes the establishment of the United Nations emergency force.

SEC. 2. It is the sense of the Congress that—

(a) A force of a similar character should be made a permanent arm of the United Nations;

(b) Such a force should be composed of units made available by members of the United Nations: *Provided,* That no such units should be accepted from permanent members of the Security Council;

(c) Consideration should be given to arrangements whereby individuals would be allowed to volunteer for service with such a force; *Provided,* That individuals who are nationals of permanent members of the Security Council should not be acceptable;

(d) Equipment and expenses of such a force should be provided by the United Nations out of its regular budget.[20]

Several days later, President Eisenhower put this idea before a special session of the General Assembly.

William Frye, after an earnest study of the matter, was convinced of the need in the world community for a permanent organization not unlike UNEF.

Another time, if the UN is confronted with a crisis like that of November, 1956, the very least that would be useful would be a guide book, a disstillation of knowledge and experience. In addition, the world organization would speak with more authority and act with more practical effect if it had at its fingertips a permanent police force, ready to do at least the limited kind of noncombatant duties that were assigned to UNEF.[21]

He felt that a permanent force could be built on a stand-by basis with the expenditure of no more than a few hundred thousand dollars. These were his explicit suggestions: national states should be asked to earmark portions of their forces for use by the United Nations to keep the peace if and when a crisis develops; a corps of officers should be set up under the Secretary-General's authority to plan in advance swift mobilization in an emergency; another small corps of men—perhaps two hundred in number—should be kept in readiness to be flown to a crisis area immediately for the purpose of showing the United Nations flag and helping to preserve quiet until the international army arrives. Frye lists several past situations faced by the world organization where a UNEF-type force, in his opinion, would have been useful in restoring peace and security.

Critics of a permanent military institution for the United Nations, however, are also numerous. Some of the small states fear the expense involved. Countries such as Portugal and the Union of South Africa emphasized the emergency nature of the international troops in Egypt and hoped, as far back as 1958, that it would be possible to disband UNEF in the near future.[22] Other countries have viewed a permanent force as a possible method of intervention and pressure by a United Nations majority and, therefore, a menace to state sovereignty. Members of the Soviet bloc were agreed with Albania that

establishment of the Force [UNEF] constituted a dangerous precedent, for certain countries might well try to use those armed forces to threaten the sovereignty of small states. In that respect, the efforts of certain countries to make the Force permanent were disquieting. The United Nations should not embark upon that course.[23]

Indeed, the failure or the refusal of many countries to pay their allotted shares of the expenses of UNEF (and, more importantly, ONUC), combined with the poor voluntary-giving by some states favoring these forces, raises the questions of whether the United Nations can, or should, undertake similar operations in the future. The problem entails stronger political than economic considerations, for the major portion of the deficits in the Special Accounts are due to states which are unwilling, not unable, to pay. "This would suggest that there is no political consensus within the United Nations on the utilization of the organization as an instrument of what Dag Hammarskjold called 'preventive diplomacy,' at any rate when this involves the mustering and maintenance of significant peacekeeping forces. Since financial support presumably implies approval and refusal of support may be taken as evidence of disapproval, it seems clear that no solid political basis exists for such United Nations operations as those undertaken in the Middle East and in the Congo." [24]

Should the United Nations, then, terminate its peacekeeping operations as soon as possible and abandon the idea of creating new para-military forces or a permanent force in the future? To do so would suggest the adoption of an attitude of "prudent concern" and the belief that "the effect of the United Nations requires or suggests that the organization not court financial disaster by undertaking activities that are not firmly supported by the bulk of its membership, including, most importantly, the major powers." [25] Should the United Nations, contrarily, try to override political opposition if necessary and foster the performance of certain peacekeeping functions despite powerful opposition on the part of certain states or blocs? The adoption of such a position would reflect the view that the United Nations must serve not merely as static conference machinery, but as "a dynamic instrument of governments," carrying out "executive action."

On the other hand, would it not be desirable for the United Nations to adopt a middle-ground policy and initiate action when necessary despite opposition, so long as the limits of consensus are not clearly visible or absolutely rigid? To espouse such a policy would require a willingness on the part of a majority of Member States to balance the risk of damaging the United Nations by pushing it beyond the limits of consensus against the risk of failing to use the Organization when it is needed and necessary for the maintenance of international peace and security. As I. L. Claude writes: "There is a strong case for probing the limits of consensus, in the hope of discovering that restrictive views of the organization's role are not firmly held, or that opposition in principle to United Nations executive action is qualified in the particular instance by appreciation of its potential contribution to political stability. If this probing goes too far, the precipitation of financial crisis may result, as one aspect of the political overextension of the United Nations. If it does not go far enough, the United Nations will be doomed to the underdevelopment of its capabilities for service to member states. The decision as to how far to go should not necessarily be determined by considerations related to the financial health of the United Nations." [26]

In regard to the establishment of a permanent international force, however, the view of the former Secretary-General is certainly important. Dag Hammarskjold did not favor the establishment of a standing United Nations military force.

In his summary study of the experience derived from the operation of UNEF, he emphasized the special circumstances attendant to the creation and functioning of the Force. "Those circumstances definitely limit any detailed application of that experience to the general problem of United Nations operations of this character." [27] He pointed out that when UNEF actually entered Egyptian territory the governments concerned had already agreed to a cease-fire. As a result, the Force was never in a position to require rights and responsibilities other than those necessary for such an interposed force under cease-fire conditions. For example, UNEF was never in a position to *enforce* withdrawal of foreign forces. The Emergency Force, moreover, functioned under a clear-cut mandate which has kept it entirely aloof from involvement in any internal or local problems, and enabled it to remain neutral in relation to international political issues. It was in response to these special factors that the composition, deployment, legal status, and effectiveness of the Force were largely determined.

The Secretary-General also stressed the unique legal position of the area in which the United Nations Emergency Force was called upon to operate. Because of the special status of Gaza and other regions under the Armistice Agreement, the question of infringement of sovereign rights by the Force had never been raised; UNEF has always functioned on the understanding that it is in Egypt, at the invitation of the Egyptian government and in accordance with Assembly decisions, to maintain quiet on the frontier around the Gaza Strip and along the international line to the south. The Egyptian government has cooperated in helping UNEF to function successfully; military units of the Egyptian army have been kept away from the areas where the Emergency Force is deployed.

Hammarskjold doubted that these unique circumstances—which help to explain UNEF's success—could reasonably be duplicated elsewhere. In fact, subsequent experience in Jordan and Lebanon seemed to him to provide proof of this point.

Neither in Lebanon nor in Jordan would it have been possible to interpose a United Nations force between conflicting parties. Nor would it have been possible in either of those situations to preserve a natural distinction between the presence and functions in various areas of any United Nations force and the presence and functions of government troops. In Lebanon, it is unlikely that a United Nations force could have operated without soon becoming a party to the internal conflicts among nationals of the country. In Jordan, the presence of a United Nations force has been regarded by the Government as difficult to reconcile with its own exercise of full sovereignty. . . .[28]

Hence, the Secretary-General was of the opinion that "far-reaching and firm arrangements—as, for example, the maintenance of a nucleus United Nations force of the type generally envisaged—

would be without great practical value and certainly would not warrant the substantial sacrifices involved." Each case which arises is highly variable, requiring different personnel, specialists, and supporting units.[29] Hammarskjold advised the Assembly to consider very general stand-by arrangements for collective military operations. These would consist "of an approval of those general conclusions regarding principles which can be reached in the light of the UNEF experience. . . ."[30]

Hammarskjold did well to urge the Assembly to adopt a series of principles on a UN peace and security force. As effective "stand-by arrangements," however, are principles adequate preparation? Perhaps the Secretary-General's statement was designed to forestall any definitive efforts to create a permanent force before it was manifestly clear that such a move would be acceptable not only to the majority of states in the Assembly, but to all the permanent members of the Security Council. But was not Hammarskjold unduly pessimistic in discounting the usefulness of a nucleus force-in-being? Such a force would stand as a powerful deterrent.

Had a United Nations Emergency Force existed in 1956, the invasion of Egypt might have been prevented altogether. "Official" reasons for attack would have lost their meaning: Britain and France would not have been able to justify their actions by declaring the United Nations inadequately equipped to deal with the crisis. Few, if any, nations would have been willing to flout world opinion and attack a UN symbol—an almost holy international cause.

With a permanent force standing by at a time of crisis, improvisation would be eliminated, mistakes avoided, and noticeable advantages gained. UNEF was swiftly mobilized and set into action; in another emergency, however, almost *immediate* arrival of United Nations troops in the trouble zone might prove essential to peace. Advance preparations would also have pushed UNEF's timetable ahead. The resolution of November 1–2 calling for a cease-fire might well have included the provisions for the police force, which did not come until November 4, 5, and 7. The Secretary-General's discussions with contributing states would have been shortened; his negotiations with President Nasser could have occurred immediately. During the tense days of November 1 and 2, 1956, when many states feared another world war, when bombs were descending upon Port Said, when Soviet support of Egypt had not yet crystallized, the Secretary-General and the Assembly would have been able, conceivably, to obtain far-reaching terms from the Egyptian President. With UNEF standing in the background, supported by the entire international organization, Prime Minister Ben-Gurion might likewise have looked more favorably upon compromise measures. Equipped with a police force, the General Assembly in 1956 certainly would have had a wider choice of alternative actions. A strong push by the Assembly and the Secretary-General toward the negotiation of the major issues of friction in the Middle East might, indeed, have succeeded.

Hammarskjold's emphasis upon the special circumstances of the UNEF operation is also unduly strong. Each crisis which may arise and which may warrant the use of a peace force will, of course, contain its own special elements. The case of the Congo has proven this point. But thorough and careful advance planning would be useful in any area. Certainly, the Congo operation seems to have been aided by the skills, experiences, and precedents derived from the United Nations Emergency Force. And UNEF itself has taught invaluable lessons in respect to the need for preparations in peace and security endeavors.

During the early days of November 1956, would matters not have been greatly facilitated had the Secretary-General and his staff known where to find aerial reconnaissance troops, large transport aircraft, a staging area near Suez, the necessary support-personnel? Would it not have been useful to have at hand blueprints for a well-balanced and effective force, *before* approaches to governments were made and public troop-offers were forwarded? Prior preparation for UNEF would have smoothed over both military and political issues, saved ruffled feelings, and promoted efficiency. Countless administrative details would have been determined beforehand, leaving the Secretary-General free to concentrate on the political aspects of the situation. Advance planning might conceivably have prevented such problems as the establishment of a Special Account for UNEF's expenses.

What kind of force, then, can reasonably be envisaged in the light of UNEF experience and against the background of many years of relative frustration? If a permanent nucleus force is created, it will conceivably be done on the basis of an Assembly or Council resolution. Hence, the general consent of United Nations Members becomes vitally important. Although it would seem quite unrealistic to envisage a military group with enforcement responsibilities, it may be reasonable to foresee an international force with wider powers than those of UNEF—a force which, although functioning mainly to secure a cease-fire, maintain law and order, supervise an armistice, patrol a frontier, or oversee a plebiscite, would not be limited to use of weapons solely for purposes of self-defense. In the realm of composition and organization of a permanent United Nations force, the application of conservative principles may be foreseen.

While there are appealing arguments for a force composed of persons individually recruited, equipped, trained and maintained by the UN itself, the practical difficulties in the way of organizing and maintaining such a force seem prohibitive. There would be the necessity of a permanent base or bases and a larger budget than probably could be politically possible, to mention only two of the difficulties that would be encountered. It probably will be necessary to settle for a force composed of national contingents maintained and supported, when not on UN missions, as units of national armed forces. These contingents should preferably be contributed by members other than the permanent members of the Security Council.[31]

The force would be a permanent one in the sense that the commander and his staff would be regular members of the Secretariat, appointed by the Council or Assembly and subject to their jurisdiction. These arrangements would thus go further than the mere adoption of principles suggested by Hammarskjold. UN officials would make plans for the use of the force and would negotiate model agreements specifying the terms of national contributions, the terms of entry of the troops into member territory, and the legal status of the force in such territory. Trouble areas would be studied by them and military advice extended to the Secretary-General, as well as assistance in interpretation and implementation of cease-fire, truce, and armistice agreements. Furthermore, they would assume command responsibilities at those times when a force for specific purposes were established. Member States would be expected to pledge in advance the use of their national contingents to constitute this force. From these pledges, the Secretary-General, acting upon the advice of the commander and his staff, would draw a list of participants suitable to the particular purpose for which the Assembly or the Council had created an international command.[32]

A force of this nature is still comparatively modest. Fulfillment of hopes for the creation of a truly effective international instrument of peace enforcement, capable of action wherever and whenever peace may be threatened or disturbed, must await the time when Member States will be willing not only to grant a supranational agency power over their military forces, but also provide the necessary men, money, and facilities to this agency. It is the political value of an operation like UNEF that will remain substantially pertinent. Such a force will forever symbolize United Nations interest and international presence, it will insert itself between two or more belligerents in order to discourage warfare, and will report back to the world an unbiased account of the situation. It will bring into a potentially bilateral struggle the principles and purposes and rules of the Charter. It will always be an international and neutral operation: thus, for similar purposes, forces derived from any of the security and regional organizations such as NATO and SEATO could hardly serve the same impartial end. "Some sort of U.N. force, then, becomes a crucial component of the 'spectrum of possibilities,' the military 'mix,' which needs to be created to deal with the situations most likely to endanger world politics short of overt . . . military aggression." [33]

In the meantime, the United Nations Emergency Force continues to function and to symbolize growing community interest in a peaceful and settled world. This first international police force has dampened passions, softened national humiliations, promoted peaceful settlement, and shown itself a useful model of United Nations military mediation. Heralding future and greater efforts in this realm, UNEF relays once more Santayana's dictum that "those who do not remember the past are condemned to relive it."

HISTORICAL APPENDIX

A look at modern history shows great concern with the concept
of international police, but no success in its firm and continued
establishment in reality. As early as the year 1000, French princes of
the Church declared their willingness to make "war against war" by
the intervention of collective military forces under religious leadership.[1] A little later, Archbishop Aimon of Bourges who "may, in fact,
be considered as the earliest predecessor of the commander of a
modern international armed force," [2] led a number of punitive ex-
peditions with an international army of priests against groups of
recalcitrant knights. In the thirteenth century, the Church Council
of Toulouse passed a strong resolution ordering every person over
fourteen years of age to solemnly renounce war, and proclaiming
that any violator of this pledge would be immediately punished by
collective action.[3]

The ideal of universal peace, the notion of war as fundamentally
evil, came to the fore at the beginning of the fourteenth century.
Thereafter, a great number of proposals—among them those of
Dante, the Duc de Sully, William Penn, the Abbé de Saint-Pierre,
and J.-J. Rousseau [4]—began to be made as to the best means of
achieving this aim. Most of these projects envisaged a system of
world government or a stringent order of collective security backed
by an international army. But from these larger principles would
inevitably emerge the concept of a small international force, useful
for limited purposes, functioning in the aid of peace. The idea of a
large world army and the idea of a small police force are fundamentally linked.

Actual practical arrangements were also instituted. For example, dissension in the Low Countries between Britain, Austria, and the States General in 1715 came to be regulated by a treaty which designated a section of the Austro-French frontier where Dutch soldiers, functioning as international police, would buttress the peace.[5] The Concert of Europe was perhaps the "most elaborate attempt at peace preservation prior to the twentieth century"; [6] an international army was not instituted during the "Era of Metternich" but national forces were made to act in the name of the whole alliance. And, at the time of the Boxer Rebellion in 1900, an allied force of 18,600 men, representing five countries, was sent to the aid of foreign legations in Peking. Authority over these forces was in the hands of the commanders of the national contingents; cooperative conferences were held, however, and decisions were taken by majority vote.[7]

The question of international police as an instrument in the machinery of peace enforcement claimed the attention of innumerable statesmen, military authorities, and scholars throughout the first part of the twentieth century. This was the Hague Period, a time when the idea of peace enforcement was strong. Theodore Roosevelt spoke often about the desirability of an international system of collective security.[8] T. W. Kinkaid, Commander of the United States Navy, declared in 1911: "The criticism that the Hague Tribunal has no military support need not always exist. The object of this brief paper is to suggest that the leading nations of the world unite for the formation and maintenance of an international navy." [9] Fundamentally supporting the views of his colleague, U.S. Rear Admiral C. F. Goodrich wrote an article entitled: "Wanted—An International Police." [10] Nicholas Murray Butler and Andrew Carnegie espoused the cause of a police force, drawn from many countries, to act as international sheriff in keeping the peace. And the United States Congress passed a joint resolution in June 1910, appointing a five-member commission to consider, among other things, the expediency "of constituting the combined navies of the world an international force for the preservation of universal peace."

In many parts of the world these ideas were voiced. Urging the Dutch government in 1910 to make a positive and masterful contribution to the Third Peace Conference at the Hague by formulating a new "Deed" for a world organization, C. Van Vollenhoven, Professor of Law in the University of Leyden, discussed an international army in all its aspects of *pro* and *con*. During a public debate on international police in May 1913, the Dutch professor elaborated his views in terms that seem quite "modern" today, although inordinately optimistic:

As long as the current view was—as in Grotius's days and a long time afterwards—,that quarrels between states could only be peacefully settled by the other states themselves, the question of impartial international arbitration was indeed insolvable. But it has become easy, since it has proved possible to have international differences settled by a separate tribunal, created, it is true, by the states themselves, and therefore in accordance with their sovereignty, but composed not of states, but of independent individuals. The same thing exactly applies to an impartial international police. This institution will only be possible, if directed by a board, created by sovereign states and maintained by them, but consisting of independent individuals, and therefore withdrawn from the influence of national interests and national secretaries of foreign affairs.[11]

Rafael Erich of Finland likewise urged creation of an army composed of forces from several nations, independent as far as possible from the authority of particular states, and exercising its function in the name of the "Community of States." The army would operate only upon appeal from a state needing protection, an independent authority would decide upon such an appeal, and an international agreement would settle the terms by which the international executive force would be used:

The circumstance that the different States would make unequal contributions to the international force, would make no difference in their claim upon it, as it would be in no wise at the service of individual States;

but at that of their Community. Although the force, put together in this way, would form a power, independent of the States lending national contingents to it, yet, upon general principles of justice, it follows that the portion of the force contributed by a State would never be used against that State.[12]

But the first decade of the twentieth century failed to see either a police force or a workable system of peace established. A whirlwind of armament races and international crises gained sway and the peace projects which had been so earnestly forwarded were swept away in the course of events. After the commencement of the First World War, however, proposals for an international *gendarmerie* or a multi-national police force became even more numerous: [13] for, the horrors of war and the destruction perpetrated, engendered a belief that "If we do not try to end war, war will end us"; [14] and one of the means of eliminating war was peace enforcement. Lord Bryce [15] and David Davies [16] in England, the British League of Nations Society,[17] and the American League to Enforce Peace [18] (supported by President Wilson, William Howard Taft, Charles E. Hughes, among others), the American League of Free Nations Association,[19] the Fabian Society of England,[20] and many more persons and groups in Europe and in the United States formulated explicit plans for the avoidance of war and each, in one way or another, envisaged the use of military sanctions or an international police. Likewise, the great majority of drafts for the Covenant of the League of Nations—the proposals of Phillimore, Smuts, Cecil, and Hurst Miller and the programs of the German and Italian governments [21]—contained provisions for the use of international military forces.

One of the most carefully formulated and advanced proposals on this matter was submitted by the French government during the discussions in Paris on the drafting of the League Covenant. The French plan entrusted the execution of military sanctions to an international force or to one or more Powers of the League.[22] It was envisaged that the troops, distributed over the globe and commanded by a permanent staff, would be directly responsible to the "International Body," although the Member States themselves would supply the force with adequate strength to uphold League decisions. The "International Body" would determine the total magnitude and the composition of the force and would be empowered to control the activities of the national armies.

In 1919, however, neither the British nor the Americans favored the organization of such military measures. Indeed, President Wilson was firm in his avowal that "the United States would never ratify any treaty which put the force of the United States at the disposal of such a group or body." [23] Consequently, an international armed force to guarantee compliance with League decisions was not directly authorized in Articles 10 and 16 of the Covenant; and in no way was the Council expressly empowered to employ military sanctions for definitive purposes or under deliberate conditions.

PROPOSALS AND USES DURING THE
LEAGUE PERIOD

Nevertheless, after the Polish-led occupation of Vilna in 1920, the League attempted to establish an international police force, not for purposes of peace enforcement, but "to ensure a well-ordered and fair expression of opinion" in the impending plebiscite.[24] The force, instituted by a Council resolution of November 21, 1920, was to have consisted of 1,800 men composed of Belgian, British, Spanish, French, Danish, Dutch, Norwegian, and Swedish troops supplied by the contributing states.[25] But the entire project was abandoned by the Council on March 3, 1921, when it became evident that a plebiscite could not be expected while Polish occupying forces were still in the area, while disagreement between the parties remained rife, and while Russia objected to settlement of the question by the League.[26] The dispatch of troops to Vilna by the League of Nations would, according to the Soviet Union, have constituted a danger to Soviet security and, had Lithuania let such forces enter, Russia would have considered it an unfriendly act.[27]

In 1934 the League Council again created an international force which operated, with the consent of France and Germany, to ensure order before, during, and after the plebiscite in the Saar Territory.[28] This time the endeavor was a success and, indeed, presaged the experiment of UNEF. Authorized by a resolution of November 11, the Saar Force was primarily intended as an emergency reserve exercising by its mere presence a restraint on any use of violence by the interested parties.[29] Effective policing of the Territory during the plebiscite constituted a problem which had caused concern in many quarters. Diverse political groups were maneuvering for position during the pre-plebiscite campaign; rumors of a *Putsch* were abundant. Observers expected that by the time of the election itself, political fervor would be raised to fever pitch. For, hatred between political adversaries in the Territory was exceptionally acute, complaints of boycott, pressure and terrorism on the part of political extremists were often voiced, and para-military organizations were numerous. The idea of a neutral police force, primarily intended as an emergency reserve to keep the peace, evolved in discussions on the plebiscite.

A Committee of Three, appointed by the League Council and assisted by a sub-committee, formulated specific recommendations concerning the functions, composition, organization, and finances of the police force which was placed under British Command and was directly responsible to the Governing Commission of the Saar Territory.[30] National contingents totaling 3,300 men were contributed by the United Kingdom, Italy, the Netherlands, and Sweden.

The main task of the international force was to uphold order in the territory and to keep peace between the contending parties in the plebiscite. In the early stages of the operation, the soldiers were asked to show themselves to the local population, and to be ready to appear immediately, if necessary, at any spot where disturbances threatened. At five different times mobile parties were dispatched to areas where trouble appeared to be brewing, but it seems that the mere show of force dampened overzealous spirits and, in effect, no military action had to be taken.[31] On the day of the vote, members of the international force were asked to guard polling stations and urns, to escort lorries carrying the ballot boxes, and to be on hand in the event of conflict.[32]

Colonel A. H. Burne, an officer of the British contingent, reported that not a single shot was fired while the Force operated in the Saarland.[33] Whether orders were or were not given to use weapons in the event of trouble is not known. We do know that the same general principles of action were observed throughout:

(1) To make an imposing parade of force *before* the trouble breaks out.

(2) To keep the troops hidden away during the actual period of tension, leaving the maintenance of order, in the first instance, to the Police. . . .[34]

(3) To maintain a large mobile reserve.[35]

Carefully coordinated and imposed by Headquarters, this "British Method" of troop employment was adopted in place of the "Continental Method" (also propounded at the time), which "consisted in the main of placing machine guns, etc., at street corners." [36] If necessary, however, would machine guns have been used? There is no record that the League Council actually discussed or authorized enforcement measures.

After having attained the consent of Germany, France, and the contributing states to the operation, the League Council remained the ultimate source of creation and control; the Council decided when the Force should enter the Territory, what it would do there, who would command, and when withdrawal would be effectuated. The troops were thus truly international soldiers serving the interest of the world community; for, the Governing Commission of the Saar Territory continued as the responsible authority for the maintenance of order and the Force was subject to its rules and decisions, while emergency powers were vested in the commander-in-chief, who controlled the staff officers of each national unit.

It was a well-organized and carefully planned force. Each contingent consisted of infantry, armored cars, and ancillary troops, and Member States were asked to grant every facility for the transit through their territory of the soldiers and their supplies.[37] Furthermore, the League Council authorized the Governing Commission

to enact the legislation necessary to exempt the international force and its members from all responsibility for any act accomplished in the performance of their mission and to confer on itself in case of need the power of requisition for the accommodation, maintenance and transport of the said force.[38]

Exemption from the jurisdiction of the courts of the Saar was granted to the command of the Force, its organs and services and members. Only the Supreme Plebiscite Tribunal (a League creation) was declared "competent to judge breaches of penal law committed against the international force or its members. . . ."[39]

In regard to the financing of the Force, the principle adopted by the Council, just as in the plans for the Vilna project, was that the contributing states would be reimbursed for the cost of all expenditures which exceeded those sums normally spent by them for maintenance of their contingents—that is, the costs of transport and costs of maintenance resulting from expatriation.[40] These expenses would be charged to a fund for expenditures in connection with the plebiscite.[41]

On June 4, 1934, the Council had decided that the German and French governments were to advance five million French francs respectively and the Governing Commission of the Saar was to advance one million French francs as immediate advances to cover the expenses of the plebiscite. These sums were to be placed in a special account, apart from the ordinary funds of the League. The future government of the Saar, to be established as a result of the plebiscite, was to incur the obligation for compensation of lost or damaged material belonging to the international force as well as payment of death or invalidity pensions "which may have to be paid in respect of the death or invalidity of members of the international force as a result of their service, in accordance with the most favorable rules embodied in the legislation in force in the four participating countries. . . ." [42] It was firmly decided that in no case were the resources proper of the League to be drawn upon "either for payments which are not reimbursable, or for advances from the Working Capital Fund." [43] These financial arrangements were very different indeed from those made in 1956 for UNEF.

However, the fiscal principles adopted were in line with general League policy, for many of the League's Commissions and special projects were not directly supported by the Organization but were charged to those states for whom the expenses of the programs had been incurred. This was true, for example, of the Manchurian Commission, the Chaco Commission, and the High Commissioner for Danzig. It was true as well for the two peace and security operations planned by the League—operations which, perhaps, represent significant precedents to those Members of the United Nations today who would like to see UNEF and ONUC financed solely by the countries benefiting directly from the existence of the two police forces.

The multinational Force for the Saar worked efficiently and effectively. Colonel A. H. Burne, a participant and close observer, asked whether the International Police was in fact justified by the results obtained and whether the experience promoted the acceptability of a permanent police force. The answer to the first question was emphatic: the "experiment was a complete and unqualified success"; the League's prestige was raised; since tension between Nazi and *status quo* parties was high, the local police would have been inadequate to meet the situation and, if French troops had been called upon to deal with the mounting pressures, would certainly have been exacerbated; indeed, "in the opinion of many, this would have led to open conflict between the French and Germans. The expressed opinion of many prominent Germans on the Saar that the presence of the Saar Force averted a European war may therefore not be devoid of substance." [44]

But Colonel Burne found it difficult to answer the second question pertaining to a permanent force. He attributed the success of the Saar experiment mainly to the British character of the High Command, to the personality of the Force Commander, the good personal relations between Headquarters and the contingents, the short period that the Force was in existence, the adoption of British methods, and the personality of one of the Englishmen leading the Force. These factors were unlikely to be duplicated in a future situation.* Commenting on Colonel Burne's remarks, Captain B. H. Liddell Hart was especially struck by the difficulty of drawing many conclusions from the Saar policing episode:

It is a fact that the Force as organized fulfilled its task without trouble, and so we can at least draw the conclusion that a force of this kind is practicable in conditions that do not develop into war or an armed outbreak.

But any deductions as to difficulties which a force of different composition or one acting under different conditions might suffer from are necessarily speculative.[45]

As a truly international force created and controlled by a world organization, the Force, however, may be considered as a precursor of the United Nations Emergency Force. Like UNEF, the Saar Police Force had no coercionary powers and functioned mainly as an international representative, keeping order by its mere presence and prestige. Consent of the parties concerned was considered a strict prerequisite to the formation of both groups and an advisory committee assisted in their creation and organization. Similarities in the legal regulation of the two groups, their structure and control, are many. The difference lies primarily in the scope of the two operations, the nature of the crises, and the functions performed. The aim of the Saar Force was to keep order during a time when a plebiscite

* In his summary study on UNEF, Secretary-General Hammarskjold similarly pointed out that the circumstances attendant to the Force in Egypt were unlikely to be duplicated once more. Yet there are many similarities between the Saar Force and UNEF and, in turn, between UNEF and the UN force for the Congo. See above, Chapter VIII.

was in progress. UNEF was entrusted with much more delicate and responsible tasks: to supervise a cease-fire, to guide the withdrawal of powerful military forces from foreign territory, and to oversee an armistice. The political situation of 1956 in regard to the Middle East was decidedly more disturbed and incendiary than that of 1934 in respect to the Saarland. And the UNEF operation may be considered, in its entirety, not only more extensive and vital than that of the Saar Force, but more closely planned and organized. However, by propagating the idea of an international police, by demonstrating its success even in limited circumstances, the Saar expeditionary force of the League may have furthered in a small way the entire concept of a military force for the international community of states and may have provided a precedent in a general way for the organization of the Emergency Force in 1956.*

MILITARY FORCES AND THE UNITED NATIONS

Even before the time of the Saar plebiscite, another plan for the creation of a permanent police force to prevent war was proposed by France at the Disarmament Conference in 1932.[46] The police force was to be always on hand "with complete freedom of passage to occupy in times of emergency areas where a threat of war has arisen"; each of the contracting parties was to furnish contingents "in a proportion to be determined," while command arrangements were to be made by the League. A primary contingent of mobile forces was to bring immediate assistance to any victim of aggression.[47] For, the new era of air power required advance planning which aimed toward the *immediate* use of aircraft and personnel when it should be needed. The First World War days of military planning, focusing upon supremacy on the seas, had passed. As a result, France also made concrete proposals for placing civil aviation, bombing aircraft, and certain matériel of land and naval forces at

---

* There is, however, no reference to the Saar Force in any of the Secretary-General's reports or in the Assembly debates on the United Nations Emergency Force.

the disposal of the League. Although coolly received at the time, these suggestions later formed the essence of Articles 43 and 45 of the Charter of the United Nations.

Indeed the Disarmament Conference, accompanied as it was by Hitler's swift rise to power, perhaps marked the beginning of the end of the League; and no real efforts toward military enforcement of peace by world organization were made again until the Dumbarton Oaks Conference in 1944. Multi-national armed forces were harnessed during the Second World War and their experience and organization provided (as did later the NATO experience) a precedent upon which the creators of UNEF could lean. But the war operations were not executed by international military forces serving a world organization, but of one or the other party to the war. And, actually, there is no indication that these were "precedents," relied upon by UNEF's architects.

At Dumbarton Oaks, the United States submitted proposals [48] not unlike those of the French government in 1932, which were accepted in substance by the other delegations at the conference, and later formed Chapter VII of the United Nations Charter. By the terms of this chapter the Security Council "may take such action by air, sea, or land forces as may be necessary to maintain or restore international peace and security."

In order that the Security Council may operate effectively, Article 43 of the Charter commits Members of the United Nations to make available to the Council "armed forces, assistance, and facilities, including rights of passage," in accordance with special agreements, for the purpose of maintaining international peace and security. A Military Staff Committee, composed of the Chiefs of Staff of the permanent members of the Council or their representatives, is to advise and assist the Council on all questions relating to these military requirements and on the employment and command of forces placed at its disposal. The permanent members of the Council, however—particularly the Soviet Union and the United States—were unable to come to terms on the basic principles to govern an international force and, as a result, agreements were never concluded between Member States and the Security Council.[49] The impasse was a political rather than a technical one: although the members of the Military Staff Committee wrangled over the various ideological and practical aspects of an international military force, it was the growth of the "cold war" which helped to produce the fundamental deadlock. The debates in the committee revealed the extent to which each major power would endeavor to obtain maximum influence over a UN army and hence compete on the questions of organizing and of stationing such a force. The problem of creating an international military operation cannot be divorced from the unified political purpose it is to serve. Deadlock, then, prevented the Security Council from obtaining the military means to enforce its decisions. And one of the essential provisions of the Charter remained unfulfilled.

Since there was no immediate hope of agreement between the Great Powers on the establishment of an enforcement army, a number of schemes for a small armed force outside the framework of Article 43 of the Charter and without enforcement powers were considered at the United Nations. Upon the request of the UN Mediator in Palestine, more than a hundred military officers from the armed forces of Sweden, Belgium, France, and the United States were sent to the Middle East as military observers in 1948.[50] During July of the same year, Secretary-General Trygve Lie proposed the creation of "a small United Nations Guard Force" of 1,000 to 5,000 men "which could be recruited by the Secretary-General and placed at the disposal of the Security Council and the General Assembly." [51] The "primary positive purpose" of the Guard was "to be representative of United Nations authority in support of United Nations Missions in the field and to provide a limited protection to United Nations personnel and property." [52] Mr. Lie stated that "such a force would not be used as a substitute for the Force contemplated in Articles 42 and 43. It would not be a striking force, but purely a guard force. It could be used as a constabulary under the Security

Council or the Trusteeship Council in cities like Jerusalem and Trieste during the establishment of international regimes. It might also be called upon by the Security Council under Article 40 of the Charter, which provides for provisional measures to prevent the aggravation of a situation threatening the peace."

Faced with considerable opposition in the Assembly to the Guard Force, Secretary-General Lie initiated a more modest plan which the Assembly accepted, on November 22, 1949, by the establishment of a United Nations Field Service of 300 communication technicians and guards to form a normal unit of the Secretariat and aid the operation of UN Field Missions.[53] This was undoubtedly a useful institution, but fell far short of being a police force of international military units whose aid the United Nations could enlist for functions of pacific settlement or for enforcement action to prevent or suppress acts of aggression.

Thus military forces were not immediately available for use by the world organization when the Security Council on June 25, 1950, determined that a breach of the peace had been committed in Korea.[54] Unable to act under Article 42, the Council recommended that Member States "furnish such assistance to the Republic of Korea as may be necessary to repel the armed attack" and invited the United States to establish a unified command.[55] Fortunately, the United States government had substantial forces in close proximity to the area of the North Korean attack and favored their immediate use to repel the invasion. "If it had not been for this special juxtaposition of circumstances, it is quite unlikely that assistance would have been rendered to the Republic of Korea in time to halt the North Korean attack." [56]

Indeed, the Korean operation undoubtedly demonstrated the weakness of the United Nations system of enforcement action, without advance preparation by governments to place their forces at the disposal of the UN and without adequately training, organizing, and equipping them for this specific use. Members of the United Nations other than the United States acted slowly in contributing military assistance to the UN Command in Korea. Difficulties were encountered in regard to the strategic direction of the international force. And it became apparent that

when one state assumes a major responsibility initially for aiding the victim of aggression, largely on its own and not as part of a prepared plan of collective action, the whole operation fails to acquire a truly collective character, because the state bearing the major responsibility almost necessarily exercises a dominant control over the whole operation.[57]

The drawbacks inherent in the improvised and unilateral procedure of the Korean operation were important factors in leading Members of the United Nations to pass the "Uniting for Peace" resolution of November 3, 1950, in which the Assembly recommended that "each Member maintain within its national forces elements so trained, organized and equipped that they could promptly be made available . . . for service as a United Nations unit or units, upon recommendation by the Security Council or the General Assembly." [58] The resolution also established a Collective Measures Committee which would undertake the preparation of basic principles and plans of action to guide and facilitate the application of collective measures. Although this Committee made extensive studies of the question [59] and submitted a number of significant proposals on the matter to the General Assembly, it was soon evident that most Member States were unwilling to undertake specific commitments for the future.[60] The failure of the Security Council to establish an effective system of collective security had caused many of them to provide for their mutual defense by means of special arrangements for collective self-defense and hence they were anxious to determine their future course of action in the light of these commitments and the circumstances of the particular situation. Leland Goodrich and Anne Simons assert that the efforts of the Collective Measures Committee and the Assembly's deliberations and resolutions did not seem to "have had any direct or immediate effect on preparatory measures taken by Members to strengthen 'international peace and security.' " [61] Actually, those states whose response was most favorable never "indicated any intention of taking new steps on the basis of this institution alone." [62]

Thus efforts to earmark military forces for United Nations use, although persistently made in the past, had not matured at the time of the Suez crisis in November 1956. The reasons for this are many and probably lie most fundamentally in the continuous opposition of sovereign states to international control. "Broadly speaking, international (or better, supernational) ways of thinking, feeling, and acting cannot be simply superimposed on national ways. The larger mode will not embrace the smaller; it must replace it by means of a thorough permeation." [63] In the period since the establishment of the United Nations, the postwar world—with its bipolar-power system, cold war, emphasis on regional alliances, and lack of trust in world organization—has been so constituted as to engender profound differences between the Great Powers on the basic considerations to govern an international military force. Yet developments in atomic and hydrogen weapons, space and intercontinental ballistic missiles have made the fear of war so overwhelming that keen attention has been paid to every situation which might, if left unchecked, lead to global disaster. Consequently, "What we faced in the Assembly last November [1956] was the necessity of organizing quickly a force, not to fight but to ensure that fighting would not be resumed." [64] There was no attempt during the Middle Eastern emergency to establish a large army with coercionary powers. But even the establishment of a small para-military group required considerable foresight and planning. The few limited experiences of the past, as well as the myriad schemes for an international military force, were probably more valuable in their function of furthering and spreading the idea of international policing than in their practical nature as precedents to guide the architects of UNEF. Hence, the United Nations Emergency Force emerges as a distinct pioneering effort.

NOTES

INTRODUCTION

1. "Report of the Secretary-General," U.N. Doc. A/3943, October 9, 1958.

2. "Introduction to the Annual Report of the Secretary-General on the Work of the Organization, 16 June 1959–15 June 1960," General Assembly, *Official Records*, 15th Session (1960–61), Supp. No. 1A, p. 4. See also Chapter VIII.

3. Lester B. Pearson, "Force for U.N.," *Foreign Affairs*, XXXV (April, 1957), 402.

4. William R. Frye, *A United Nations Peace Force*, p. 32.

5. *Ibid.*

6. Lester B. Pearson, "Force for U.N.," *Foreign Affairs*, XXXV (April, 1957), 401.

I: POLITICAL BACKGROUND

1. From an address by Clarence A. Berdahl at the Conference of National Organizations called by the American Association for the United Nations, March 9 and 10, 1958.

2. One possible exception is the Saar Force created by the League of Nations, but the differences between this military group and UNEF are, nonetheless, considerable. See Historical Appendix.

3. Percy E. Corbett, "Power and Law at Suez," *International Journal*, XII (Winter, 1956–57), 1.

4. From statement by Francisco Urrutia, representative of Colombia, speaking in the Assembly (November 1, 1956). General Assembly, *Official Records*, 1st Emergency Special Session, 562d meeting (November 1, 1956), p. 15.

5. "Statement in the British House of Commons by Prime Minister Eden, October 30, 1956," reprinted in U.S. Department of State, *United States Policy in the Middle East*, p. 139.

6. Farid Zeineddine of Syria, General Assembly, *Official Records*, 11th Session, Plenary meeting 639 (January 17, 1957), Vol. II–III, p. 898.

7. Israel interpreted the military agreement between Egypt, Jordan, and Syria, signed October 25, 1956, which provided for unified military command in case of war with Israel, as evidence, "in the words of *Al Gamhouria* on October 27, that the Arab peoples were endeavoring to tighten the noose

around their enemy and to strangle him." See statement by Israel's Ambassador to London, *The Times* (London), November 3, 1956.

8. See L. L. Leonard, "The United Nations and Palestine," *International Conciliation*, No. 454 (October, 1949); Shabtai Rosenne, *Israel's Armistice Agreements with the Arab States; A Juridical Interpretation;* and Security Council, *Official Records*, 4th year (1959), Special Supp. Nos. 1–4.

9. The United Nations, in addition to establishing an organization entrusted with supervision of the armistice (UNTSO), created the Palestine Conciliation Commission in November 1947 to work out terms for a permanent settlement. The Commission has been unsuccessfully engaged in this work ever since. See J. C. Hurewitz, "The United Nations Conciliation Commission for Palestine," *International Organization*, VII (1953), 482–97, and the reports of the Commission to the United Nations.

10. Among the most fundamental of the political problems outstanding between Israel and the Arab States were: the border regulations and the status of Jerusalem; the repatriation of Arab refugees, compensation for property, freeing of blocked accounts; and the creation of an international water authority to deal with the problems of the Jordan and Yarmuk Rivers. Consult George Lenczowski, *The Middle East in World Affairs.*

11. *Ibid.*, p. 358.

12. On October 19, 1955, an elaborate and comprehensive law dealing with the economic boycott of Israel was enacted by Egypt. It provides, in part, that "no person, or other legal entity, is permitted to conclude an agreement, directly or indirectly, with institutions or persons in Israel, or persons acting on her behalf in another country. This covers any commercial, financial or other transactions." *Journal Officiel* (Cairo), October 23, 1955.

13. L. M. Bloomfield, *Egypt, Israel and the Gulf of Aqaba*, p. 7.

14. Specific regulations regarding the Suez Canal and the Gulf of Aqaba were "partly achieved by means of administrative regulations embodied in documents such as Notices to Mariners and Notices to Airmen . . . but occasionally legislative action" was taken. An example of such legislative action was the amendment in November 1953, to the Decree on the Procedure of Ship and Aircraft Searches and of Seizure of Contraband Goods in connection with the Palestine War, whereby foodstuffs were added to the list of contraband goods and whereby all items on the list were to be considered as war contraband even when only passing through Egyptian territorial waters en route elsewhere. *Ibid.*, pp. 7–8. For administrative regulations, see *Journal de Commerce et de la Marine* (Alexandria), August 19, 1955.

15. The measure was announced in a memorandum, dated January 28, 1950, which was read at the 659th meeting of the Security Council on February 15, 1954. See Security Council, *Official Records*, 9th year, 659th meeting (February 15, 1954), p. 19.

16. For enumeration of these incidents, see Bloomfield, *Egypt, Israel and the Gulf of Aqaba*, pp. 11–15.

17. On four different occasions Egypt's regulations were discussed by the Security Council, notably during October–November 1950; July 26, 1951–September 1, 1951; February 5, 1954–March 29, 1954; and November 3, 1954–January 13, 1955.

18. U.N. Doc. S/2322, September 1, 1951.

19. Composed of United Nations observers whose task it was to watch the borders. See Chapter IV.

20. U.N. Doc. S/2194, June 13, 1951.

21. In 1956, Israel claimed that "some 90 per cent of the trade which would have normally flowed through the Canal to and from Israel in the past years has been effectively obstructed." See letter dated October 13, 1956, from the representative of Israel to the President of the Security Council, U.N. Doc. S/3673.

22. Several of these raids, particularly those executed against the Arab settlements of Kibya and Nahalin in Jordan during 1953 and 1954, against Egyptian headquarters in Gaza during 1955, and against a Syrian village near the Sea of Galilee at the end of 1955, assumed major proportions. For details of Kibya question, see Security Council, *Official Records*, 8th year, 629th–643d meetings (October 27–November 25, 1953). The incident of Nahalin concerned the Council during the 665th–671st meetings (April 8–May 12, 1954), *ibid.*, 9th year (1954); see *ibid.*, 10th year, 692nd–696th meetings (March 4–30, 1955) for discussion of the 1955 Gaza raid; and *ibid.*, 10th year, 709th meeting (December 22, 1955); *ibid.*, 11th year, 710th–715th meetings (January 12–19, 1956) for details of the incident near Lake Tiberias.

23. Mohammed Fadhil Jamali of Iraq, General Assembly, *Official Records*, 11th Session (1956–57), Plenary meeting 639 (January 17, 1957), Vol. II–III, p. 906.

24. The Arab governments have constantly denied connection between the *fedayeen* and Egypt's regular armed forces. Deriving their name from the Arabic word meaning "sacrificers," the *fedayeen* are said to serve as volunteers, usually in units of three to four men. Israel was convinced, however, that these bands, though consisting mainly of Palestinian Arab refugees, were trained, armed and financed by the Egyptian War Ministry and operated from permanent sites within Egypt.

25. See U.N. Doc. S/3575, April 4, 1956 and Joseph P. Lash, *Dag Hammarskjold*, p. 71.

26. U.N. Doc. S/3596, May 9, 1956.

27. U.N. Doc. S/3600, May 25, 1956.

28. For summary of discussion, see *Yearbook of the United Nations 1956*, pp. 9–11. Lash, *Dag Hammarskjold*, p. 74, declares that Soviet objections might have been less strong had the resolution been negotiated by means of a four-power approach, but the United States had been anxious to exclude the USSR from these proceedings.

29. U.N. Doc. S/3600/Rev. 2, June 4, 1956.

30. See the *Yearbook of the United Nations 1956*, pp. 11 and ff.

31. Lash, *Dag Hammarskjold*, p. 76.

32. Security Council, *Official Records*, 11th year, 749th meeting (October 30, 1956), p. 8.

33. For further details of the postwar policies of Britain, France, Israel, and the United States, see G. F. Hudson, "The United Nations Emergency Force: A Notable Precedent," *Current History*, XXXVIII (June, 1960), 327–30; and John Marlowe, *Arab Nationalism and British Imperialism*.

34. Republic of Egypt, Ministry for Foreign Affairs, *White Paper on the Nationalization of the Suez Maritime Canal Company,* published by the government of Egypt (Cairo, Government Press, August 12, 1956), pp. 3–13.

35. A statement issued July 19, 1956, read: "Developments [since the U.S. offer was announced on December 17, 1955] . . . have not been favorable to the success of the project. . . . Agreement by the riparian states [Sudan, Ethiopia, and Uganda on a division of the Nile waters] has not been achieved, and the ability of Egypt to devote adequate resources to assure the project's success has become more uncertain than at the time the offer was made." U.S. Department of State *Bulletin,* XXXV (July 30, 1956), 188. For discussion, see Anthony Eden, *Memoirs.*

36. The British government immediately declared that nationalization by Egypt "constitutes a serious threat to the freedom of navigation on a waterway of vital importance." New York *Times,* July 27, 1956. Eden in the House of Commons on July 30 announced that Britain will not accept the "unfettered control of a single power" over the Suez Canal, *ibid.,* July 31, 1956. *The Times* (London) declared on July 28 that, "Interference with Britain's free use of the Suez Canal would cut at the roots both of her domestic economy and her survival as a great Power. It would mean the severance of her strategic sea links with Asia, the Far East and Australasia."

French anxiety revolved mainly about the effects upon the Algerian conflict of President Nasser's defiance of the West.

Secretary of State Dulles felt bound to say on July 29 that nationalization "strikes a grievous blow at international confidence . . . it could affect the operation of the canal itself. That would be a matter of deep concern to the United States as one of the maritime nations." Press Release 415, U.S. Department of State *Bulletin,* XXXV (August 6, 1956), 221.

37. For text of the Charter given to the Company in 1856, see *ibid.,* pp. 21–27; and *Suez Canal, A Documentary Study* (New Delhi, Lak Sabha Secretariat, 1956), pp. 38–44.

38. New York *Times,* August 22, 1956. India proposed that operation of the Canal remain in the hands of an Egyptian board of control, advised by an international body.

39. A detailed account of the Menzies Mission is found in Eden, *Memoirs,* pp. 507–28.

40. *Parliamentary Debates: House of Commons Official Report,* 5th Series, Vol. 558 (September 12, 1956), pp. 10–11.

41. A statement and a declaration, issued on September 21 and providing for a Suez Canal Users' Association (SCUA), announced that the Association "will seek the cooperation of the competent Egyptian authorities pending a solution of the larger issues. . . . The Conference considers that recourse should be had to the United Nations whenever it seems that this would facilitate a settlement." The declaration authorized the SCUA to "seek the cooperation of the competent Egyptian authorities for this purpose. . . . To receive, hold and disburse the revenues accruing from dues . . . which any user of the Canal may pay to SCUA." See Press Release 502, U.S. Department of State *Bulletin,* XXXV (October 1, 1956) 507–8.

The weakness of this arrangement and the lack of firmness shown towards Nasser were severely criticized by many observers. See *The Times* (London), September 22, 1956, the New York *Times*, September 23, 1956, *Le Monde* (Paris), September 24, 1956, and *Le Figaro* (Paris), September 23, 1956.

See also, U.S. Department of State Publication 6392, *The Suez Canal Problem, July 26–September 22, 1956: A Documentary Publication* and U.S. Department of State, *United States Policy in the Middle East.*

42. Actually, the nationalized Canal had been working efficiently and without incident for over two months. Accidents due to inexperienced pilotage had not occurred. There had been no delays due to inefficient administration, no discrimination (except against Israel), and no increases in tolls.

43. The principles were: "(a) There should be free and open transit through the Canal without discrimination, overt or covert—this covers both political and technical aspects; (b) The sovereignty of Egypt should be respected; (c) The operation of the Canal should be insulated from the politics of any country; (d) The manner of fixing tolls and charges should be decided by agreement between Egypt and the users; (e) A fair proportion of the dues should be allotted to development; (f) In case of disputes, unresolved affairs between the Universal Suez Maritime Canal Company and the Egyptian Government should be settled by arbitration, with suitable terms of reference and suitable provisions for the payment of sums found to be due." U.N. Doc. S/3671. For discussion at the United Nations, see Security Council, *Official Records,* 11th year, 742d and 743d meetings (October 13, 1956).

44. See U.N. Doc. S/3712, October 30, 1956. Official United States reaction to the ultimatum, knowledge of which, it appears, was obtained only through press reports, manifested itself in an urgent personal message from President Eisenhower to Prime Minister Eden and Premier Mollet expressing "his earnest hope that the United Nations Organization would be given full opportunity to settle the items in the controversy by peaceful means instead of by forceful ones." U.S. Department of State, *United States Policy in the Middle East,* p. 142.

45. U.N. Doc. S/3706, October 30, 1956.

46. Security Council, *Official Records,* 11th year, 749th meeting (October 30, 1956), p. 31.

Eden explained the veto by declaring his unwillingness to support a resolution which in effect condemned Israel as an aggressor. "Throughout recent months," Eden told the Commons, "and, in particular since the seizure of the Canal, the Egyptian Government have kept up a violent campaign against Israel, against this country and against the West. The Egyptian Government have made clear over and over again, with increased emphasis since the seizure of the Canal, their intention to destroy Israel, just as they have made plain that they would drive the Western Powers out of the Middle East. That is what has been happening and that is the background to understand what is happening. It is from these Egyptian policies that much of the present crisis has sprung and to ignore them is to shun reality." Statement in the House of Commons, *Parliamentary Debates: House of Commons Official Report,* 5th Series, Vol. 558 (October 31, 1956), p. 1450.

47. *Ibid.*

48. Eden, *Memoirs,* p. 588.

49. For discussion, consult the New York *Times,* November 1, 1956.

50. See editorial, "Over the Brink," in *The Times* (London), November 1, 1956; also, "Labour Forces a Division in the Commons," "To War," "Sir Anthony Eden on Aim to Stop War," *ibid.;* "Britain's Act of Aggression," *New Statesman and Nation,* November 3, 1956; "Conditional Cease-fire," *Manchester Guardian Weekly,* November 8, 1956; "Britons Divided on Move in Egypt," New York *Times,* November 1, 1956.

51. For summary of governmental attitude toward the problem, see "Une large majorité a approuvé l'action du gouvernement," *Le Monde* (Paris), November 7, 1956.

52. Nehru declared that the attack against Egypt would have far-reaching results in Asia and Africa and might lead to war on a large scale. New York *Times,* November 1, 1956; see also, "Clear and Naked Aggression," *Hindu Weekly Review,* November 5, 1956. Other hostile reactions in Asia are reported in "Asians Rally to Egypt's Cause and Ignore Satellites," New York *Times,* November 4, 1956.

53. Joseph and Stewart Alsop reporting from Washington, D.C., New York *Herald Tribune,* November 2, 1956.

54. The United Kingdom and French governments were also convinced, on the basis of intelligence reports, that the regimes in Jordan, Syria, and Iraq were being threatened by groups of officers stimulated by Egyptian propaganda and, to some extent, even financed by Egypt. Were a successful revolution to occur in these lands, a military and political alliance aimed toward the liquidation of Israel would certainly follow. One of the goals of British policy was to prevent such an alliance and its probable concomitant war. See Eden, *Memoirs,* p. 469; and the report of Drew Middleton in the New York *Times,* November 1, 1956.

55. New York *Times,* November 1, 1956.

56. Sherman Adams, *Firsthand Report,* p. 256.

57. This proposal was rejected by the Council on November 5, 1956, Security Council, *Official Records,* 11th year, 755th meeting (November 5, 1956), pp. 4–14.

58. New York *Times,* November 6, 1956.

59. *Ibid.*

60. White House news release, U.S. Department of State, *United States Policy in the Middle East,* p. 182.

61. The vote on the draft resolution calling for an emergency special session of the Assembly was as follows: In favor: China, Cuba, Iran, Peru, USSR, U.S., Yugoslavia; Against: France, U.K.; Abstaining: Australia, Belgium. Security Council, *Official Records,* 11th year, 751st meeting (October 31, 1956), p. 22.

II: CREATION OF THE FORCE

1. Phrases used by Stanley Hoffmann, "Sisyphus and the Avalanche: The United Nations, Egypt, and Hungary," *International Organization,* XI (Summer, 1957), 452.

2. Security Council, *Official Records,* 11th year, 751st meeting (October 31, 1956).

3. See Leland M. Goodrich, *Korea: A Study of U.S. Policy in the United Nations.*

4. General Assembly, *Official Records,* 1st Emergency Special Session, 562d meeting (November 1, 1956), p. 26.

5. *Ibid.,* 561st meeting (November 1, 1956), p. 9.

6. *Ibid.,* 562d meeting (November 1, 1956), p. 28.

7. *Ibid.,* 561st meeting (November 1, 1956), p. 10.

8. "Radio and Television address by President Eisenhower, October 31, 1956," U.S. Department of State, *United States Policy in the Middle East,* p. 149. Cf. Adams, *Firsthand Report,* p. 255: "The next day, October 31, the President learned to his astonishment that British bombers from Cyprus had attacked the Egyptian airfields. The news caught the President by surprise and the suddenness shocked him. He had received no previous warning from the British and French and no advance information from our intelligence sources in Europe or in the Mediterranean."

9. Eden's *Memoirs,* p. 588.

10. "Statement in the British House of Commons by Prime Minister Eden, October 31, 1956," U.S. Department of State, *United States Policy in the Middle East,* p. 146.

11. See "Radio and Television Address by President Eisenhower, October 31, 1956," *ibid.,* pp. 148–51 and "Statement in the United Nations General Assembly by Secretary of State Dulles, November 1, 1956," *ibid.,* pp. 151–57.

12. "Radio and Television Address by President Eisenhower, October 31, 1956," *ibid.,* pp. 149–50.

13. Adams, *Firsthand Report,* p. 262.

14. During his address to the Assembly, the delegate of Australia observed: "In Australia we believe that the strength of the United Nations rests principally upon two foundations: on the one hand, the participation of the wide range of Members throughout the world and, secondly, on the close friendship and close cooperation of the United States, the United Kingdom and France. It is with very heavy heart that we recognize the division of opinion, the very deep division of opinion, that has developed regarding the practical measures that should be taken at this time to deal with the tragic situation in the Middle East." General Assembly, *Official Records,* 1st Emergency Special Session, 562d meeting (November 1, 1956), p. 27.

15. *Ibid.,* p. 34. At the same meeting, the representative of the Philippines, Felixberto Serrano, outlined a detailed "conciliatory" procedure.

16. *Ibid.,* 561st meeting (November 1, 1956). The words quoted are those of the delegate of Ceylon, R. S. S. Gunewardene.

17. *Ibid.,* 562d meeting (November 1, 1956), p. 18.

18. Statement of the Jordanian representative, Abdul Monem Rifa'i, *ibid.,* p. 15.

19. Hoffmann, "Sisyphus and the Avalanche," *International Organization,* XI (Summer, 1957), 452.

20. Canada, Department of External Affairs, Information Division, *Statement*

and Speeches, Excerpts from a Statement by the Hon. L. B. Pearson, in the Fourth (Special) Session of Parliament on November 27, 1956.

21. U.N. Doc. A/3256, November 1, 1956; subsequently became Resolution 997 (ES-I).

22. General Assembly, *Official Records,* 1st Emergency Special Session, 562d meeting (November 1, 1956), p. 36.

23. Lash, *Dag Hammarskjold,* p. 84.

24. *Ibid.,* p. 85.

25. See letters dated November 3, 1956, from the representatives of France and the United Kingdom to the Secretary-General, U.N. Docs. A/3268 and A/3269, November 3, 1956.

26. In cablegrams to the Ministers for Foreign Affairs of France and the United Kingdom on November 4, Hammarskjold pointed out that since the Assembly established a time limit of twelve hours for a report on the cease-fire in Resolution 997 (ES-I), the General Assembly had not actually made the establishment of a UN Force a condition for the cease-fire. Furthermore, "it was a widespread view that none of the parties engaged in the present operations in the area should participate in the Force. This has a direct and obvious bearing on any possibility of stationing Anglo-French troops between the combatants. . . ." U.N. Doc. A/3287 Annexes 2 and 4, November 4, 1956.

27. U.N. Doc. A/3276, November 3, 1956; subsequently became Resolution 998 (ES-I).

28. The representatives from Indonesia, El Salvador, and India desired clarification of the phrase, "with the consent of the nations concerned," but were sympathetic to the idea. Delegates from the United States, Costa Rica, Ceylon, Mexico, and Thailand expressed forthright approval of the Canadian draft resolution. Mr. Lodge declared: "I want to say that the United States likes the Canadian draft resolution very much. We are looking for something that will meet the immediate crisis which is in front of us, as well as something that will go to the causes and into the more long-range subjects." General Assembly, *Official Records,* 1st Emergency Special Session, 563d meeting (November 3, 1956), pp. 55–71.

Frye, *A United Nations Peace Force,* p. 6, indicates that lobbying before and during the debate was intense. The British had been contacted by Canada even before the Assembly convened, the United States and Norway had been asked to participate in the planning for the Force, "and strategy had been mapped out in detail." During the debate, Pearson is said to have masterminded "the process from his seat in the Assembly Hall."

29. Abstaining were Czechoslovakia, Egypt, France, Hungary, Israel, Laos, New Zealand, Poland, Portugal, Rumania, Ukraine, Union of South Africa, USSR, United Kingdom, Albania, Australia, Austria, Bulgaria, Byelorussia. See General Assembly, *Official Records,* 1st Emergency Special Session, 563d meeting (November 3, 1956), p. 71.

30. Lash, *Dag Hammarskjold,* pp. 87–88.

31. "First report of the Secretary-General on the plan for an emergency international United Nations Force, requested in Resolution 998 (ES-I), adopted by the General Assembly on 4 November 1956," U.N. Doc. A/3289, November 4, 1956.

32. U.N. Doc. A/3290, November 4, 1956; subsequently became Resolution 1000 (ES-I). The draft resolution was adopted by 57 votes in favor, none opposed, and 19 abstentions. Abstaining were New Zealand, Poland, Portugal, Rumania, Turkey, Ukraine, Union of South Africa, USSR, United Kingdom, Albania, Australia, Bulgaria, Byelorussia, Czechoslovakia, Egypt, France, Hungary, Israel, and Laos. General Assembly, *Official Records,* 1st Emergency Special Session, 565th meeting (November 4, 1956), p. 89.

33. *Ibid.,* p. 87.

34. See Frye, *A United Nations Peace Force,* p. 3.

35. In fact, while President Eisenhower himself came to favor the idea of a personal visit from Eden to discuss the situation and was not opposed to helping Britain economically and financially during this difficult period, the State Department strongly discouraged such measures. See Adams, *Firsthand Report,* p. 262.

36. "A Second and final report of the Secretary-General on the plan for an emergency international United Nations Force requested in Resolution 998 (ES-I), adopted by the General Assembly on 4 November 1956," U.N. Doc. A/3302, November 6, 1956. The report was final only in the sense that it was the last report issued under the Assembly's mandate of November 4, which asked for compliance within forty-eight hours.

37. Egypt had accepted the two calls of the Assembly for a cease-fire on November 2 (U.N. Doc. A/3266) and November 4 (U.N. Doc. A/3287, Annex 6); Israel, which had declared on November 3 (A/3279) that it would agree to an immediate cessation of hostilities on condition that Egypt would do the same, confirmed its acceptance on November 5 (A/3301); Britain and France announced on November 5 that they would discontinue all military measures as soon as Egypt and Israel accepted a UN plan for an international force with certain prescribed functions (A/3294 and A/3293). These governments were informed by the Secretary-General on the same day that in view of the Assembly's decision to set up an international force and in view of Egyptian and Israeli agreement to a cease-fire, "the conditions for a general cease-fire would thus seem to be established." (A/3310). The next day, France and the United Kingdom announced that their forces would cease fire at midnight GMT of November 6, pending confirmation of Egyptian-Israeli acceptance of an unconditional cease-fire and assurance that there would be a UN force competent to secure and supervise the attainment of the objectives of resolution 997 (ES-I) (A/3307 and A/3306). Hammarskjold promptly made known to Egypt and Israel that the cessation of hostilities would become effective on the hour of midnight and on this basis the cease-fire began at that time, November 6th. In a later study, the Secretary-General emphasized that "the General Assembly did not make the cease-fire dependent upon the creation or the functioning of UNEF. Its calls for a cease-fire and its decision to establish the Force were in separate resolutions [Resolutions 997 (ES-I) and 999 (ES-I) on the one hand, and 998 (ES-I) on the other]." See "Summary study of the experience derived from the establishment and operation of the Force: report of the Secretary-General," U.N. Doc. A/3943, October 9, 1958, General Assembly, *Official Records,* 13th Session (1958–59), Annexes, Agenda Item 65, p. 11.

38. General Assembly, *Official Records*, 1st Emergency Special Session, 567th meeting (November 7, 1956), p. 119.

39. Sixty-four votes in favor, none opposed, twelve abstentions. Abstaining were members of the Soviet bloc, Egypt, Israel, and the Union of South Africa, *ibid.*, p. 126.

40. U.N. Doc. A/3308, November 6, 1956; subsequently became Resolution 1001 (ES-I).

41. U.N. Doc. S/4387, July 14, 1960.

42. For a discussion of the question of Egyptian consent to UNEF see Chapter III.

43. Patrick O'Donovan, "How the U.N. Troops Were Mobilized," *The Reporter*, Vol. XVI, No. 1 (January 10, 1957), p. 30. The practical arrangements made in the assembling of the Force are discussed in Chapter V.

III: LEGAL BASIS

1. Preamble and Chapter I, "Purposes and Principles," of the Charter.

2. See Leland M. Goodrich and Anne P. Simons, *The United Nations and the Maintenance of International Peace and Security*, pp. 429–30.

3. Resolution 377 (V), "Uniting for Peace," November 3, 1950. For complete text, see General Assembly, *Official Records*, 5th Session (1950), Supp. No. 20, pp. 10–12. For discussion, see Julius Stone, *Legal Controls of International Conflict*, pp. 266–78; Goodrich and Simons, *The United Nations and the Maintenance of International Peace*, pp. 406–23; United Nations, *Repertory of Practice of United Nations Organs* (New York, 1955), I, 306–19; and D. H. N. Johnson, "The Effect of Resolutions of the General Assembly of the United Nations," *British Yearbook of International Law 1955–56*, XXXII (1957), 97–122.

4. On finding in the Charter the legal basis for General Assembly action, the above analysis stresses the collective measures aspect (although UNEF was set up to assist in the process of pacification and not to take coercive measures) because this is the aspect of the question emphasized by those states (the USSR and the Soviet bloc) which find UNEF's legal basis unsatisfactory.

5. U.N. Doc. A/3302, p. 20.

6. Louis B. Sohn, "The Authority of the United Nations to Establish and Maintain a Permanent United Nations Force," *American Journal of International Law*, LII (1958), 234.

Compare the opinion of Francisco Urrutia, the delegate from Colombia: "The Charter of the United Nations is very clear. It establishes two distinct procedures. One is the pacific settlement of disputes, the conciliation procedure provided for under Chapter VI, and the other is collective action, which is dealt with in Chapter VII, and is a function of the Security Council. If such action should fail because of a veto in the Security Council, then, under the resolution 377 (V), 'Uniting for Peace,' the matter passes to the General Assembly but is there subject to the conciliation procedure provided for in Chapter VI. Thus in such a case we may authorize the use of force but only, as we stated at a previous meeting, in cases of individual or collective self-defense. Apart from those cases in which we can as a mere authorization permit a state to defend itself, we cannot take any decision or order any collective measure because under Chapter VII of the Charter to do so is a function of the Security Council." General Assembly, *Official Records*, 1st Emergency Special Session (1956), 565th meeting (November 4, 1956), p. 87.

7. U.N. Doc. A/3943, p. 24.

8. "Report of the Secretary-General on arrangements concerning the status of the United Nations Emergency Force in Egypt," U.N. Doc. A/3526, February 8, 1957, General Assembly, *Official Records*, 11th Session (1956–57), Annexes, Vol. II–III, Agenda Item 66, pp. 52–53.

9. "Although UNEF is regarded in its entirety as a subsidiary organ of the General Assembly, it would also be possible for the Assembly to establish only a Command, and then *recommend* to the *member states* that they furnish troop contingents which would act in accordance with the *recommendations* of the U.N. Command. The difference is that under the latter plan, the troops would be acting as *national* units and their status would be determined solely by reference to the status of friendly foreign forces under international law . . . If, on the other hand, the troops contingents constitute part of a subsidiary organ of the General Assembly, they are entitled to the privileges and immunities of the United Nations under Article 105 of the Charter. . . ." See Dudley H. Chapman, "International Law—The United Nations Emergency Force—Legal Status," *Michigan Law Review*, Vol. LVII, No. 1 (November, 1958), pp. 59–60. See also Chapter VI, below.

10. United Nations, *Repertory of Practice of United Nations Organs* (New York, 1955), I, 661–742.

11. For example, the Special Committee on Admission of New Members, the Collective Measures Committee and the Atomic Energy Commission. See *ibid.*, p. 665.

12. *Ibid.*, pp. 666–67.

13. The UN Commissioner in Libya, for example, was appointed "for the purpose of assisting the people of Libya in the formulation of the constitution and the establishment of an independent government." In order to carry out this task, he was authorized to appoint, after consultation, the members of an advisory group representing the regions and minorities of Libya. See General Assembly Resolution 289 A (IV).

14. See Sohn, "The Authority of the United Nations to Establish and Maintain a Permanent United Nations Force," *American Journal of International Law*, LII (1958), 234.

15. General Assembly, *Official Records*, 2d Session, Plenary meeting 110 (October 13, 1947), Vol. II, pp. 753–804; *ibid.*, 111th meeting, pp. 805–22; *ibid.*, 1st Committee, 74th–78th meetings (October 14–18, 1947), pp. 129–79; 94th–97th meetings (November 5–6, 1947), pp. 307–36.

16. *Ibid.*, 5th Session, Plenary meetings 299–320 (November 1–3, 1950), Vol. I, pp. 292–347; 1st Committee, 354th–371st meetings (October 9–21, 1950), pp. 63–174.

17. *Ibid.*, 2d Session, Plenary meetings 124–126 (November 26–28, 1947), pp. 1324–79; *Ad Hoc* Com. on the Palestinian Question, 24th–31st meetings (November 20–24, 1947), pp. 147–95.

18. The UN Palestine Commission was assigned the following functions:

1) take over the administration of Palestine from Britain; 2) carry out measures for demarcation of the borders between the Arab and Jewish states and the City of Jerusalem; 3) select and establish in both states a Provisional Council of Government, to exercise general direction over it and, in time, to transfer to it responsibility for the administration of the state; 4) exercise political and military control over the armed militia in each state; and, 5) approve election regulations drawn up by the Provisional Council of Government. See United Nations, *Repertory*, p. 678.

19. Hans Kelsen, *The Law of the United Nations*, p. 137. See also Leland M. Goodrich and Edvard Hambro, *Charter of the United Nations, Commentary and Documents* (Boston, World Peace Foundation, 1949), pp. 193–94: "The basic rule for all such bodies is that their authority cannot exceed that of the General Assembly from which it is derived."

20. See Tatsuro Kunugi, "Legal Problems Derived from the Establishment and Functioning of the United Nations Emergency Force," p. 45.

21. U.N. Doc. A/3302, p. 20. Italics added.

22. U.N. Docs. A/3552 and A/3943.

23. ST/SGB/UNEF/1, Regulation 6. Italics added.

24. U.N. Doc. A/3943, p. 11.

25. International Court of Justice, *Reports* (1954), pp. 47–97.

26. *Ibid.*, pp. 48–63.

27. By establishing the Administrative Tribunal, the Assembly had not delegated the performance of its own functions; it had exercised a power which it has under the Charter to regulate staff relations.

28. International Court of Justice, *Reports* (1949), pp. 182–83.

29. Unanimity in regard to creation of subsidiary organs has not always been achieved. When the Assembly established an *ad hoc* committee on Information from Non-Self-Governing Territories on December 14, 1946, the colonial powers were strongly opposed. Yet this committee functioned nonetheless as an organ of the entire Organization.

30. General Assembly, *Official Records*, 1st Emergency Special Session, 567th meeting (November 7, 1956), pp. 127–28.

31. Actually, A. A. Sobolev declared in 1959: "The United Nations Charter, as is known, makes no provision whatsoever for the establishment of a United Nations force, but merely envisages the possibility of Member States placing armed forces at the disposal of the Security Council, in accordance with special agreements.

"Article 43 of the Charter clearly states that all Members of the United Nations undertake to make available to the Security Council, on its call and in accordance with a special agreement or agreements, armed forces necessary for the purpose of maintaining international peace and security. Thus, the Charter totally precludes the adoption by the General Assembly of any decisions regarding the establishment or operation of international armed forces." General Assembly, *Official Records*, 14th Session, Plenary meeting 842 (November 21, 1959), p. 597.

32. *Ibid.*, p. 108.

33. *Ibid.*, p. 128. Two states of the Soviet bloc—Rumania and Czechoslo-

vakia—offered contributions of national contingents to the Force (U.N. Docs. A/3302/Add. 7 and A/3302/Add. 6, p. 24.). Czechoslovakia declared, however, on November 23 that UNEF did not conform to the provisions of the Charter, General Assembly, *Official Records,* 11th Session, Plenary meeting 591 (November 23, 1956), Vol. I, p. 254.

While the Soviet bloc does not strongly oppose UNEF, it must be stressed nonetheless that on November 19, 1958, it voted against Resolution 1263 (XIII) which noted "with satisfaction the effective way in which the Force continues to function" and which requested the Fifth Committee to recommend such action as may be necessary for the continuing operation of UNEF.

See also statement by A. A. Sobolev at the 97th meeting of the Special Political Committee, October 29, 1958; and Chapter VII.

34. U.N. Doc. A/3302, p. 20.

35. See remarks of the representatives of Indonesia, El Salvador, and India, General Assembly, *Official Records,* 1st Emergency Special Session, 563d meeting (November 3, 1956), pp. 68–70.

36. U.N. Doc. A/3276, November 3, 1956; subsequently became Resolution 998 (ES-I).

37. General Assembly, *Official Records,* 1st Emergency Special Session, 563d meeting (November 3, 1956), p. 70.

38. *Ibid.,* p. 71.

39. Resolution 1001 (ES-I).

40. Legally, of course, no Member is obliged under the Charter to make national contingents available except in accordance with a special agreement with the Security Council. No state was ready at San Francisco (in the days of the Charter's inception) to subject its armed forces to international control without express agreement.

41. For discussion, see separate opinion of Judge Lauterpacht in "Voting Procedure on Questions Relating to Reports and Petitions Concerning the Territory of South-West Africa," International Court of Justice, *Reports* (1955), pp. 117–20.

42. Article 2, paragraphs 2 and 5 of the United Nations Charter.

43. "Introduction to the Annual Report of the Secretary-General on the Work of the Organization, 16 June 1960–15 June 1961," General Assembly, *Official Records,* 16th Session (1961–62), Supp. No. 1A, p. 3. See also D. H. N. Johnson, "The Effect of Resolutions of the General Assembly of the United Nations," *British Yearbook of International Law 1955–56,* XXXII (1957), 97–122.

44. Notification indicating readiness to make appropriate contributions available to the UN Command were communicated to the Secretary-General by the governments of Canada, Colombia, Denmark, Norway, Pakistan, Sweden, Finland, Ceylon, India, Czechoslovakia, Rumania, New Zealand, United States, Burma, Yugoslavia, Brazil, Iran, Ethiopia, Indonesia, Ecuador, Philippines, Peru, Afghanistan, Laos, Chile, Switzerland, and Italy. U.N. Doc. A/3302/ Additions 1–30. The American, Swiss, and Italian offers, however, were exclusively for transport and supplies. See Chapter V.

45. "Letter Dated 5 November 1956 from the Permanent Representative of

Sweden, Addressed to the Secretary-General," U.N. Doc. A/3302, Annex 7, p. 23.

46. "Letter Dated 6 November from the Permanent Representative of India, Addressed to the Secretary-General," U.N. Doc. A/3302/Add. 4/Rev. 1, Addendum, pp. 23–24.

In the Assembly on November 26, the delegate from India emphasized "acknowledgment by the Secretary-General to the effect that the conditions attached had been fully noted and that the offer was accepted. It is well known that both in private municipal law and in international law, if you make an offer with conditions and that offer is accepted, it means that the conditions are accepted." General Assembly, *Official Records,* 11th Session, Plenary meeting 596 (November 26, 1956), Vol. I, p. 332.

47. "Letter Dated 13 November 1956 from the Permanent Representative of Finland, Addressed to the Secretary-General," U.N. Doc. A/3302/Add. 21.

Indonesia made a similar reservation: "It was on this clear understanding of the temporary, emergency nature of the United Nations Emergency Force that my Government participated in it. . . . However, if the functions of the Force should be broadened or enlarged beyond its original purpose, such as linking it indefinitely with the Truce Supervision Organization, then my Government certainly would have to reserve its right to reconsider its continued participation," General Assembly, *Official Records,* 11th Session, Plenary meeting 649 (February 1, 1957), Vol. II–III, p. 1043. Indonesia withdrew its contingent from UNEF on September 12, 1957. See Chapter V.

48. Not all offers of assistance were, however, accepted. See Chapter V.

49. U.N. Doc. A/3943, Annex 1.

50. *Ibid.*

51. See Chapter V.

52. Commenting on the rights of the contributing states, C. Chaumont writes: "Mais il est admis aussi qu'ils possèdent un droit de regard spécial, sinon sur le fonctionnement interne de la Force dans le cadre tracé par les résolutions de l'Assemblée générale, du moins sur l'utilisation générale de la Force et les missions qui peuvent lui être assignées," C. Chaumont, "La situation juridique des États Membres à l'égard de la Force d'Urgence des Nations Unies," *Annuaire Français de Droit International,* IV (1958), 434. ("But one must also admit that they have a right to a special voice, if not in matters dealing with the internal working of the Force as outlined in Assembly resolutions, at least in matters pertaining to the general use of the Force and the functions which might be assigned to it.")

But cf. Maxwell Cohen, "The United Nations Emergency Force: A Preliminary View," *International Journal,* Vol. XII, No. 2 (Spring, 1957), p. 127: "Just as there is sound reason for doubting the unilateral right of Egypt to order the withdrawal of UNEF until the Assembly or the Advisory Committee have determined that UNEF's objectives have been accomplished, so equally it is doubtful if any member state contributing contingents can withdraw such contingents by unilateral decision if their recall means a serious interference with the capacity of UNEF to carry out its responsibilities, as determined by the Assembly."

53. See Sohn, "The Authority of the United Nations to Establish and Main-

tain a Permanent United Nations Force," *American Journal of International Law*, LII (1958), 237.

54. U.N. Doc. A/3302, p. 20.

55. General Assembly, *Official Records*, 1st Emergency Special Session, 565th meeting (November 4, 1956), p. 83.

56. Herbert W. Briggs, *The Law of Nations* (2d ed., New York, Appleton-Century-Crofts, 1952), p. 312. See also Charles Cheyney Hyde, *International Law* (2d ed. rev., Boston, Little, Brown, 1945), pp. 641–42: "Any act committed within the territory of a State in obedience to the command of a foreign power and contrary to the will of the territorial sovereign marks contempt for its supremacy therein. Thus, the operations or movements of foreign military or naval forces within the territory of a State, or directed against the occupants thereof from a position outside of the national domain, normally constitute a serious invasion of the rights of the territorial sovereign." See also "Draft Declaration on Rights and Duties of States," U.N. Doc. A/1251; Green Haywood Hackworth, *Digest of International Law* (Washington, D.C., Government Printing Office, 1940–44), II, 362–71; and John Bassett Moore, *A Digest of International Law* (Washington, D.C., Government Printing Office, 1906), pp. 282–306, 323–27.

57. U.N. Doc. A/3302, p. 20.

58. "Cablegram dated 5 November 1956 from the Minister of Foreign Affairs of Egypt, Addressed to the Secretary-General," U.N. Doc. A/3295, November 5, 1956, General Assembly, *Official Records*, 1st Emergency Special Session, Annexes, Agenda Item 5, p. 17.

59. "Report of the Secretary-General on basic points for the presence and functioning in Egypt of the United Nations Emergency Force," U.N. Doc. A/3375, November 20, 1956, General Assembly, *Official Records*, 11th Session, Annexes, Vol. II–III, Agenda Item 66, p. 9.

60. *Ibid.*, pp. 9–10.

61. Resolution 1121 (XI).

62. Resolution 1126 (XI). This resolution noted with approval the "Report of the Secretary-General on arrangements concerning the status of the United Nations Emergency Force in Egypt," (U.N. Doc. A/3526) which contained the Agreement.

63. "Report of the Secretary-General in pursuance of General Assembly resolution 1123 (XI)," U.N. Doc. A/3512, January 24, 1957, General Assembly, *Official Records*, 11th Session, Annexes, Vol. II–III, Agenda Item 66, p. 47.

64. *Ibid.*, p. 48. Similarly, Egyptian consent was considered necessary in order for UNEF to maintain quiet in the area of the Straits of Tiran. And deployment of the Force on both sides of the armistice demarcation line, as well as assumption by UNEF of some of the functions of UNTSO, required the consent of both Israel and Egypt, since such arrangements had not been specified in the Armistice Agreement between them.

65. General Assembly, *Official Records*, 11th Session, Plenary meeting 659 (February 22, 1957), Vol. II–III, pp. 1192–93.

66. It should, of course, be stressed that the Aide-memoire on the basis for the presence and functioning of the United Nations Emergency Force in Egypt

recognized Egypt's "sovereign rights on any matter concerning the presence and functioning of UNEF." Yet in exercising these rights, Egypt promised to act in good faith by its acceptance of the Assembly Resolution 1000 (ES-I). The problem is very much one of interpretation.

67. Charles P. Noyes, "The Problem of 'Consent' in Relation to a U.N. Force," in Frye, *A United Nations Peace Force,* pp. 151–52.

68. Sohn, "The Authority of the United Nations to Establish and Maintain a Permanent United Nations Force," *American Journal of International Law,* LII (April, 1958), 240. Cf. Chaumont, "La situation juridique des États Membres à l'égard de la Force d'Urgence des Nations-Unies," *Annuaire Français de Droit International,* IV (1958), 424: "Il n'est pas possible de poser l'intervention de la volonté de l'Etat-hôte comme une règle de droit, mais c'est un fait qu'en 1956 les choses se sont passées ainsi, et que le précédent ainsi créé fait une large place à la souveraineté de l'Etat-hôte, non seulement pour la création, mais pour la composition d'une Force d'Urgence des Nations Unies." ("It is not possible to lay down as a rule of law the host state's right to impose its will, but it is a fact that in 1956 this will was imposed and that the precedent thereby created gave an important place to the host state's sovereign power over, not only the creation, but the composition of a United Nations Emergency Force.")

69. U.N. Doc. A/3943, p. 11.

70. See E. M. Miller, "Legal Aspects of the United Nations Action in the Congo," *American Journal of International Law,* LV (January, 1961), 12–13.

71. The Secretary-General speaking to the General Assembly, *Official Records,* 11th Session, Plenary meeting 649 (February 1, 1957), Vol. II–III, p. 1040.

72. Mahmoud Fawzi at the 597th meeting of the Assembly, November 27, 1956, *ibid.,* Vol. I, p. 348. His viewpoint is shared by the Soviet Union: "It goes without saying that the United Nations forces must also withdraw from the demarcation line and from Egyptian territory in general as soon as the Republic of Egypt should consider it necessary," *ibid.,* 589th meeting (November 22, 1956), pp. 223–24. The government of India also concurs with this interpretation, *ibid.,* 596th meeting (November 26, 1956), p. 333.

Israel, of course, is adamantly opposed to the above views: "If we were to accept one of the proposals made here—namely, that the Force should separate Egyptian and Israel troops for as long as Egypt thought it convenient and should then be withdrawn on Egypt's unilateral request, we would reach a reduction to absurdity. Egypt would then be in a position to build up, behind the screen of this Force, its full military preparations and, when it felt that those military preparations had reached their desired climax, to dismiss the United Nations Emergency Force and to stand again in close contact and proximity with the territory of Israel. This reduction to absurdity proves how impossible it is to accept in any matter affecting the composition or the functions of the Force the policies of the Egyptian Government as the sole or even the decisive criterion." *Ibid.,* 592d meeting (November 23, 1956), p. 275.

Lester Pearson of Canada holds a similar position: ". . . the Force is to remain in the area until its task is completed, and that would surely be for the determination of the United Nations itself." *Ibid.,* p. 268.

73. U.N. Doc. A/3943, p. 28.

74. See "Memorandum of important points in the discussion between the Representative of Israel and the Secretary-General on 25 February 1957," U.N. Doc. A/3563, February 26, 1957, General Assembly, *Official Records,* 11th Session, Annexes, Vol. II–III, Agenda Item 66, p. 71.

75. By accepting UNEF and by concluding an agreement with the United Nations, Egypt curtailed its sovereignty and limited its freedom of action, a procedure permissible in international law. Cf. the view expressed by former Secretary of State Dulles: "once the consent has been given, then I think a good argument can be made that the consent cannot be arbitrarily withdrawn, frustrating the original project, because other people change their positions in reliance of the original consent, forces are set in motion, a chain of events has occurred. And we would question, certainly, whether Egypt has the right arbitrarily to alter and change a consent once given until the purpose of that consent has been accomplished." U.S. Department of State *Bulletin,* XXXVI (1957), 597.

76. Hackworth, *Digest,* V, 297. See also illustrative materials, pp. 297–377.

Denunciation is not provided for in any of the agreements between Egypt and the United Nations. It may be argued that the international juridical effect of these agreements is not that of a treaty *per se.* Yet, "the international juridical effect of a treaty is not dependent upon the name given to an instrument." (See Harvard Law School, *Research in International Law,* Part III, Law of Treaties, 1935, p. 710.) And it is generally recognized in international law today that the term "treaty" may be used in a very general sense. Thus, the term "embraces a great variety of instruments to many of which other names than 'treaty' are given, although there is seldom if ever any juridical distinction between them. But they differ in form, content, and in other formal respects, and as to the parties in whose name they are concluded. Some are highly formal instruments while others are not. Some are in the form of exchanges of notes and even of letters and telegrams." (*Ibid.,* p. 688.)

77. Cf. Lester Pearson's view: "In giving its consent for . . . [the presence of UNEF] the Egyptian Government accepted a limitation on its sovereignty. It is now in the prerogative of the United Nations rather than the Egyptian Government to determine when the United Nations forces have completed their task of restoring peace and when they should be withdrawn." New York *Times,* March 16, 1957.

78. See Noyes, "The Problem of 'Consent' in Relation to a UN Force," in Frye, *A United Nations Peace Force,* p. 152.

79. U.N. Doc. S/P.V. 884, August 8, 1960, pp. 9 and 10. See also, Miller, "Legal Aspects of the United Nations Action in the Congo," *American Journal of International Law,* LV (January, 1961), 1–9.

80. U.N. Doc. S/4426, August 9, 1960.

81. U.N. Doc. A/3943, p. 12.

82. (". . . la création de la Force d'urgence avait fait l'objet du consentement des trois pays, et ce consentement était içi particulièrement important, puisque la création de la Force apparaissait comme la condition mise par eux à la fin même du conflit.")

He goes on to say: "On peut discuter sur le point de savoir si cette liaison [entre le consentement et la creation] correspondait bien aux intentions de l'Assemblée générale. A notre sens, elle peut être considérée comme résultant de la qualification donnée par celle-ci à la mission de la Force: cette qualification est contenue dans la résolution 998 (ES-I) du 4 Novembre, chargeant la Force d'urgence 'd'assurer et de surveiller la cessation des hostilités,' c'est-à-dire prévoyant pour la Force une mission de contrôle à la fois a priori et a posteriori. En fait, c'est entre la présence de la Force et le retrait des troupes étrangères que la relation fut établie." ("One can argue whether this link [between consent and creation] corresponded to the will of the General Assembly. In our view, it can be considered the result of the character given by the Assembly to the mission of the Force: the nature of its mission is contained in Resolution 998 of November 4, directing the Emergency Force 'to secure and supervise the cessation of hostilities,' that is to say foreseeing for the Force a mission of control which is at once a priori and a posteriori. In fact, the presence of the Force is dependent upon the withdrawal of foreign troops.") Chaumont, "La situation juridique des États Membres à l'égard de la Force d'Urgence des Nations-Unies," *Annuaire Français de Droit International,* IV (1958), 427.

83. Noyes, "The Problem of 'Consent' in Relation to a UN Force," in Frye, *A United Nations Peace Force,* p. 152.

84. "Report of the Secretary-General," U.N. Doc. A/3694, October 9, 1957, General Assembly, *Official Records,* 12th Session, Annexes, Agenda Item 65, p. 7.

85. *Ibid.,* p. 11.

86. U.N. Doc. A/3320, p. 32. Italics added.

87. General Assembly, *Official Records,* 11th Session, Plenary meeting 592 (November 23, 1956), Vol. I, p. 275.

88. *Ibid.,* 12th Session, Plenary meeting 720 (November 22, 1957), p. 503. Compare analogous position of the delegate from India, Krishna Menon, when discussing not the establishment of the Force, but its competence: "Therefore to suggest in any way that the withdrawal is dependent upon the judgment of the United Kingdom and French Governments as to the competence of the United Nations Emergency Force, is again to seek to usurp the powers of this Assembly. Who are these two Governments to make their own judgments? . . . Therefore, whether this United Nations Emergency Force is competent, is a matter for General Burns on the one hand and the Secretary-General on the other. Constitutional responsibility for it rests in this Assembly, and my delegation denies the right of the . . . United Kingdom and France to appropriate to themselves the right to say that this Force is competent for any one purpose or another." *Ibid.,* 11th Session, Plenary meeting 596 (November 26, 1956), Vol. I, p. 331.

89. Noyes, "The Problem of 'Consent' in Relation to a UN Force," in Frye, *A United Nations Peace Force,* p. 153.

90. U.N. Resolution 1125 (XI). Since Israel refused to let UNEF operate on Israeli territory, "on" the demarcation line came to mean "on the *Egyptian* side of the demarcation line." But the Secretary-General had requested deployment of UNEF on the *Israeli* side of the line and, although the Assembly phrased the resolution cautiously, it presumably concurred with the Secretary-General. See also Chapter V, notes 29 and 49.

91. Chaumont, "La situation juridique des États Membres à l'égard de la Force d'Urgence des Nations-Unies," *Annuaire Français de Droit International,*

IV (1958), 430. ("Israel est, dans un certain sens, un Etat militaire; il n'y a pas, sur son territoire, place pour d'autres forces armées . . . que les siennes."

92. Conversations took place between these officials during a visit to Israel by Hammarskjold in the spring of 1957. See Frye, *A United Nations Peace Force,* p. 44.

93. U.N. Doc. A/3943, p. 28.

94. *Ibid.*

95. Indeed the basic agreement between the Republic of the Congo and the Secretary-General contain identical paragraphs to those in the Aide-memoire relating to UNEF. See U.N. Doc. S/4389, Add. 5 and discussion above.

96. U.N. Doc. A/3943, p. 29.

IV: FUNCTIONS AND POWERS

1. U.N. Doc. A/3302.

2. *Ibid.,* p. 21.

3. Frye, *A United Nations Peace Force,* p. 1.

4. "United Nations Emergency Force," *International Review Service,* XI (1956), 16.

5. Joseph E. Johnson, "The United Nations Emergency Force," *Hearings before the Subcommittee on International Organizations and Movements of the Committee on Foreign Affairs, House of Representatives,* 85th Congress, 2d Session, July 24, 25, 1958 (Washington, D.C., Government Printing Office, 1958).

6. U.N. Doc. A/3694.

7. U.N. Doc. A/3943.

8. General Assembly, *Official Records,* 1st Emergency Special Session, 566th meeting (November 7, 1956), p. 94. It was not intended that UNEF use initiative in employment of firearms or that it would coerce any party in the dispute to comply with Assembly resolutions. The use of weapons, however, has been authorized under certain circumstances. See discussion below.

9. General Assembly, *Official Records,* 11th Session, Plenary meeting 640 (January 18, 1957), Vol. II–III, p. 919.

10. *Ibid.,* 651st meeting (February 2, 1957), p. 1066.

11. "The United Nations Emergency Force on Duty in Egypt," *United Nations Review,* III (February, 1957), 25.

12. U.N. Doc. A/3302, p. 20.

13. Note, for example, statement of Bulgaria: "The United Kingdom and French Governments . . . now wish to make use of the United Nations Force in order to achieve one of their original objectives: the internationalization of the Canal. This is the only possible explanation of the demands of certain circles in the United Kingdom and France that the tasks and functions of the United Nations Force should be altered to make it a force of occupation rather than control." General Assembly, *Official Records,* Plenary meeting 592 (November 23, 1956), Vol. I, p. 278.

14. U.N. Doc. A/3302, p. 20.

15. *Ibid.*

16. "Report of the Secretary-General in pursuance of General Assembly

resolution 1123 (XI)," U.N. Doc. A/3512, January 24, 1957, General Assembly, *Official Records*, 11th Session, Annexes, Vol. II–III, Agenda Item 66, p. 47. See also commentary by Hoffmann, "Sisyphus and the Avalanche," *International Organization*, XI (Summer, 1957), 454–55: "Mr. Hammarskjold stated that his proposals tended to restore not the *status quo* but the *status juris*. But the distinction is a fragile one: indeed what *is* the *status juris?* . . . The *status juris* is a return to the *status quo* accompanied by hopes that the parties would in the future respect the law."

17. "Report by the Secretary-General on compliance with General Assembly resolutions calling for withdrawal of troops and other measures," U.N. Doc. A/3500 and Add. 1, January 15, 1957, General Assembly, *Official Records*, 11th Session, Annexes, Vol. II–III, Agenda Item 66, p. 44.

18. U.N. Doc. A/3302, pp. 20–21.

19. U.N. Doc. A/3694 and Add. 1, pp. 6–7.

20. U.N. Doc. A/3302, p. 20.

21. U.N. Doc. A/3500 and Add. 1, p. 43.

22. "Second Report of the Secretary-General in pursuance of General Assembly resolutions 1124 (XI) and 1125 (XI)," U.N. Doc. A/3568, March 8, 1957, General Assembly, *Official Records*, 11th Session, Annexes, Vol. II–III, Agenda Item 66, p. 73.

23. U.N. Doc. A/3943, p. 10. For analysis of the United Nations Truce Supervision Organization and the armistice system, see Rosenne, *Israel's Armistice Agreements;* Hurewitz, "The Israeli-Syrian Crisis in the Light of the Arab-Israel Armistice System," *International Organization*, V (1951), 459–79; and unpublished dissertation by David Brook, Columbia University, 1961.

24. U.N. Doc. A/3302/Add. 4/Rev. 1, pp. 23–24. See also those understandings in which other states agreed to contribute to UNEF, above Chapter III.

25. U.N. Docs. A/3268 and A/3269, November 3, 1956. See above, Chapter II.

26. U.N. Doc. A/3279, p. 9.

27. General Assembly, *Official Records*, 11th Session, Plenary meetings 591 (November 23, 1956) and 593 (November 24, 1956), Vol. I, pp. 259 and 290. See also, "Report of the Secretary-General on compliance with General Assembly resolutions 997 (ES-I) and 1002 (ES-I)," U.N. Doc. A/3384, November 21, 1956, *ibid.*, Annexes, Vol. II–III, Agenda Item 66, pp. 16–17.

28. *Ibid.*, 592d meeting (November 23, 1956), p. 275. Israel on November 8 and 21 had already informed the Secretary-General of willingness to withdraw its forces from Egypt immediately on conclusion of satisfactory arrangements with the UN in connection with UNEF. (U.N. Doc. A/3320, November 8, 1956, and U.N. Doc. A/3384, Annex 11, November 21, 1956). Therefore, in addition to the effective functioning of the Emergency Force, "the satisfactory arrangements which Israel seeks are such that will ensure Israel's security against the recurrence of the threat or danger of attack, and against acts of belligerency by land or sea."

29. For example, speech by the delegate from Indonesia at the 11th Session, 596th meeting (November 26, 1956), p. 337.

30. "Note by the Secretary-General," U.N. Doc. A/3415, December 3, 1956, General Assembly, *Official Records*, 11th Session (1956–57), Annexes, Vol. II–III, Agenda Item 66, p. 28.

31. U.N. Doc. A/3943, pp. 15–16.

32. "Declaration Made by the Government of Egypt on the Suez Canal and the Arrangements for its Operation," Cairo, April 24, 1957, United Nations, *Treaty Series,* CCLXV (1957), 300–308.

33. New York *Times,* April 27, 1957.

34. Mr. Eban at the 11th Session of the Assembly, 592d meeting (November 23, 1956).

35. Israel was, above all, anxious for reassurance that Egypt would discontinue her policy of belligerency. She addressed four questions to the Egyptian government: "Does Egypt still adhere to the position declared and maintained by it over years that it is in a state of war with Israel? Is Egypt prepared to enter into immediate negotiation with Israel with a view to the establishment of peace between the two countries as indicated in the *aide-memoire* (A/3279) of the Government of Israel of 4 November 1956 to the Secretary-General of the United Nations? Does Egypt agree to cease economic boycott against Israel and lift the blockade of Israel shipping in the Suez Canal? Does Egypt undertake to recall *fedayeen* gangs under its control in other Arab countries?" General Assembly, *Official Records,* 11th Session, Plenary meeting 638 (January 17, 1957), Vol. II–III, p. 887.

36. Mrs. Meir in the Assembly on January 17, 1957: "The Gaza Strip was an integral part of the mandated territory of Palestine, and is geographically and economically part of the Negev. . . . Throughout the Egyptian occupation of Gaza, Egypt did not annex the Gaza Strip, but treated it as occupied territory provisionally administered by the Egyptian military authorities. In a ruling given by the Cairo court of administrative jurisdiction in September 1955, it was stated that the Gaza Strip was outside Egyptian territory and that the Egyptian authorities were exercising 'a kind of control over part of the territory of Palestine.'" *Ibid.,* p. 890.

37. *Ibid.*

38. *Ibid.,* p. 891.

39. Aouney Dejany of Saudi Arabia speaking at the Assembly's 595th meeting, November 26, 1956.

40. "Note by the Secretary-General transmitting an aide-memoire on the Israel position on the Sharm el-Sheikh area and the Gaza Strip," U.N. Doc. A/3511, January 24, 1957, General Assembly, *Official Records,* 11th Session, Annexes, Vol. II–III, Agenda Item 66, p. 46.

Israel's position was that since Egypt had continuously violated the Armistice and had been in a state of war with Israel, incompatible with the Armistice Agreement, that Agreement could not be invoked to bring Egypt back to Gaza.

41. *Ibid.,* Plenary meeting 642 (January 19, 1957), Vol. II–III, p. 956.

42. U.N. Doc. A/3512, p. 47.

43. "The Armistice Agreement was signed by both parties and, according to Article XII, remains in force until a peaceful settlement between them is achieved. It was approved by the Security Council. Whatever arrangements the United Nations may now wish to make in order to further progress toward peaceful conditions, the Agreement must be fully respected by it." *Ibid.,* p. 48.

44. *Ibid.*

45. The Assembly's authorization for the deployment of the Force and Egyptian agreement thereto had been only for Egypt's side of the armistice line.

46. (Statement by Sir Percy Spender of Australia.) General Assembly *Official Records,* 11th Session, Plenary meeting 638 (January 17, 1957), Vol. II–III, p. 882.

47. *Ibid.,* 639th meeting (January 17, 1957), p. 904.

48. *Ibid.,* 651st meeting (February 2, 1957), p. 1084.

49. See *ibid.,* 639th meeting (January 17, 1957), p. 898 and 650th meeting (February 2, 1957), p. 1050.

Mason, "The United Nations Emergency Force," *International Law and the Middle East Crisis,* p. 28, declares that the United States-Latin American bloc would only support resolutions which did not spell out precise interpretations, apparently for reasons of United States foreign policy. "According to one report, the Latin Americans were also disinclined to vote with the Asian-Arab bloc because this bloc had given very poor support to Latin American anti-Soviet resolutions in the Hungarian issue. The height of the Hungarian crisis had to be tackled by the Assembly concurrently with the invasion of Egypt."

50. General Assembly, *Official Records,* 11th Session, Plenary meeting 641 (January 18, 1957), Vol. II–III, p. 930. See also, *ibid.,* 651st meeting (February 2, 1957), p. 1070: ". . . the Force can be placed only on both sides of the armistice demarcation line. . . . The line goes from Rafah, on the other side of the Gaza Strip, down to a point just below Elath, on the Gulf of Aqaba. . . . But there is no suggestion, and there can be no suggestion, that foreign forces, which are United Nations forces, can be stationed anywhere on Egyptian territory."

51. *Ibid.,* 649th meeting (February 1, 1957), p. 1043. The Indonesian contingent withdrew from the Force on September 12, 1957.

52. *Ibid.,* 638th meeting (January 17, 1957), pp. 892–93.

53. *Ibid.,* 646th meeting (January 29, 1957), pp. 1002–3. See also, *ibid.,* 652d meeting (February 2, 1957), p. 1077.

54. *Ibid.,* 650th meeting (February 2, 1957), p. 1053.

55. Resolution 1125 (XI), February 2, 1957.

56. Hamilton Fish Armstrong, "The U.N. Experience in Gaza," *Foreign Affairs,* XXXV (1956–57), 609–10.

57. A United States memorandum to Israel of February 11 stated that "Israeli withdrawal from Gaza should be prompt and unconditional, leaving the future of the Gaza Strip to be worked out through the efforts and good offices of the United Nations." The Assembly should seek that UNEF "move into this area and be on the boundary between Israel and the Gaza Strip. The United States will use its best efforts to help to assure this result, which we believe is contemplated by the Second Resolution of February 2, 1957." Quoted were assurances given by Egypt in regard to Aqaba. Furthermore, the United States "is prepared to exercise the right of free and innocent passage, and to join with others to secure general recognition of this right." U.S. Department of State, *United States Policy in the Middle East,* p. 290.

58. General Assembly, *Official Records,* 11th Session, Plenary meeting 659 (February 22, 1957), Vol. II–III, pp. 1192–93.

59. *Ibid.,* 660th meeting (February 26, 1957), p. 1204.

60. A draft resolution of February 22, 1957, sponsored by Afghanistan, Indonesia, Iraq, Lebanon, Pakistan and Sudan, would have condemned Israel for its non-compliance with Assembly resolutions and would have called upon all states to deny military, economic or financial assistance and facilities to Israel in view of its continued defiance of the resolutions. See U.N. Doc. A/3557, General Assembly, *Official Records,* 11th Session, Annexes, Vol. II–III, Agenda Item 66, p. 62.

61. General Assembly, *Official Records,* 11th Session, Plenary meeting 666 (March 1, 1957), Vol. II–III, p. 1276.

62. Of course, Israel's "assumptions" and "expectations" constitute part of her diplomacy, that is, an effort to stake out a position for further action in case these "expectations" were not fulfilled. They do not, therefore, necessarily represent what the Israel Government really expected.

63. General Assembly, *Official Records,* 11th Session, Plenary meeting 666 (March 1, 1957), Vol. II–III, p. 1277.

64. "Gratified" by Israel's decision to withdraw, President Eisenhower declared "that Israel will have no cause to regret having thus conformed to the strong sentiment of the world community as expressed in the various United Nations Resolutions relating to withdrawal." The President again confirmed the American view that "after the withdrawal there should be a united effort by all of the nations to bring about conditions in the area more stable, more tranquil, and more conducive to the general welfare than those which existed heretofore. Already the United Nations General Assembly has adopted Resolutions which presage such a better future. Hopes and expectations based thereon were voiced by your Foreign Minister and others. I believe that it is reasonable to entertain such hopes and expectations and I want you to know that the United States, as a friend of all of the countries of the area and as a loyal member of the United Nations, will seek that such hopes prove not to be in vain." "Letter to Israeli Prime Minister Ben-Gurion from President Eisenhower, March 2, 1957," U.S. Department of State, *United States Policy in the Middle East,* pp. 332–33.

65. U.N. Doc. A/3694 and Add. 1, pp. 5–6.

66. General Assembly, *Official Records,* 11th Session, Plenary meeting 659 (February 22, 1957), Vol. II–III, p. 1192.

67. Armstrong, "U.N. Experience in Gaza," *Foreign Affairs,* XXXV (July, 1957), 614–16.

68. *Ibid.,* p. 614.

69. *Ibid.,* p. 600.

70. *Ibid.,* p. 616.

71. Colonel Carl Engholm had organized the administrative posts of the territory by setting up a number of municipal councils. UNRWA had assumed administration of education, public health, and social welfare.

72. See the New York *Times,* March 12, 1957. Note commentary by the newspaper's correspondent in Gaza, *ibid.,* March 17: "Colonel Nasser's announcement caused surprise and anger in the West. 'It wasn't so much what he said, but the way he said it,' one diplomat observed. However, none here questioned Egypt's legal right to return to the civil administration of Gaza."

73. Actually, on March 12, Ralph Bunche pointed out that the UN had

"never questioned Egypt's legal rights in Gaza" and denied UN intention to internationalize the Strip. *Ibid.*, March 12, 1957.

74. *Ibid.*, March 24, 1957.

75. *Ibid.*, March 30, 1957. Hammarskjold held "informative exploratory talks" in Cairo with government officials during the end of March. Among the understandings resulting from the visit were: "1. Egypt is making known effectively to the refugees and other inhabitants of the Strip that it is Egyptian policy to prevent infiltration across the demarcation line. 2. . . . The role of UNEF in assisting in the prevention of infiltration will be made . . . known to the population of the Gaza Strip. . . ." *Ibid.*, March 31, 1957.

76. Armstrong, "U.N. Experience in Gaza," *Foreign Affairs,* XXXV (July, 1957), 601.

77. *Ibid.*, pp. 601–2.

78. "At one time Israel had offered to take back and resettle 100,000 Palestinian refugees; later she indicated that the offer had lapsed, but some observers thought that this was the moment to insist that she receive some such number from Gaza and that she compensate the remainder. In 1953 Egypt had favored a plan to make available a large tract in Sinai near the Suez Canal for settlement of Gaza refugees, the irrigation and other expenses to be financed through UNRWA. Deterioration of Egyptian-Israeli relations had caused the project to be dropped. Might it not be revived?" *Ibid.*, p. 602. A number of proposals were open for the UN to explore in regard to the refugees. An international commission, or UNRWA, might have consulted the wishes of the population and supervised its movement to either Israel or Egypt, whichever its option.

79. *Ibid.*, p. 617.

80. For example, see Security Council, *Official Records,* 6th year, 558th meeting (September 1, 1951).

81. General Assembly, *Official Records,* 11th Session, Plenary meeting 638 (January 17, 1957), Vol. II–III, p. 889.

82. U.N. Doc. A/3512, p. 49.

83. *Ibid.*

84. *Ibid.*, p. 50.

85. The delegate from Australia said (11th Session, 638th meeting [January 17, 1957], p. 884): "The positions evacuated by Israel forces should be occupied forthwith by the United Nations Emergency Force troops, who should, during their occupations, ensure that the status of the gulf as an international waterway was safeguarded and respected. The gulf serves no less than four littoral states . . . all of which should without discrimination be able to use this waterway for their own peaceful purposes."

The viewpoint of the United States government was essentially similar, though expressed in more cautious terms: "We feel it is important that the United Nations Emergency Force move in immediately behind the withdrawing Israel forces in order to assure the maintenance of the cease-fire and to safeguard the armistice agreement. This is particularly important at this final stage of the withdrawal because the areas in question have been major sources of tension and the sites of many hostile actions in the past. We believe that the United Nations Emergency Force should be so deployed as to be in a position to prevent a recurrence of such hostile activities." General Assembly, *Official*

Records, 11th Session, Plenary meeting 639 (January 17, 1957), Vol. II–III, p. 898.

86. "I want to say here that any emendation, any enlargement of the functions of the United Nations Emergency Force would require basic reconsideration, consultation and agreement by all the parties concerned. Already we have a situation where an army is functioning without any restraint from a legislature or a government, and we ourselves would not want to find ourselves in a position where this army would be assuming responsibilities involving the use of lethal weapons without the previous commitment of our Governments." Declaration by the delegate from India, *ibid.,* 641st meeting (January 18, 1957), p. 930.

87. "The Israel delegation has just suggested the possibility of entrusting the United Nations troops with the task of guaranteeing the innocent passage of ships through the Gulf of Aqaba. The problem is much more complex than it appears at first sight. Even if Egypt agreed to any such solution, a ruling would still be required on the proper interpretation of 'innocent passage.' The Israel delegation quoted the draft resolution submitted in the Security Council two years ago (S/3188 and Corr. 1), for which my country voted. The Israel delegation also quoted an opinion given by the International Court of Justice. I do not know whether this is applicable in the present case, because it must not be forgotten that, even if the Gulf of Aqaba can be considered an international waterway, international law recognizes that coastal states have the right to special protection." *Ibid.,* 638th meeting (January 17, 1957), p. 892.

88. The delegate from Iraq stated: "Therefore the contentions of Israel that no forces should provoke it from Arab lands and that it wants free passage through the Suez and Aqaba should be balanced with its holding of our property, with its denial of the rights of the Arabs to return to their own homes, with its occupation of Arab territory, and with its refusal to internationalize Jerusalem. When Israel wants to claim something, it must give other things. Israel cannot have it all its own way." *Ibid.,* 639th meeting (January 17, 1957), p. 906.

89. U.N. Doc. A/3512, p. 50.

90. New York *Times,* March 17, 1957.

91. U.N. Doc. A/3563, p. 71.

92. U.N. Doc. A/3568, p. 72.

93. Security Council, *Official Records,* 4th year (1949), Special Supp. No. 3. Furthermore, the Armistice Agreement declares: "No element of the land, sea or air military or para-military forces of either Party, including non-regular forces, shall commit any warlike or hostile act against the military or para-military forces of the other Party, or against civilians in territory under the control of that Party."

94. See Hurewitz, "The Israeli-Syrian Crisis in the Light of the Arab-Israel Armistice System," *International Organization,* V (1951), 459.

95. *Ibid.,* p. 462. The Egypt-Israel Commission is composed of seven members. Each of the parties chooses three of these members, while UNTSO's Chief of Staff (or a senior aide designated by him) chooses the seventh.

96. *Ibid.*

97. As J. C. Hurewitz reports, however, the "Egyptian-Israel MAC very

early formed mixed patrols, comprising officers and enlisted men of the two countries to prevent border violations." "The Israeli-Syrian Crisis in the Light of the Arab-Israel Armistice System," *International Organization*, V (1951), 464. But in the years immediately before the Suez crisis, these patrols seem to have been little effective against *fedayeen* ambushes or reprisal attacks. See Chapter I.

98. U.N. Doc. A/3500 and Add. 1, p. 43.

99. U.N. Doc. A/3943, p. 43.

100. "Letter dated 25 January 1957 from the Permanent Representative of Israel, addressed to the Secretary-General," U.N. Doc. A/3527, Annex V, February 11, 1957, General Assembly, *Official Records,* 11th Session, Annexes, Vol. II–III, p. 62.

101. Quoted by Abba Eban from a speech by Prime Minister Ben-Gurion in the Knesset on January 23, 1957, *ibid.*

102. U.N. Doc. A/3512, p. 47.

103. U.N. Doc. A/3943, p. 17.

104. U.N. Doc. A/3512, p. 48.

105. U.N. Doc. A/3527, p. 59.

106. U.N. Doc. A/3943, p. 17.

107. "Report of the Secretary-General on the work of the Force," U.N. Doc. A/4210 and Add. 1, September 10, 1959, General Assembly, *Official Records,* 14th Session (1959), Annexes, Agenda Item 28, pp. 23–25.

108. Seventy such posts existed in September 1962. "United Nations Emergency Force, Report of the Secretary-General," U.N. Doc. A/5172, August 22, 1962, *ibid.*, 17th Session (1962), p. 7.

109. Statement by a UNEF public relations official in Christopher Rand, "Our Far-Flung Correspondent," *The New Yorker*, XXXV (May 9, 1959), 118. (A.D.L. signifies Armistice Demarcation Line.)

110. The Secretary-General reported in August 1961 that in one particular sector, where it was found that more patrolling was necessary, a special track was made by the UNEF engineers, U.N. Doc. A/4857, August 30, 1961, p. 7.

111. U.N. Docs. A/3694, A/3899, A/4210, A/4857, and A/5172.

112. Frye, *A United Nations Peace Force*, p. 15.

113. For example, the incident reported in the New York *Times* on February 2, 1957: UNEF headquarters made known that five Israeli soldiers opened fire on a Swedish patrol west of Rafah camp at the Gaza Strip; the patrol returned the fire but, according to a communiqué, no casualties occurred; upon protest by Major General Burns, the Israel Government extended its apologies for the incident.

114. For figures from UNEF headquarters regarding number and type of incidents, see U.N. Doc. A/3694 and Add. 1, p. 6; U.N. Doc. A/3899, p. 6; U.N. Doc. A/4210, p. 26; and U.N. Doc. A/5172, Annexes.

115. U.N. Doc. A/5172, p. 10.

116. U.N. Doc. A/3943, p. 31.

117. "Report by Major-General H. T. Alexander, DSO, OBE Chief of Defence Staff," U.N. Doc. S/4445, August 19, 1960, Annex II.

118. "Observations by the Special Representative of the Secretary-General in the Republic of the Congo on the Memorandum by Major-General H. T. Alexander," U.N. Doc. S/4451, August 21, 1960.

119. U.N. Doc. S/4445.

120. U.N. Doc. S/4451.

121. *Ibid.*

122. Whether UNEF will continue to function satisfactorily is of course a moot question. With the greater threat to the peace in the area eliminated, the Force might be withdrawn *before* the fulfillment of *all* its functions—i.e., functions aiming toward the scrupulous maintenance of the Armistice Agreement and "the implementation of other measures as proposed in the Secretary-General's report" of January 24, 1957.

123. U.N. Doc. A/3694 and Add. 1, p. 7.

124. "Annual Report of the Secretary-General on the Work of the Organization, 16 June 1960–15 June 1961," General Assembly, *Official Records,* 16th Session (1961–62), Supp. No. 1.

125. General Assembly, *Official Records,* 12th Session, Plenary meeting 720 (November 22, 1957), pp. 496–97.

126. *Ibid.,* p. 497.

127. *Ibid.* See also 721st meeting (November 22, 1957) and the records of the 5th Committee at the 14th Session of the Assembly (1959). France and Argentina, however, during the Assembly's 16th Session, felt that consideration should be given to reducing UNEF's strength and, consequently, its financial costs. A/C.5/SR.899, December 13, 1961, p. 10, and A/C.5/SR.902, December 16, 1961, p. 10.

128. *Ibid.,* p. 494.

129. General Assembly, *Official Records,* 13th Session, Special Political Committee, 99th meeting (November 3, 1958), p. 59.

130. *Ibid.,* 97th meeting (October 29, 1958), p. 51.

131. General Assembly, *Official Records,* 12th Session, Plenary meeting 720 (November 22, 1957), p. 500.

132. Chaumont, "La situation juridique des États Membres à l'égard de la Force d'Urgence des Nations-Unies," *Annuaire Français de Droit International,* IV (1958), 410.

133. Cohen, "The United Nations Emergency Force: A Preliminary View," *International Journal,* XII (Spring, 1957), 109–27.

134. General Assembly, *Official Records,* 13th Session, Special Political Committee, 97th meeting (October 29, 1958), p. 52.

135. Hoffmann, "Sisyphus and the Avalanche," *International Organization,* XI (Summer, 1957), 453.

136. *Ibid.,* pp. 454–55. Stanley Hoffmann's remarks on this question are interesting. Asking what the *status juris* really is, he writes: "The parties disagree, and this disagreement itself explains in part the collapse of the armistice agreements. For the Israelis, the law includes not only the end of border raids, or the scrupulous observance of articles VII and VIII of the Israel-Egypt armistice agreement, dealing with the armistice lines, but also the end of the blockade of the Suez Canal and the Gulf of Aqaba. For the Egyptians, this is not the case, and in his report of January 24 the Secretary-General (who has constantly refused to answer Israel's questions concerning Egypt's policy of belligerency) was only able to say about the Gulf of Aqaba that 'any possible claims of belligerent rights . . . if asserted, should be limited to clearly non-

controversial stiuations.' In his report of January 24, he defined the return to the *status juris* as 'a withdrawal of troops, and . . . the relinquishment or nullification of rights asserted in territories covered by the military action and depending upon it.' The *status juris* is a return to the *status quo* accompanied by hopes that the parties would in the future respect the law."

137. Cf., Armstrong, "U.N. Experience in Gaza," *Foreign Affairs*, XXXV (July, 1957), 603.

138. *Ibid.*, pp. 608–9.

139. *Ibid.*, p. 609.

140. General Assembly, *Official Records*, 1st Emergency Special Session, 561st meeting (November 1, 1956), p. 2.

141. *Ibid.*, 562d meeting (November 1, 1956), p. 36.

142. *Ibid.*, p. 43.

143. U.N. Doc. A/3272, November 3, 1956, General Assembly, *Official Records*, 1st Emergency Special Session, Annexes, Agenda Item 5, p. 6.

144. U.N. Doc. A/3273, November 3, 1956 in *ibid.*, pp. 6–7.

145. Armstrong, "U.N. Experience in Gaza," *Foreign Affairs*, XXXV (July, 1957), 604–5.

146. Hoffmann, "Sisyphus and the Avalanche," *International Organization*, XI (Summer, 1957), 454.

147. See *ibid.*

148. Cf. Armstrong, "U.N. Experience in Gaza," *Foreign Affairs*, XXXV (July, 1957), 601.

V: COMPOSITION, ORGANIZATION, CONTROL

1. U.N. Doc. A/3302.

2. See Leland M. Goodrich, *Korea: A Study of U.S. Policy in the United Nations*, Chapter V.

3. See identical letters to the Secretary-General, November 5, 1956, U.N. Docs. A/3293 and A/3294, General Assembly, *Official Records*, 1st Emergency Special Session, Annexes, Agenda Item 5, pp. 16–17.

4. U.N. Resolution 1000 (ES-I).

5. For further biographical data on Major General Burns, see "Confirmation of the appointment of Major General E. L. M. Burns as Chief of the United Nations Command for the emergency international Force," U.N. Doc. A/3317, November 8, 1956, General Assembly, *Official Records*, 1st Emergency Special Session, Annexes, Agenda Item 5, pp. 31–32.

6. U.N. Doc. A/3302, p. 20.

7. Frye, *A United Nations Peace Force*, p. 12.

8. U.N. Doc. A/3302, p. 21.

9. *Ibid.*, Add. 1 to 16, pp. 22–26; also, U.N. Doc. A/3302/Add. 17 to 30, pp. 3–7.

10. U.N. Doc. A/3943, p. 14.

11. See *ibid.*, p. 11.

12. General Assembly, *Official Records*, 1st Emergency Special Session, 566th meeting (November 7, 1956), p. 100, italics added.

13. Noyes, "The Problem of 'Consent' in Relation to a UN Force" in Frye,

A *United Nations Peace Force,* p. 151; Henry L. Mason, "The United Nations Emergency Force," *International Law and the Middle East Crisis: A Symposium,* Tulane Studies in Political Science, IV (1957), 49. In accepting UNEF, however, the Egyptian government must have considered the Force valuable for its own national interest. Therefore, Egyptian pressure upon the Secretary-General in regard to UNEF's composition must have been tempered by the realization that, if no Force were established, Egypt herself would be the loser.

14. See U.N. Doc. A/3694 and Add. 1, p. 2.

15. Leland M. Goodrich and Gabriella E. Rosner, "The United Nations Emergency Force," *International Organization,* XII (1957), 424. Cf. comment by Frye, *A United Nations Peace Force,* p. 23: "Pakistan wanted to serve, too, and Bunche would have been glad to have had them. Among other things, their unit included an excellent military band. But the Pakistan prime minister had attacked Nasser publicly; Pakistan was a member of the Baghdad Pact; and India was not eager to have Pakistani troops in UNEF. So Pakistan was not considered suitable."

16. Yugoslavia, for example, is on record as being willing to collaborate in maintaining the Force until it had accomplished the task assigned to it at its establishment, *and as long as Egypt thought it useful.* It is, therefore, likely that, were Egypt to retract her approval of UNEF, the Yugoslav contingent would be withdrawn. General Assembly, *Official Records,* 13th Session, Special Political Committee, 98th meeting (October 31, 1958), p. 55.

17. U.N. Doc. A/3694 and Add. 1, p. 2.

18. *Ibid.,* Rotation of national contingents takes place at varying intervals according to national practice.

19. United Nations Emergency Force, "Report of the Secretary-General," U.N. Doc. A/3899, August 27, 1958. General Assembly, *Official Records,* 13th Session, Annexes, Agenda Item 65, p. 4. On August 15, 1958, the Force numbered 5,445 men.

20. U.N. Doc. A/5172, p. 5.

21. U.N. Doc. A/3943, p. 13.

22. O'Donovan, "How the U.N. Troops Were Mobilized," *The Reporter,* XVI (January 10, 1957), 31.

23. *Ibid.,* p. 30.

24. *Ibid.*

25. The quantities of rations brought into Egypt by airlift were inadequate in the early stages and procurement was obtained from the Egyptian Army. "In the early days of an operation such an UNEF it is imperative to have an assured source that can produce most of the supplies required by modern troops in the field. Once a 'pipeline' has been established, attention can be given to developing alternative sources that may be cheaper or more satisfactory in other ways." U.N. Doc. A/3943, p. 19.

26. *Ibid.,* p. 15.

27. This base was closed in January 1958 and the Royal Canadian Air Force Communication Flight withdrawn; subsequently, a liaison officer and a movement control attachment were maintained at Pisa to care for logistics requirements.

28. For positions and deployment during 1959, 1960, and 1961, see, U.N.

Doc. A/4210 and Add. 1, pp. 23–24; U.N. Doc. A/4486, pp. 9–10; U.N. Doc. A/4857, pp. 7–9; and U.N. Doc. A/5172, pp. 8–9.

Limited health services are provided by some of the national contingents for their own troops, but more extensive medical facilities have been established at Rafah, under joint Canadian-Indian management. Arrangements have also been made to provide emergency cases, requiring specialized care, with ready access to outside facilities.

29. Resolution 1125 (XI). See also, Chapter III, note 90.

30. U.N. Doc. A/3943, p. 12.

31. *Ibid.*, p. 13.

32. U.N. Doc. A/AC.89/R.1.

33. Day-to-day tasks of administration were handled by the Commander of UNEF assisted by senior Secretariat officials assigned by the Secretary-General to the Force, and by the Headquarters staff. Secretariat staff serving with the Force are (1) Officers, such as the Chief Administrative Officer, who reports to the Commander and to United Nations Headquarters in New York and who is assisted by a Chief Procurement Officer, a Chief Finance Officer and a Personnel Officer; (2) Officials such as the Legal Advisor and the Public Information Officer, who form part of the staff of the Chief Administrative Officer, but work directly with the Commander; (3) Personnel providing services not readily available from military sources or needing special training and knowledge, as for example, the Field Operations Service. See U.N. Doc. A/3943, p. 18.

34. U.N. Doc. A/3302, p. 22. During the Lebanon crisis in 1958, the Secretary-General went even further in defining the breadth of his powers. Announcing that he would send reinforcements to the United Nations Observation Group in Lebanon as requested, Mr. Hammarskjold declared that it was "in keeping with the philosophy of the Charter that the Secretary-General also should be expected to act without any guidance from the Assembly or the Security Council should this appear to him necessary towards helping to fill any vacuum that may appear in the systems which the Charter and traditional diplomacy provide for the safeguarding of peace and security." S/PV.837 (July 22, 1958), p. 11.

In the Congo crisis of 1960, however, Dag Hammarskjold has been victim of sharp criticism of his policy and initiative by members of the Soviet bloc. Faced with an extremely delicate internal situation in the new African Republic and confronted with a series of broad and vague resolutions which required interpretation, the Secretary-General once more found it necessary to use a good deal of personal initiative in putting the Assembly's decisions into effect. See Chapter VIII.

35. See Mason, "The United Nations Emergency Force," in *International Law and the Middle East Crisis*, p. 38.

36. Ahmed S. Bokhari, "Parliaments, Priests and Prophets," *Foreign Affairs*, XXXV (April, 1957), 406–7.

37. Security Council, *Official Records*, 11th year, 751st meeting (October 31, 1956), pp. 1–2.

38. Elmore Jackson, "The Developing Role of the Secretary-General," *International Organization*, XI (1957), 440.

39. Some dissatisfaction had been expressed with the composition of the Advisory Committee. Uruguay, for example, felt that "perhaps the representation of the European countries might have been differently conceived," General Assembly, *Official Records,* 1st Emergency Special Session, 566th meeting (November 7, 1956), p. 99. Poland at the 567th meeting, *ibid.,* p. 108, objected to the omission of a country from Eastern Europe in the Committee and suggested the inclusion of Czechoslovakia.

40. Resolution 1001 (ES-I). See explanation by the representative from Ecuador at the First Emergency Special Session: "instead of the General Assembly's having to be convened frequently to deal with administrative questions and immediate action to be taken by this emergency army, this committee, presided over by the Secretary-General, would be able to take the necessary steps and would call for a meeting of the General Assembly only if there were questions of sufficient importance to warrant doing so." General Assembly, *Official Records,* 1st Emergency Special Session, 566th meeting (November 7, 1956), p. 94.

41. U.N. Doc. A/3943, p. 31. Unfortunately, there remains a dearth of official information on the means employed by the Committee to fulfill its tasks and on the specific issues with which it has dealt. Meetings are private and official reports have not been released. Interesting, however, is Mr. Cohen's commentary on the Committee, "The United Nations Emergency Force: A Preliminary View," *International Journal,* XII (Spring, 1957), 120–21: "In early statements and interpretations, Mr. Hammarskjold had not employed the Advisory Committee to any serious extent. Probably he found it a useful device to ratify his policies but not to control them. From the time of Israeli withdrawal on March 7, and the unexpected return of Egyptian Civilian Administration to Gaza after March 14, the Advisory Committee became a more significant instrument, very likely because the Secretary-General needed support for situations that had not been foreseen."

42. U.N. Doc. A/3943, p. 31. If an important, urgent disagreement arose between the Secretary-General and the Committee, it would probably have to be solved by the Assembly itself. See Sohn, "Authority of the UN to Establish and Maintain a Permanent UN Force," *American Journal of International Law,* LV (April, 1958), 235.

43. "Regulations for the United Nations Emergency Force," U.N. Doc. ST/SGB/UNEF/1, February 20, 1957, p. 3.

44. U.N. Resolution 1442 (XIV), December 5, 1959.

45. See, U.N. Doc. A/3943, p. 17.

46. U.N. Doc. ST/SGB/UNEF/1, pp. 3–5.

47. U.N. Doc. A/3943, p. 17.

48. *Ibid.,* p. 13.

49. The question of liaison representation in Tel Aviv was left in abeyance for some time. Israel thought such representation unnecessary because UNEF was not to be stationed on the Israeli side of the armistice demarcation line. But, Pearson, UN officials, and many delegates interpreted Resolution 1129 (XI), whereby UNEF was to be placed "on" the armistice line, as including both sides of the line. See also note 29, above.

50. U.N. Doc. A/3943, p. 18.

51. *Ibid.*, p. 19.
52. *Ibid.*, p. 29.
53. *Ibid.*, p. 30.
54. *Ibid.*, p. 31.
55. Pearson, "Force for U.N.," *Foreign Affairs*, XXXV (April, 1957), 401–2.
56. U.N. Doc. A/3943, p. 32.
57. See above, note 34.

VI: STATUS IN INTERNATIONAL LAW

1. This agreement was effected by exchange of letters on February 8, 1957 between the Secretary-General, on behalf of the United Nations, and the Minister for Foreign Affairs of Egypt. It was approved by the General Assembly in Resolution 1121 (XI). For text of agreement, see U.N. Doc. A/3526.

2. "Text of Letter Dated June 21, 1957 from the Secretary-General to the States Providing Contingents," U.N. Doc. A/3943, Annex 1, p. 33.

3. For text, see "Resolutions Adopted by the General Assembly during the First Part of its First Session from 10 January to 14 February, 1946," U.N. Doc. A/64, July 1, 1946, pp. 25–33.

4. U.N. Doc. ST/SGB/UNEF/1. These rules were issued by the Secretary-General after consultation with the Advisory Committee, the participating states, and the Commander of UNEF. National contingents provided for UNEF serve under these Regulations.

5. According to the Convention, the United Nations also enjoys the following privileges and immunities: inviolability of premises; immunity from search, requisition, confiscation, expropriation and any other form of interference (whether by executive, administrative, judicial or legislative action); inviolability of archives; freedom from financial controls; right to hold funds; exemption of assets and income and other property from all direct taxes; exemption from custom duties and prohibition of restrictions on imports and exports needed for official purposes; most-favored nations treatment as to communications and use of communication facilities without censorship. See Joseph L. Kunz, "Privileges and Immunities of International Organizations," *American Journal of International Law*, XLI (1947), 850. From these privileges and immunities of the larger organization seem to follow those of its subsidiary organ, i.e., UNEF.

6. U.N. Doc. A/3526, p. 55.

7. *Ibid.*, p. 53. Italics added.

8. *Ibid.*, p. 54.

9. *Ibid.*, p. 56.

10. U.N. Doc. A/3943, p. 27.

11. U.N. Doc. ST/SGB/UNEF/1, p. 2.

12. U.N. Doc. A/3526, p. 56.

13. *Ibid.*

14. U.N. Doc. A/64, p. 26.

15. Article 18 of the Convention.

16. See Kunz, "Privileges and Immunities of International Organizations," *American Journal of International Law*, XLI (1947), 856.

17. Article 27 of the Convention.

18. U.N. Doc. A/3526, p. 55.

19. "This immunity from legal process shall continue to be accorded notwithstanding that the persons concerned are no longer employed on missions for the United Nations. . . ." Article VI of the Convention.

20. U.N. Doc. A/3526, p. 55. Neither these Secretariat members nor officers of the UNEF command enjoy immunity from civil, administrative, and police jurisdiction in connection with acts of their private lives.

21. U.N. Doc. ST/SGB/UNEF/1, p. 2.

22. *Ibid.*, p. 6.

23. *Ibid.*, p. 5.

24. *Ibid.*

25. Staff Rules and Regulations of the United Nations, U.N. Doc. UN/SGB/94, Regulation 1.4.

26. Clarence Wilfred Jenks, "Some Problems of an International Civil Service," *Public Administration Review*, III (Spring, 1943), 95.

27. Of course, it is still unclear whether Secretariat members are also, in the last analysis, totally independent of the approval of their national government. Certainly experience has shown that under certain circumstances the influence of the national government can bring about dismissal. See S. M. Schwebel, "The International Character of the Secretariat of the United Nations," *British Yearbook of International Law 1953*, XXX, 71–115; "Report of the Secretary-General on Personnel Policy," U.N. Doc. A/2364, January 30, 1953.

28. U.N. Doc. A/3526, p. 53.

29. "The possible conflict of jurisdiction is analyzed as follows: each state has exclusive jurisdiction over all security offenses (such as treason or sabotage) which are punishable by its law but not by the law of the other state. The sending state has the primary right to exercise jurisdiction over a member of its forces wherever the offense is solely against its property or security, or solely against the person or property of another member of that force or a civilian component or dependent, or where the offense arises out of any act or omission done in the performance of official duty. In all other cases the receiving state has the primary right to exercise jurisdiction." Murray L. Schwartz, "International Law and the NATO Status of Forces Agreement," *Columbia Law Review*, LIII (1953), 1091. See also J. H. Rouse and G. B. Baldwin, "The Exercise of Criminal Jurisdiction Under the NATO Status of Forces Agreement," *American Journal of International Law*, LI (January, 1957), 29–62. For text of NATO Agreement, see Lord Ismay, *NATO: The First Five Years*, pp. 204–7.

30. See Archibald King, "Jurisdiction Over Friendly Armed Forces," *American Journal of International Law*, XXXVI (1942), 539–67.

31. "Agreement Between the United States of America and Egypt Respecting Jurisdiction over Criminal Offenses Committed by the Armed Forces of the United States in Egypt, March 2, 1943," *United States Statutes at Large*, LVII, 1197–98.

32. In the one case the Foreign Minister of Egypt made a point of noting that special wartime conditions necessitated his extraordinary grant. King, "Ju-

risdiction Over Friendly Armed Forces," *American Journal of International Law*, XXXVI (1942), 539–67.

33. Rouse and Baldwin, "The Exercise of Criminal Jurisdiction under the NATO Status of Forces Agreement," *American Journal of International Law*, LI (January, 1957), 32.

34. U.N. Doc. A/3943, p. 26.

35. *Ibid.*, Annex 1, p. 33.

36. U.N. Doc. A/3526, p. 53.

37. Should the Commander give notice that a member of UNEF is prevented, "because of official duties or authorized absence to protect his interests in a civil proceeding in which he is a participant, the Egyptian court or authority shall at his request suspend the proceeding until the elimination of the disability, but for not more than ninety days." Another right of a UNEF member is to keep property, which the Commander has certified as necessary for the fulfillment of his duties, free from seizure for the satisfaction of a judgment, decision or order, together with other property not subject thereto under the law of Egypt. In no case can members of the Force be deprived of or restricted in their personal liberty by an Egyptian court or authority in a civil proceeding, "whether to enforce a judgment, decision or order, to compel an oath of disclosure, or for any other reason." *Ibid.*, pp. 53–54.

38. General Assembly, *Official Records*, 11th Session, Plenary meeting 659 (February 23, 1957), Vol. II–III, p. 1192.

39. *Ibid.*

40. U.N. Doc. ST/SGB/UNEF/1, p. 5.

41. U.N. Doc. A/3526, p. 56.

42. *Ibid.* In the NATO Status of Forces Agreement claims of one party against another for damage to any property are waived if caused by a member of an employee of the armed services of the other in connection with the operation of the North Atlantic Treaty. In case of damage caused to other property the issue of liability is determined and the amount of damage is assessed by a sole arbitrator, unless the parties agree otherwise. See Article VIII.

43. U.N. Doc. A/3943, p. 26. Most of the property used by the Force for its headquarters, camps and premises, were provided free of charge by the Egyptian government. Some privately-owned land was utilized, however, and claims for compensation or rentals for this property were submitted to the Emergency Force through the Egyptian Liaison Office. The policy of the Force has been to pay for damages to real property arising out of negligence or other causes not specifically connected with the official functions of UNEF.

Following upon consultation between the Egyptian authorities and the Secretary-General, a procedure has been adopted in regard to privately-owned land whereby the Emergency Force surveys the sites with local authorities and, "on that basis and on the assumption that it is established that the Egyptian government would have honored the claim, makes payment to the owners, reserving its rights under the Agreement and the possibility, in due course, of raising with the government such demands for reimbursement as those rights warrant." *Ibid.*

44. "Report of the Secretary-General on Administrative and Financial Ar-

rangements for the United Nations Emergency Force," U.N. Doc. A/3883 and Rev. 1, November 21, 1956, General Assembly, *Official Records*, 11th Session, Annexes, Vol. II–III, Agenda Item 66, p. 15.

45. This commercial insurance, covering death and dismemberment of UNEF soldiers from all causes, was taken out on a temporary basis for a minimum period of one month starting from November 12, 1956. It provided that compensation for any one member of the Force would be limited to $25,000 at a cost of $25 per month per member, commencing with initial travel (from the home country) in each case. See *ibid.;* also, "Thirty-Fifth Report of the Advisory Committee on Administrative and Budgetary Questions: possible claims in respect of death or disability attributable to service with the United Nations Emergency Force," U.N. Doc. A/3456, December 14, 1956, General Assembly, *Official Records*, 11th Session, Annexes, Vol. II–III, Agenda Item 66, p. 32.

46. See Resolution 1122 (XI); U.N. Doc. A/3456, p. 32.

47. For exact figures, see *ibid.*

48. U.N. Doc. A/3694 and Add. 1, p. 11.

49. U.N. Doc. A/5172, p. 11.

50. U.N. Doc. A/3694 and Add. 1, p. 11.

51. See Advisory Opinion of April 11, 1949, "Reparations for Injuries Suffered in the Service of the United Nations," International Court of Justice, *Reports*, 1949, p. 174.

52. For further discussion, see Clyde Eagleton, "International Organization and the Law of Responsibility," in Academie de Droit International, *Recueil des Cours*, LXXVI (1950), 385 *et seq.*

53. U.N. Doc. A/3456, pp. 32–33.

54. U.N. Doc. A/3694 and Add. 1, p. 11.

55. Eagleton, "International Organization and the Law of Responsibility," *Recueil des Cours*, LXXVI (1950), 393. See also Guenter Weissberg, *The International Status of the United Nations* (New York, Oceana, 1961).

56. All claims have, in practice, been settled informally.

57. U.N. Doc. A/3526, pp. 56–57; U.N. Doc. A/3943, Annex 1, p. 33.

58. *Ibid.*

59. The provisions of the agreement dealing with the settlement of disputes, however, are to remain in force "until all claims arising prior to the date of termination of these arrangements, and submitted prior to or within three months following the date of termination, have been settled," U.N. Doc. A/3526, p. 57.

60. U.N. Doc. A/3943, p. 29.

61. *Ibid.*

VII: FINANCING THE FORCE

1. Frye, *A United Nations Peace Force*, p. 19.

2. "Report of the Secretary-General on administrative and financial arrangements for the United Nations Emergency Force," U.N. Doc. A/3383 and Rev. 1, November 21, 1956, General Assembly, *Official Records*, 11th Session (1956–

57), Annexes, Vol. II–III, Agenda Item 66, pp. 13–15. Earlier, the Secretary-General had declared that the question of financing UNEF required further study. He did, however, suggest that a basic rule could be applied provisionally, namely "that a nation providing a unit would be responsible for all costs for equipment and salaries, while all other costs should be financed outside the normal budget of the United Nations." He suggested that the Assembly, in the first instance, vote a general authorization for the cost of the Force on the basis of the general principles he had suggested. See U.N. Doc. A/3302, par. 15. The Assembly, in resolution 1001 (ES-I), approved *provisionally* the basic rule concerning the financing of the Force laid down in par. 15 of Hammarskjold's report.

3. For 1957, this resolution was 1084 (XI), December 21, 1956.

4. U.N. Doc. A/3943, p. 21.

5. *Ibid.,* pp. 21–22.

6. U.N. Resolution 1122 (XI). Pending receipt of funds for the Special Account, the Secretary-General was also authorized to advance necessary funds from the Working Capital Fund.

7. General Assembly, *Official Records,* 11th Session, 5th Committee, 538th meeting (November 27, 1956), pp. 32–33.

8. "Twenty-second report of the Advisory Committee on Administrative and Budgetary Questions: Administrative and Financial arrangements for the United Nations Emergency Force," U.N. Doc. A/3402, November 30, 1956, General Assembly, *Official Records,* 11th Session (1956–57), Annexes, Vol. II–III, Agenda Item 66, pp. 23–25.

9. The Fifth Committee, while discussing this question, requested and received assurances from the Secretary-General that he would draw on such accounts—as, for example, that of the United Nations Children's Fund and the Special Account for the Expanded Programme of Technical Assistance—only as a last resort and only if not immediately required by the agency in question. Some members of the Committee felt, however, that they could not support such a move, which would set a precedent for diversion of funds provided for specific purposes. See "Report of the Fifth Committee," U.N. Doc. A/3560 and Add. 1, February 25, 1957, General Assembly, *Official Records,* 11th Session (1956–57), Annexes, Vol. II–III, Agenda Item 66, p. 64. To date, the Secretary-General's authority in this realm has not been utilized.

10. These suggestions of the Advisory Committee were approved by the Fifth Committee at its 541st meeting (December 3, 1956) and by the Assembly in resolution 1122 (XI). Thereafter, the Secretary-General, in consultation with the Advisory Committee, established provisional financial rules for UNEF: U.N. Doc. ST/SGB/UNEF/2.

11. U.N. Doc. A/3402, p. 24.

12. See debate of the Fifth Committee at its 541st meeting, December 3, 1956.

13. Fifth Committee, 541st meeting, December 3, 1956, p. 47.

14. *Ibid.,* 545th meeting, December 6, 1956, p. 70.

15. *Ibid.,* p. 69.

16. *Ibid.,* 546th meeting, December 6, 1956, pp. 76–77.

17. *Ibid.,* 553rd meeting, December 17, 1956, p. 116.

18. *Ibid.*, 544th meeting, December 5, 1956, p. 67, and 545th meeting, December 6, 1956, p. 70.

19. *Ibid.*, 544th meeting, December 5, 1956, p. 67.

20. See remarks of delegate from Saudi Arabia, *ibid.*, 546th meeting, December 6, 1956, p. 75.

21. *Ibid.*

22. *Ibid.*

23. "In support of their own plan, which was designed to combine the method advocated by the Secretary-General with the voluntary contributions scheme, the Latin American representatives felt it their duty to recall that, at the United Nations Conference on International Organization held at San Francisco, during the discussions in the General Assembly which had resulted in the adoption of resolution 337A (V), entitled 'Uniting for Peace,' and in the reports of the Collective Measures Committee, it had been acknowledged that it was not yet possible to establish a mathematically accurate system for the proportional allocation of the heavy expenses to which the maintenance of mobile military forces would give rise. Undoubtedly, the responsibility for the maintenance of international peace and security devolved principally upon the permanent members of the Security Council. The Latin American countries considered that the Charter, in awarding that responsibility to the permanent members simultaneously with the privilege established by Article 27, gave implicit recognition to an indisputable fact, namely the concentration of vast economic, political, financial and military power in the hands of a very small number of states." Fifth Committee, 547th meeting, December 10, 1956, p. 82.

24. *Ibid.*, 557th meeting, December 20, 1956, p. 143. Against: Byelorussia, Czechoslovakia, Poland, Rumania, Ukraine, USSR, Albania, Bulgaria; Abstaining: Cambodia, Egypt, El Salvador, Greece, Haiti, Turkey, Union of South Africa, Argentina, Bolivia.

25. See "Report of the Committee appointed by the General Assembly at its 632nd Plenary Session, 21 December 1956," Annex of U.N. Doc. A/3560 and Add. 1, p. 69.

26. Fifth Committee, 594th meeting, February 22, 1957.

27. *Ibid.*, p. 349.

28. U.N. Doc. A/3560 and Add. 1.

29. These sources were to include other funds under the Secretary-General's control, provided that the repayment of any such advances of loans to the Special Account should constitute a first charge against contributions as they are received, and on condition that such loans should not affect current operational programs.

30. This reimbursement was a question provoking some thought; the Secretary-General finally decided that the United Nations would assume this obligation for the initial six-months service, which would amount to another $2,000,000. Reimbursement of extra and extraordinary costs relating to pay and allowances beyond the six-month period was estimated at an additional $4,-500,000. For further discussion, see section below.

31. See U.N. Doc. A/3694, Annex A, pp. 13–16.

32. Including the salary of the Special Advisor to the Secretary-General and travel and subsistence in respect of the Special Advisor and his staff of three

military officers; salaries and wages of (a) 4 international staff members recruited for services with UNEF (b) 42 staff members detailed to UNEF from Headquarters and other United Nations offices (c) 63 Field Service personnel serving in the mission area (d) 790 locally recruited staff in the mission area (e) 31 posts established in New York and Geneva to alleviate the additional workload caused by UNEF operations; and common staff costs providing for dependency allowances, education grants and related travel, etc.

33. Including transportation to leave centers by sea and air, leave center facilities, purchase of recreational and sports supplies, printing of air letters, rental of films, live shows.

34. Most of the costs under this heading have been borne in the form of voluntary contributions, but expenditures in regard to the initial transportation to Egypt of the Yugoslav contingent, plus the rotation of several contingents and military personnel, had yet to be met.

35. This sum is based on the payment of a daily allowance of 86 cents to approximately 6,000 officers and other ranks, paid from Dec. 17, 1956 in accordance with the principle decided upon by the Fifth Committee at its 541st meeting on December 3, 1956.

36. Mostly telecommunications, engineering, signal, and medical equipment.

37. Includes a great variety of technical, general and defense supplies, such as tents, fencing, cots, blankets, tools, medical and dental supplies, and communication.

38. Normal rations are calculated on the basis of $2 per day per man. In considering this level, the Assembly was asked to take into account the nature, size and composition of the Force, as well as its location. Because of the various national groups represented, special attention must be paid to national dietetic requirements. Since only a limited number of items are locally available, the bulk of provisions must be imported.

39. Railroads are frequently utilized since the Gaza harbor is not equipped for freight handling and the ports of Beirut and Port Said are used instead. Thus extra expense is involved.

40. For example, flags, newspapers, periodicals; cost of uniforms and clothing; contractual maintenance costs in connection with uniforms and personal equipment.

41. A commercial insurance policy (costing $110,000) in respect of the troops was carried during the period November 12–December 20, 1956. The Force has certain third-party vehicular coverage and certain protective cargo marine insurance.

42. Under this heading were placed foreseen expenditures (such as rotation of the Canadian contingent), which could not be calculated in advance; unforeseen expenditures (such as compensation claims which possibly would be presented); and cost of obligations already incurred, but which were in the process of verification and review.

43. U.N. Doc. A/3694, p. 8.

44. *Ibid.*, p. 9.

45. The British contribution has been treated as a reduction of its claim against the Special Account for equipment and supplies provided to the Force.

46. A condition of the United States contribution is that other Member States contribute an equal amount to the Special Account.

47. In addition, a request was made for the amount "as may be authorized or required with reference to reimbursement of costs to Governments providing contingents, it being understood that, so long as UNEF continues on its present basis of operations, the expenses of maintaining the Force would not normally exceed $2 million for any single month." U.N. Doc. A/3694, p. 12.

48. *Ibid.*

49. General Assembly, *Official Records,* 12th Session, Plenary meetings 720 and 721 (November 22–23, 1957).

50. U.N. Doc. A/3745, November 19, 1957, General Assembly, *Official Records,* 12th Session, Annexes, Agenda Item 65, p. 17.

51. Thus, by the addition of the $16.5 million authorized in Resolution 1090 (XI), a total of $30 million was approved for the expenses of the Force during the first financial period.

52. "Report of the Committee on Contributions," General Assembly, *Official Records,* 12th Session (1957), Supp. No. 10, pp. 2–3. The scale of assessments for subsequent years is very similar, although somewhat lower, due to admission of new United Nations Members.

53. U.N. Doc. A/3943, p. 22.

54. See. U.N. Doc. A/3694, p. 10.

55. *Ibid.*

56. Equipment which has been destroyed, worn out, or has deteriorated beyond what was provided for under normal depreciation schedules and which could be assessed at the conclusion of the total period of service of a government's contingent. *Ibid.,* p. 11.

57. U.N. Resolution 1151 (XII).

58. U.N. Doc. A/3943, p. 23.

59. A recommendation that formal budgets for UNEF be prepared was first submitted by the Advisory Committee on Administrative and Budgetary Questions in its twenty-sixth report, U.N. Doc. A/3761, December 31, 1957, General Assembly, *Official Records,* 12th Session, Annexes, Agenda Item 65. This Committee has reported annually to the Assembly, giving suggestions and comments regarding possible ways of reducing UNEF costs. See also, "Second Report of the Advisory Committee on Administrative and Budgetary Questions," U.N. Doc. A/3839, July 3, 1958 and "Twenty-fifth report of the Advisory Committee . . . ," U.N. Doc. A/4002, November 19, 1958, General Assembly, *Official Records,* 13th Session, Annexes, Agenda Item 65, pp. 1–4, 34–37; "Second report of the Advisory Committee on Administrative and Budgetary Questions to the General Assembly at its fifteenth Session," U.N. Doc. A/4409, July 21, 1960, General Assembly, *Official Records,* 14th Session, Annexes, Agenda Item 28.

60. The Assembly appropriated a maximum of $19 million for UNEF in 1959 (Resolution 1337 [XIII]), while the Secretary-General had prepared a budget estimate of $19,369,000. Likewise, a maximum of $20 million for the continuing operation of UNEF during 1960 was approved by the Assembly (Resolution 1441 [XIV]), while Secretariat estimates had amounted to $20,206,000.

61. Budget estimates are quoted for this period. Since the Assembly had authorized $25 million in December 1957 (Resolution 1151 [XII]), and budget estimates were not made until later, there was no need for adjusting estimates to appropriations. See United Nations Emergency Force, "Budget Estimates for the period 1 January to 31 December 1958," U.N. Doc. A/3823, General Assembly, *Official Records,* 13th Session (1958), Supp. No. 5A.

62. For details, see United Nations Emergency Force, "Budget for the period 1 January to 31 December 1959," U.N. Doc. A/4098, Supp. No. 5C.

63. United Nations Emergency Force, "Budget for the period 1 January to 31 December 1960," U.N. Doc. A/4355, Supp. No. 5B.

64. The figures for the years 1961 and 1962 are budget estimates. "United Nations Emergency Force Cost Estimates for the Maintenance of the Force. Report of the Secretary-General," U.N. Docs. A/4396, July 8, 1960 and A/4789, July 13, 1961, General Assembly, *Official Records,* 14th Session, Annexes, Agenda Item 28.

65. U.N. Doc. A/4486, September 13, 1960, *ibid.,* 15th session, Annexes, p. 21.

66. Resolution 1575 (XV), December 20, 1960. Voluntary contributions of $3.2 million from the United States and $275,000 from the United Kingdom to the Special Account resulted in a 50 percent reduction of the assessments for 1960 of all Members with the exception of the five having the largest assessments. These latter states—United States, United Kingdom, USSR, France, and China—received a reduction of $5,635 in comparison with an assessment of $1,001,239.

67. U.N. Doc. A/4857, p. 18.

68. As of 15 June 1961, the following countries owed assessments in full for the year 1960: Afghanistan, Albania, Argentina, Bolivia, Bulgaria, Byelorussia, Chile, China, Colombia, Costa Rica, Cuba, Czechoslovakia, El Salvador, Ethiopia, Greece, Guatemala, Haiti, Honduras, Hungary, India, Iraq, Jordan, Lebanon, Liberia, Libya, Mexico, Morocco, Nepal, Pakistan, Panama, Paraguay, Peru, Philippines, Poland, Rumania, Saudi Arabia, Spain, Sudan, Ukraine, USSR, U.A.R., Uruguay, Venezuela, Yemen. As of July 31, two of these governments had paid their obligations. U.N. Doc. ST/ADM/SER.B/145, June 15, 1961.

69. See U.N. Doc. A/4857.

70. See John G. Stoessinger, "Financing the United Nations," *International Conciliation,* No. 535 (November, 1961), pp. 23–32.

71. General Assembly Resolution 1590 (XV), December 20, 1960.

72. General Assembly Resolution 1619 (XV), April 21, 1961.

73. Fifty-two nations voted for the resolution, 32 abstained, the Soviet bloc and France voted against the measure, and 9 delegates were absent from the meeting. France declared that the Assembly could only *request* a Member State to pay its assessments, not *require* it to do so, for recognition of a requirement would transform the UN into a "world government." The USSR delegate denounced the bond issue as "illegal" and reaffirmed his government's intention not to recognize any opinion rendered by the ICJ. See the New York *Times,* December 21, 1961.

74. The resolution on UNEF was adopted by 57 votes to 9 (Ukraine, USSR,

Albania, Byelorussia, Czechoslovakia, Hungary, Mongolia, Poland, Rumania),
with 13 abstentions (U.A.R., Upper Volta, Yemen, Afghanistan, Belgium,
China, Ethiopia, France, Iraq, Lebanon, Peru, Philippines, Sudan). U.N. Doc.
A/C.5/SR.905, December 20, 1961.

75. See also, section above.

76. U.N. Doc. A/5172, p. 17.

77. The Court rendered its opinion by a majority of nine votes to five. International Court of Justice, *Certain Expenses of the United Nations (Article 17, paragraph 2, of the Charter), Advisory Opinion of 20 July 1962: I.C.J. Reports, 1962.* The Court's opinion appeared after the manuscript for this book was in press. Hence, a summary only is presented here. For further details, see forthcoming volume of The Brookings Institution, *Financing the United Nations.*

78. *Ibid.*, p. 162.

79. *Ibid.*, pp. 165–67.

80. *Ibid.*, p. 165.

81. *Ibid.*, p. 167.

82. *Ibid.*, p. 168.

83. For example, Cuba is of the opinion that, while all Members should contribute to the cost of maintaining the Force, it was not equitable to distribute those costs according to the proportion which Members contribute to the budget of the Organization. A more satisfactory system of financing should be found that would not overburden the budgets of countries in the process of economic development. The Force could, for example, be financed by means of a special emergency fund for the maintenance of peace, which could be raised by voluntary contributions. General Assembly, *Official Records,* Special Political Committee, 13th Session, 98th meeting (October 31, 1958), pp. 56–57. See also opinion of Spain, *ibid.*, 99th meeting (November 3, 1958), p. 60; declaration of Argentina in the 12th Session of the Assembly, Plenary meeting 720 (November 22, 1957), pp. 501–2.

84. For example, Guatemala and Mexico at the 12th Session of the Assembly, November 22, 1957; Venezuela in the Special Political Committee, October 31, 1958. The position of Guatemala is particularly interesting. Recognizing UNEF as an institution which is necessary for peace in the Middle East, as the basis for the evolution of a permanent United Nations military force, and as an organ to which all Members must financially contribute, Guatemala nevertheless has serious objections to the assessment system adopted. She believes that, since the Emergency Force became necessary owing to the individual action of certain Powers, these same Powers are primarily responsible for its financing. Moreover, those states with particular material interests in the Middle East, as well as the countries of the area itself ("owing to the tensions and instability prevailing among them"), have more direct responsibility than do others. Likewise, the permanent members of the Security Council, endowed with greater privileges than other United Nations Members, possess greater responsibilities not only in the political, but also in the financial realm. Guatemala also argues that the increase of the small countries' contribution by 50%—"for that is what the effort demanded of us amounts to—entails extraordinary sacrifices; this same increase is but 'a drop in the financial torrent' of

the military appropriations of the great Powers." It should also "be borne in mind that the Emergency Force paradoxically seems to relate to a permanent emergency. . . ."

Guatemala made "formal reservation with regard to any obligations to which this draft resolution may give rise if it is adopted . . . [subsequent U.N. Resolution 1151 (XII)]. I would also extend this reservation to the doubtful interpretation whereby a draft resolution such as that proposed may be held to place obligations upon Member States under Article 19 of the United Nations Charter."

85. "La situation juridique des États Membres à l'égard de la Force d'Urgence des Nations-Unies," *Annuaire Français de Droit International*, IV (1958), 417–19.

86. They have stated their position in Plenary Sessions on November 26, 1956; November 22, 1957; November 14, 1958; in the Fifth Committee on December 3, 1956; December 6, 1957; December 2, 1958; December 3, 1958; November 29, 1959; December 16, 1960; and October 5–December 22, 1961; and in the Special Political Committee on October 29, 1958 and October 31, 1958.

87. See, for example, remarks by Albert F. Bender in the Fifth Committee, U.N. Doc. A/C.5/SR.895, December 8, 1961, p. 10.

88. Discussion by the delegate from Bulgaria, *ibid.*, pp. 10–11.

89. "The Secretary-General holds to the view which he has previously expressed to the General Assembly that decisions which are taken by the Assembly itself and which have important financial consequences carry with them an obligation on the part of all Member Governments to make available the requisite resources or other means for their implementation." U.N. Doc. A/3694, p. 12.

90. For example, during the time of the creation of the Trusteeship Council, which moreover is a principal organ of the United Nations, the Soviet Union protested its constitution on the basis of the agreements adopted by the Assembly under Article 79. (See Goodrich and Hambro, *The Charter of the United Nations*, pp. 437–40). The Committee on Non-Self-Governing Territories, established by the Assembly on December 14, 1946 was considered illegal by the administering powers. The Soviet bloc did not recognize the Assembly's Interim Committee, established in 1948, or the Collective Measures Committee, created on November 3, 1950.

91. See Chaumont, "La situation juridique des États Membres à l'égard de la Force d'Urgence des Nations-Unies," *Annuaire Français de Droit International*, IV (1958), 420.

92. U.N. Doc. A/3964, p. 12. Italics added.

93. U.N. Doc. A/4408, p. 9.

94. From a working paper by Eric Stein for the Brookings Institution's United Nations Financing Project, May 1962.

VIII: UNEF: WEAPON FOR PEACE

1. Cohen, "The United Nations Emergency Force," *International Journal*, XII (Spring, 1957), 126. This development may prove, however, to be dis-

advantageous to a Secretary-General. Hammarskjold's role in the Congo situation elicited much criticism.

2. See New York *Times*, March 16, 1957, and February 14, 1960.

3. See Jay Waltz, reporting from Cairo in the New York *Times*, February 14, 1960.

4. Hoffmann, "Sisyphus and the Avalanche," *International Organization*, XI (Summer, 1957), 457.

5. *Ibid.*

6. General Assembly, *Official Records*, 11th Session, Plenary meeting 652 (February 2, 1957), Vol. II–III, p. 1079.

7. *Ibid.*, italics added.

8. New York *Times*, April 11, 1957.

9. See Inis L. Claude, "The United Nations and the Use of Force," *International Conciliation*, No. 532 (March, 1961).

10. "First Report by the Secretary-General on the Implementation of Security Council Resolution S/4387 of 14 July 1960," U.N. Doc. S/4389, July 18, 1960.

11. On July 17, 1960, the Congolese government declared that it would call "Soviet Russian troops" into the Congo to deal with the situation if the United Nations did not effect withdrawal of Belgian troops within seventy-two hours. In response, the United States quickly served notice on the Soviet Union that it "will do whatever may be necessary" to prevent intrusion of any military forces into the Congo other than those authorized by the UN. Note comparative problems at the time of the Suez crisis, Chapter II, above.

12. See Chapter IV, above.

13. U.N. Doc. S/4389.

14. ONUC, however, relied heavily on "sister African nations" for contingents.

15. "Second Report by the Secretary-General on the Implementation of the Security Council Resolutions of July 14 and 22, 1960, Relating to the Congo," reprinted in *United Nations Review*, VII (September, 1960), 21.

16. The Secretary-General speaking to the Council on July 20, 1960. See *ibid.*, p. 59.

17. For quotations from statements of other delegates, see Frye, *A United Nations Peace Force*, pp. 69–70.

18. Pearson, "Force for U.N.," *Foreign Affairs*, XXXV (April, 1957), 403.

19. Sir Leslie Munro, "The Case for a Standing U.N. Army," New York *Times Magazine*, July 27, 1958.

20. "United Nations Emergency Force," *Hearings before the Subcommittee on International Organization and Movements of the Committee on Foreign Affairs House of Representatives*, 85th Congress, 2d Session (July 24, 1958).

21. Frye, *A United Nations Peace Force*, p. 32.

22. General Assembly, *Official Records*, 13th Session, Special Political Committee, 98th meeting (October 31, 1958), pp. 56–57.

23. *Ibid.*, p. 56.

24. Inis L. Claude, "The Political Framework of the United Nations Financial Problem" (Chapter I of a future publication of the Brookings Institution: *Financing the United Nations*).

25. *Ibid.*

26. *Ibid.*

27. U.N. Doc. A/3943, p. 27.

28. *Ibid.*

29. The Secretary-General illustrated this point by showing that, for UNEF, it was possible to make use of enlisted men with short military experience under the command of experienced officers. Recruitment of the United Nations Observation Group in Lebanon, however, was limited largely to officers who did not have to be carefully screened. And for service in Jordan, only a very limited number of military officers, rigorously chosen, were needed. Variations existed as well in regard to material requirements: on the one hand, UNEF was serviced by a relatively small number of aircraft and vehicles; UNOGIL, on the other hand, required a much higher ratio of planes and vehicles to the men involved. *Ibid.*, p. 28.

30. *Ibid.*

31. Goodrich and Rosner, "The United Nations Emergency Force," *International Organization*, XI (Summer, 1957), 429–30.

32. *Ibid.*, p. 430.

33. Lincoln P. Bloomfield, *The United Nations and U.S. Foreign Policy*, p. 69.

HISTORICAL APPENDIX

1. Stefan T. Possony, "Peace Enforcement," *Yale Law Journal*, LV (August, 1946), 910.

2. *Ibid.*

3. Sémichon, *La Paix et la Trêve de Dieu*, 2d ed. (1869), p. 35 *et seq.*

4. Dante Alighieri, *On World Government; or, De Monarchia;* Sylvester John Hemleben, *Plans for World Peace Through Six Centuries*, pp. 1–4; Maximilien de Béthune, duc de Sully, *The Grand Design of Henry IV from the Memoirs of the Duke of Sully, and The United States of Europe;* William Penn, *An Essay Towards the Present and Future Peace of Europe, by the Establishment of an European Diet, Parliament or Estate;* Abbé de Saint-Pierre, *A Project for Establishing the General Peace of Europe, by a More Equal Partition than has hitherto been Proposed;* Jean-Jacques Rousseau, "Extrait du projet de paix perpetuelle, de M. l'abbé de Saint Pierre." in *Oeuvres Complètes.*

5. Possony, "Peace Enforcement," *Yale Law Journal*, LV (August, 1946), 919.

6. *Ibid.*

7. A. S. Daggett, *America in the China Relief Expedition* (Kansas City, Hudson-Kimberly Publishing Company, 1903), pp. 55–59.

8. For excerpts, see *War Obviated by an International Police*, A Series of Essays Written in Various Countries, pp. 145–57.

9. *Ibid.*, p. 159.

10. An article in *The Nineteenth Century* (July, 1911), p. 24 *et seq.*

11. *War Obviated by an International Police*, p. 64.

12. *Ibid.*, p. 141.

13. See Theodore Marburg, *Development of the League of Nations Idea;* see also, Hemleben, *Plans for World Peace*, pp. 138–81. For comprehensive

bibliography, consult Mid-West Debate Bureau, *An International Police Force*.

14. Viscount James Bryce, Introduction to Viscount Grey *et al., The League of Nations* (London, 1918, 1919), p. 18.

15. Viscount Bryce, *Proposals for the Prevention of Future Wars* (London, George Allen and Unwin, 1917).

16. David Davies, *The Problem of the Twentieth Century*.

17. See Hemleben, *Plans for World Peace*, pp. 143–46.

18. William H. Short, *Program and Policies of the League to Enforce Peace: A Handbook for Officers, Speakers and Editors* (New York, League to Enforce Peace, 1916); see also, Hemleben, *Plans for World Peace*, pp. 146–58.

19. League of Free Nations Association, *Statement of Principles* (New York, 1916).

20. Edward R. Pease, *The History of the Fabian Society* (New York, International Publishers, 1926); and Leonard S. Woolf, *International Government* (New York, Brentano's, 1916).

21. David Hunter Miller, *Drafting of the Covenant* (2 vols., New York, Putnam's, 1928).

22. For text, see *ibid.*, Vol. II, pp. 241–46.

23. Quoted in Possony, "Peace Enforcement," *Yale Law Journal*, LV (August, 1946), 928.

24. League of Nations, *Official Journal*, Special Supplement No. 4 (December, 1920).

25. The national states were to supply their contingents with necessary equipment and were to advance sums for transport and maintenance. All expenses exceeding those normally expended in maintaining the troops in their own country (transport, billeting, additional ration allowances, office expenses), would be repaid to the contributing states by the League of Nations out of its Budget of 1922. Thus the international nature of the force was emphasized. Eventually, Poland and Lithuania were to reimburse the League for any monies advanced by the Organization to cover the expenses of the plebiscite. "Report on the Organization of the International Force for Vilna, Approved by the Council of the League, November 25th, 1920," League of Nations, *Official Journal*, Second Year, No. 1 (January–February, 1921), p. 6.

26. See resolution adopted by the Council on March 3, 1921, League of Nations, *Official Journal*, Second Year, No. 2 (March–April, 1921), pp. 181–82.

27. F. P. Walters, *A History of the League of Nations*, p. 142.

28. The Saar Annex of the Treaty of Versailles had provided that, fifteen years after the coming into force of the Treaty, a plebiscite would be held in the Saar Territory in order to ascertain the wishes of the population: would they maintain an international regime in the Saar, unite with Germany, or join the French Republic? For text of relevant paragraphs, see League of Nations, *Official Journal*, Fifteenth Year, No. 2 (February, 1934), p. 161. For creation of force, see *ibid.*, No. 12, Part II, Fourth Meeting (December 8, 1934), p. 1730.

29. An excellent account of the Saar question is to be found in Sarah Wambaugh, *The Saar Plebiscite*. See especially Chapter VI.

30. See League of Nations, *Official Journal*, Fifteenth Year, No. 12, Part II (December, 1934).

31. Colonel A. H. Burne, D.S.O., R.A., "The International Force in the Saar," reprinted in *Policing the Saar,* p. 10.

32. Wambaugh, *The Saar Plebiscite,* pp. 302–3.

33. Burne, "The International Force in the Saar," p. 5.

34. The local police, who were very few in number, are referred to. *Ibid.,* p. 9.

35. *Ibid.*

36. *Ibid.*

37. "International Force for the Saar Territory: Report of the Subcommittee Provided for under the Council Resolution of December 8th, 1934, Approved by the Committee of the Council on December 12th, 1934," Annex 1525a, C. 553.M.254 (1934), VII, League of Nations, *Official Journal,* Fifteenth Year, No. 12, Part II (December, 1934), pp. 1841–42.

38. *Ibid.,* Seventh Meeting (December 11, 1934), p. 1763.

39. *Ibid.,* for detailed information on the court, see Wambaugh, *The Saar Plebiscite,* pp. 175–76.

40. "International Force for the Saar Territory . . . ," Annex 1525a, pp. 1841–42.

41. For text of resolution, see minutes of Council's seventh meeting (December 11, 1934), pp. 1762–63. In this resolution, the Council declared that it would "consider at a later date in what manner the cost of the plebiscite should finally be met." "Final Report of the Committee of the Council, dated June 2nd, 1934," C.209.1934 (VII), League of Nations, *Official Journal,* Fifteenth Year, No. 6, Part II (June, 1934), p. 650.

42. Seventh Meeting (December 11, 1934), p. 1763.

43. *Ibid.* If or when the special fund proved insufficient, the French and German governments were to be asked to make supplementary payments. Compare with principles adopted in the case of UNEF, see Chapter VII.

44. Burne, "The International Force in the Saar," p. 13.

45. *Ibid.,* p. 3.

46. Conference for the Reduction and Limitation of Armaments, "Proposals of the French Delegation," *Conference Documents,* Vol. I, pp. 113–16.

47. *Ibid.,* p. 115.

48. U.S. Department of State, *Postwar Foreign Policy Preparation, 1939–1945,* Publication 3580 (Washington, D.C., Government Printing Office, 1949), pp. 602–3.

49. The disputed questions centered primarily on the nature and size of the force (the Soviet Union, France, and the United Kingdom favored a small armed body, while the United States insisted upon a rather large, mobile force which could bring to bear "the maximum armed force in the minimum time"); the contributions of the five permanent members (the USSR was emphatic in its wish for equal contributions, while France, China, the United Kingdom, and the United States proposed that each state contribute those elements which it was best able to provide); and the principle to govern withdrawal of the forces (the majority view was that no rigid restrictions should be defined, but the Russian spokesman urged that withdrawal of forces should be effected 30 to 90 days after fulfillment of the measures envisaged in Article 42). See "Report of the Military Staff Committee," Security Council, *Official Records,*

Second Year, Special Supplement No. 1 (April 30, 1947), pp. 1–32; Leland M. Goodrich and Anne P. Simons, *The United Nations and the Maintenance of International Peace and Security.*

50. U.N. Doc. S/1025, September 16, 1948. A proposal to create a small armed force, outside the framework of Article 43, in order to help settle the Palestine crisis, was rejected. See Working Paper by the United Nations Secretariat, U.N. Doc. A/AC.21/13, February 9, 1948, pp. 7–11.

51. "Annual Report of the Secretary-General on the Work of the Organization 1 July 1947—30 June 1948," General Assembly, *Official Records*, 3d Session (1948–49), Supp. No. 1, pp. xvii–xviii. See also, Stephen M. Schwebel, "A United Nations 'Guard' and a United Nations 'Legion,'" in Frye, *A United Nations Peace Force*, pp. 195–202.

52. "United Nations Guard: Report of the Secretary-General," U.N. Doc. A/656, September 28, 1948, p. 7.

53. See, "Report of the Special Committee on a United Nations Guard," General Assembly, *Official Records*, 4th Session (1949), Supp. No. 13; and Schwebel, in Frye, *A United Nations Peace Force*, pp. 202–8.

54. For comprehensive analysis of the question, consult Leland M. Goodrich, *Korea: A Study of U.S. Policy in the United Nations.*

55. Text of relevant resolutions in *ibid.*, pp. 222–23.

56. Goodrich and Simons, *The United Nations and the Maintenance of International Peace*, p. 405.

57. *Ibid.*, p. 406.

58. Resolution 377A (V), General Assembly, *Official Records*, 5th Session (1950–51), Supp. No. 20, pp. 10–12.

59. "Report of the Collective Measures Committee," U.N. Doc. A/1891, General Assembly, *Official Records*, 6th Session (1951–52), Supp. No. 13 and "Report of the Collective Measures Committee," U.N. Doc. A/2215, *ibid.*, 7th Session (1952–53), Supp. No. 17.

60. See replies by governments to inquiries regarding the availability of their armed forces for UN use, *ibid.* For summary of Assembly opinion, see Goodrich and Simons, *The United Nations and the Maintenance of International Peace*, pp. 411–13.

61. *Ibid.*, p. 414. The Secretary-General's plan for a United Nations Legion, also considered briefly by the Collective Measures Committee, was left pending "for the time being," eventually "to yield to the dual pressures of the depreciation or disinterest of Members, and the doubts of his Secretariat colleagues most closely concerned," Schwebel, in Frye, *A United Nations Peace Force*, p. 216.

Stanley Hoffmann denies the usefulness of the Collective Measures Committee in the Suez crisis because of the vagueness of its recommendations ("it tried to design measures that could fit as many circumstances as possible") and because it used the Korean case as an example ("The whole effort of the Committee was orientated toward collective enforcement against a transgressor. The Committee thus neglected the cases in which there would be need for a supervisory force but not for a shooting one. . . . Also, the work of the Committee . . . was based on the hypothesis of a clear-cut case of aggression; the other hypothesis [a 'breach of the peace' which is not a clear-cut aggression] got lost."). See Hoffmann, "Sisyphus and the Avalanche: the United

Nations, Egypt and Hungary," *International Organization,* XI (Summer, 1957), 450–51.

62. Goodrich and Simons, *The United Nations and the Maintenance of International Peace,* p. 414.

63. William Aylott Orton, *The Liberal Tradition. A Study of the Social and Spiritual Conditions of Freedom* (New Haven, Yale University Press, 1945), p. 255.

64. Pearson, "Force for U.N.," *Foreign Affairs,* XXXV (April, 1957), 401.

BIBLIOGRAPHY

UNITED NATIONS OFFICIAL RECORDS

General Assembly, *Official Records*, First Emergency Special Session (1956), Plenary Meetings, 561st–572d Meetings (Nov. 1–Nov. 10, 1956).

—— *Official Records*, Eleventh Session (1956–57), Plenary Meetings, Vol. I, 581st–597th Meetings (Nov. 16–Nov. 27, 1956); Vols. II–III, 624th–668th Meetings (Dec. 18, 1956–March 8, 1957).

—— *Official Records*, Eleventh Session (1956–57), Fifth Committee, 538th–596th Meetings (Nov. 27, 1956–Feb. 25, 1957).

—— *Official Records*, Twelfth Session (1957), Plenary Meetings, 720th–729th Meetings (Nov. 22–Dec. 13, 1957).

—— *Official Records*, Twelfth Session (1957), Fifth Committee, 639th Meeting (Dec. 6, 1957) and 646th Meeting (Dec. 12, 1957).

—— *Official Records*, Thirteenth Session (1958–59), Plenary Meetings, 780th Meeting (Nov. 14, 1958) and 790th Meeting (Dec. 13, 1958).

—— *Official Records*, Thirteenth Session (1958–59), Fifth Committee, 697th–705th Meetings (Dec. 2–Dec. 11, 1958).

—— *Official Records*, Thirteenth Session (1958–59), Special Political Committee, 96th–100th Meetings (Oct. 28–Nov. 5, 1958).

—— *Official Records*, Fourteenth Session (1959–60), Plenary Meetings, 804th–809th Meetings (Sept. 24–Sept. 25, 1959).

—— *Official Records*, Fourteenth Session (1959–60), Fifth Committee, 749th–759th Meetings (Nov. 24–Dec. 4, 1959).

UNITED NATIONS DOCUMENTS

GENERAL ASSEMBLY, *Official Records*, FIRST EMERGENCY SPECIAL SESSION (1956), ANNEXES, AGENDA ITEM 5

A/3267, Nov. 3, 1956, "Report of the Secretary-General submitted in pursuance of resolution 997 (ES-I), par. 5, adopted by the General Assembly on 2 November 1956."

A/3268, Nov. 3, 1956, "Letter dated 3 November 1956 from the Alternate Permanent Representative of France, addressed to the Secretary-General."

A/3270, Nov. 3, 1956, "Communication dated 3 November 1956 from the Permanent Representative of Egypt, addressed to the President of the General Assembly and to the Secretary-General."

A/3272, Nov. 3, 1956, "United States of America: draft resolution."

A/3277, Nov. 3, 1956, "Letter dated 3 November 1956 from the Permanent Representative of Israel, addressed to the President of the General Assembly."

A/3278, Nov. 4, 1956, "Letter dated 3 November 1956 from the Permanent Representative of Syria, addressed to the President of the General Assembly."

A/3279, Nov. 4, 1956, "Aide-memoire dated 3 November 1956 from the Permanent Representative of Israel, addressed to the Secretary-General."

A/3284, Nov. 4, 1956, "Second report of the Secretary-General submitted in pursuance of resolution 997 (ES-I), par. 5, adopted by the General Assembly on 2 November 1956."

A/3287, Nov. 4, 1956, "Report of the Secretary-General on communications with the Governments of France, Egypt, Israel and the United Kingdom of Great Britain and Northern Ireland concerning implementation of General Assembly resolutions 997 (ES-I) and 999 (ES-I) dated 2 and 4 November 1956."

A/3288, Nov. 4, 1956, "Letter dated 4 November 1956 from the Permanent Representative of Egypt, addressed to the Secretary-General."

A/3289, Nov. 4, 1956, "First report of the Secretary-General on the plan for an emergency international United Nations Force requested in resolution 998 (ES-I) adopted by the General Assembly on 4 November 1956."

A/3291, Nov. 5, 1956, "Letter dated 4 November 1956 from the Permanent Representative of Israel, addressed to the Secretary-General."

A/3293, Nov. 5, 1956, "Letter dated 5 November 1956 from the Permanent Representative of Great Britain and Northern Ireland, addressed to the Secretary-General."

A/3296, Nov. 5, 1956, "Third Report of the Secretary-General submitted in pursuance of resolution 997 (ES-I), par. 5, adopted by the General Assembly on 2 November 1956."

A/3298, Nov. 5, 1956, "Letter dated 5 November 1956 from the Permanent Representative of the Union of Soviet Socialist Republics, addressed to the Secretary-General."

A/3302 and Add. 1 to 16, Nov. 6, 1956, "Second and final report of the Secretary-General on the plan for an emergency international United Nations Force requested in resolution 998 (ES-I), adopted by the General Assembly on 4 November 1956."

A/3310, Nov. 7, 1956, "Aide-memoire dated 5 November 1956 from the Secretary-General, addressed to the Governments of France and the United Kingdom of Great Britain and Northern Ireland."

A/3313, Nov. 7, 1956, "Letter dated 7 November 1956 from the Secretary-General, addressed to the Minister of Foreign Affairs of France."

A/3317, Nov. 8, 1956, "Confirmation of the appointment of Major-General E. L. M. Burns as Chief of the United Nations Command for the emergency international force."

GENERAL ASSEMBLY, *Official Records*, ELEVENTH SESSION (1956–57), ANNEXES, VOL. II–III, AGENDA ITEM 66

A/3375, Nov. 20, 1956, "Report of the Secretary-General on basic points for the presence and functioning in Egypt of the United Nations Emergency Force."

A/3376, Nov. 20, 1956, "Report of the Secretary-General on the clearing of the Suez Canal."

A/3380, Nov. 21, 1956, "Letter dated 21 November 1956 from the Permanent Representative of Egypt, addressed to the Secretary-General."

A/3383 and Rev. 1, Nov. 21, 1956, "Report of the Secretary-General on administrative and financial arrangements for the United Nations Emergency Force."

A/3384 and Add. 1 and 2, Nov. 21, 1956, "Report of the Secretary-General on compliance with General Assembly resolutions 997 (ES-I) and 1002 (ES-I).

A/3395, Nov. 26, 1956, "Exchange of letters between the Minister for Foreign Affairs of Israel and the Secretary-General."

A/3402, Nov. 30, 1956, "Twenty-second report of the Advisory Committee on Administrative and Budgetary Questions: administrative and financial arrangements for the United Nations Emergency Force."

A/3410, Dec. 1, 1956, "Letter dated 1 December 1956 from the Permanent Representative of Israel, addressed to the Secretary-General."

A/3415, Dec. 3, 1956, "Note by the Secretary-General."

A/3425, Dec. 4, 1956, "Letter dated 3 December 1956 from the Permanent Representative of Israel, addressed to the Secretary-General."

A/3456, Dec. 14, 1956, "Thirty-fifth report of the Advisory Committee on Administrative and Budgetary Questions: possible claims in respect of death or disability attributable to service in the United Nations Emergency Force."

A/3466, Dec. 18, 1956, "Memorandum dated 17 December 1956 from the Minister for Foreign Affairs of Egypt, addressed to the Secretary-General."

A/3479, Dec. 21, 1956, "Letter dated 18 December 1956 from the Permanent Representative of Israel, addressed to the Secretary-General."

A/3483, Dec. 31, 1956, "Letter dated 31 December 1956 from the Permanent Representative of Israel, addressed to the Secretary-General."

A/3491, Jan. 10, 1957, "Note by the Secretary-General, transmitting a report dated 3 December 1956 on the situation in the Gaza area."

A/3492, Jan. 10, 1957, "Second report of the Secretary-General on the clearing of the Suez Canal."

A/3500 and Add. 1, Jan. 15, 1957, "Report by the Secretary-General on compliance with General Assembly resolutions calling for withdrawal of troops and other measures."

A/3511, Jan. 24, 1957, "Note by the Secretary-General transmitting an aide-memoire on the Israel position on the Sharm el-Sheikh area and the Gaza Strip."

A/3512, Jan. 24, 1957, "Report of the Secretary-General in pursuance of General Assembly resolution 1123 (XI)."

A/3526, Feb. 9, 1957, "Report of the Secretary-General on arrangements concerning the status of the United Nations Emergency Force in Egypt."

A/3527, Feb. 11, 1957, "Report of the Secretary-General in pursuance of General Assembly resolutions 1124 (XI) and 1125 (XI)."

A/3560 and Add. 1, Feb. 25, 1957, "Report of the Fifth Committee."

A/3563, Feb. 26, 1957, "Note by the Secretary-General." (Includes

Memorandum of important points in the discussion between the Representative of Israel and the Secretary-General on 25 February 1957.)

A/3568, March 8, 1957, "Second report of the Secretary-General in pursuance of General Assembly resolutions 1124 (XI) and 1125 (XI)."

GENERAL ASSEMBLY, *Official Records,* TWELFTH SESSION
(1957), ANNEXES, AGENDA ITEM 65

A/3694 and Add. 1, Oct. 9, 1957, "Report of the Secretary-General."

A/3761, Dec. 3, 1957, "Twenty-sixth report of the Advisory Committee on Administrative and Budgetary Questions."

A/3790, Dec. 12, 1957, "Report of the Fifth Committee."

GENERAL ASSEMBLY, *Official Records,* THIRTEENTH SESSION
(1958–59), ANNEXES, AGENDA ITEM 65

A/3839, July 3, 1958, "Second report of the Advisory Committee on Administrative and Budgetary Questions. Budget estimates for the period 1 January to 31 December 1958."

A/3899, Aug. 27, 1958, "Report of the Secretary-General."

A/3943, Oct. 9, 1958, "Summary study of the experience derived from the establishment and operation of the Force: report of the Secretary-General."

A/3989, Nov. 11, 1958, "Report of the Special Political Committee."

A/4002, Nov. 19, 1958, "Twenty-fifth report of the Advisory Committee on Administrative and Budgetary Questions: Budget estimates for the period 1 January to 31 December 1959."

A/4072, Dec. 11, 1958, "Report of the Fifth Committee."

GENERAL ASSEMBLY, *Official Records,* FOURTEENTH SESSION
(1959), ANNEXES, AGENDA ITEM 28

A/4160, July 23, 1959, "Cost estimates for the maintenance of the Force: report of the Secretary-General."

A/4171, July 31, 1959, "Budget estimates for the maintenance of the Force: report of the Advisory Committee on Administrative and Budgetary Questions."

A/4176 and Add. 1 and 2, Sept. 10, 1959, "Manner of financing the Force: report of the Secretary-General on consultations with Governments of Member States."

A/4210 and Add. 1, Sept. 10, 1959, "Progress report of the Secretary-General on the United Nations Emergency Force."

A/C.5/800, Nov. 12, 1959, "Supplementary estimates for 1959: revised estimates for 1960: report of the Secretary-General."

A/4284, Nov. 17, 1959, "Supplementary estimates for 1959: revised estimates for 1960: report of the Advisory Committee on Administrative and Budgetary Questions."

A/4335, Dec. 4, 1959, "Report of the Fifth Committee."

A/4396, July 8, 1960, "United Nations Emergency Force. Cost estimates for the Maintenance of the Force. Report of the Secretary-General. Budget estimates for the period 1 January to 31 December 1961."

A/4409, July 21, 1960, "United Nations Emergency Force: budget estimates for the period 1 January to 31 December 1961. Second report of the Advisory Committee on Administrative and Budgetary Questions to the General Assembly at its fifteenth session."

GENERAL ASSEMBLY, *Official Records,*
FIFTEENTH, SIXTEENTH AND SEVENTEENTH SESSIONS
(1960–61) (1961–62) (1962–63), ANNEXES

A/4486, Sept. 13, 1960, "United Nations Emergency Force. Report of the Secretary-General."

A/4857, Aug. 30, 1961, "United Nations Emergency Force. Report of the Secretary-General."

A/5172, Aug. 22, 1962, "United Nations Emergency Force. Report of the Secretary-General."

LEAGUE OF NATIONS OFFICIAL RECORDS

League of Nations, *Official Journal,* Special Supplement No. 4 (Dec., 1920).

—— *Official Journal,* Second Year, No. 1 (Jan.–Feb., 1921) and No. 2 (March–April, 1921).

—— *Official Journal,* Fifteenth Year, No. 2 (Feb., 1934); No. 6 (Part II) (June, 1934); No. 12 (Part II) (Dec., 1934).

—— *Official Journal,* Sixteenth Year, No. 3 (March, 1935).

BOOKS, ARTICLES, MONOGRAPHS

Adams, Sherman. *Firsthand Report*. New York: Harper, 1961.

Armstrong, H. F. "U.N. Experience in Gaza," *Foreign Affairs*, XXXV (July, 1957), 600–619.

Béthune, Maximilien de, duc de Sully. *The Grand Design of Henry IV from the Memoirs of the Duke of Sully, and the United States of Europe*. Translated by Edward Everett Hale. Boston: Published for the International School of Peace, Ginn, 1909.

Bloomfield, L. M. *Egypt, Israel and the Gulf of Aqaba in International Law*. Toronto: Carswell Co., 1957.

Bloomfield, Lincoln P. *The United Nations and U.S. Foreign Policy*. New York: Little, Brown, 1961.

Bokhari, Ahmed S. "Parliaments, Priests and Prophets," *Foreign Affairs*, XXXV (April, 1957), 405–11.

Burne, A. H. "The International Force in the Saar," in *Policing the Saar*. London: New Commonwealth Publication, Series A, No. 8, April, 1936.

Cambell, John C. *Defense of the Middle East*. Revised ed. New York: Council on Foreign Relations, 1960.

Chapman, Dudley H. "International Law—The United Nations Emergency Force—Legal Status," *Michigan Law Review*, LVII (November, 1958), 56–81.

Chaumont, C. "La situation juridique des états membres à l'égard de la Force d'Urgence des Nations–Unies," *Annuarie français de Droit International*, IV (1958), 399–440.

Childers, Erskine B. *Common Sense About the Arab World*. New York: Macmillan, 1960.

Cohen, Maxwell. "The United Nations Emergency Force: A Preliminary View," *International Journal*, XII (Spring, 1957), 109–27.

Corbett, Percy E. "Power and Law at Suez," *International Journal*, VII (Winter, 1956–57), 1–12.

"Criminal Jurisdiction Over American Armed Forces Abroad," *Harvard Law Review*, LXX (April, 1957), 1043–67.

Dante Alighieri. *On World Government; or De Monarchia*. Translated by Herbert W. Schneider, New York: Liberal Arts Press, 1949.

Davies, David. *The Problem of the Twentieth Century*. London: Ernest Benn Limited, 1930.

Dayan, Moshe. "Israel's Border and Security Problems," *Foreign Affairs*, XXXIII (January, 1955), 250–67.

Eagleton, Clyde. "International Organization and the Law of Responsibility," in Académie de Droit International, *Recueil des Cours*, LXXVI (1950), 323–423.

Eden, Anthony. *The Memoirs of Anthony Eden. Full Circle*. Cambridge: Riverside, 1960.

Frye, William R. *A United Nations Peace Force*. New York: Oceana for the Carnegie Endowment for International Peace, 1957.

Goodrich, Leland M. *Korea: A Study of U.S. Policy in the United Nations*. New York: Council on Foreign Relations, 1956.

Goodrich, Leland M., and Anne P. Simons. *The United Nations and the Maintenance of International Peace and Security*. Washington, D.C.: Brookings Institution, 1955.

Goodrich, Leland M., and Gabriella E. Rosner. "The United Nations Emergency Force," *International Organization*, XI (Summer, 1957), 413–30.

Gross, Leo. "Passage through the Suez Canal of Israel Bound Cargo and Israel Ships," *American Journal of International Law*, LI (1957), 530–68.

Hackworth, Green Hayward. *Digest of International Law*. Vols. I and II. Washington, D.C.: Government Printing Office, 1941.

Hemleben, Sylvester John. *Plans for World Peace Through Six Centuries*. Chicago: University of Chicago Press, 1943.

Hoffmann, Stanley. "Sisyphus and the Avalanche: The United Nations, Egypt, and Hungary," *International Organization*, XI (Summer, 1957), 446–69.

Huang, Thomas T. F. "Some International and Legal Aspects of the Suez Canal Problem," *American Journal of International Law*, LI (1957), 277–307.

Hurewitz, Jacob C. "Arab-Israeli Tensions," *Proceedings of the Academy of Political Science*, XXIV (January, 1952), 73–81.

—— "The Israeli-Syrian Crisis in the Light of the Arab-Israel Armistice System," *International Organization*, V (1951), 459–79.

―――― "The United Nations Conciliation Commission for Palestine," *International Organization*, VII (1953), 482–97.

Hutchison, E. H. *Violent Truce*. New York: Devin-Adair, 1956.

Jackson, Elmore. "The Developing Role of the Secretary-General," *International Organization*, XI (Summer, 1957), 446–69.

Johnson, D. H. N. "The Effect of the Resolutions of the General Assembly of the United Nations," *British Yearbook of International Law*, XXXII (1955–56), 97–122.

Kelsen, Hans. *The Law of the United Nations*. London: Stevens and Sons, 1950.

King, Archibald. "Jurisdiction Over Friendly Armed Forces," *American Journal of International Law*, XXXVI (1942), 539–67.

Kunugi, Tatsuro. "Legal Problems Derived from the Establishment and Functioning of the United Nations Emergency Force." Unpublished master's essay. Ithaca: Cornell University, June, 1959.

Kunz, Joseph L. "Privileges and Immunities of International Organizations," *American Journal of International Law*, XLI (1947), 328–62.

Kunzmann, K. H. "Actuelle Vorshlage für eine Friedenstruppe der Vereinten Nationen," *Europa Archiv*, XIII (June 20, 1958), 10811–26.

Lash, Joseph P. *Dag Hammarskjold*. New York: Doubleday, 1961.

Lenczowski, George. *The Middle East in World Affairs*. 2d ed. Ithaca: Cornell University Press, 1956.

Marburg, Theodore. *Development of the League of Nations Idea*. New York: Macmillan, 1932.

Marlowe, John. *Arab Nationalism and British Imperialism*. New York: Praeger, 1961.

Mason, Henry L. "The United Nations Emergency Force," in Tulane Studies in Political Science, Vol. IV, *International Law and the Middle East Crisis*, New Orleans: Tulane University, 1957.

Mezerik, A. G., ed. "The United Nations Emergency Force (UNEF): Precedents, Creation, Evolution," *International Review Service*, III (May, 1957), 1–55.

Mid-West Debate Bureau. *An International Police Force*. Jacksonville, Ill.: n.d.

Miller, David-Hunter. *Drafting the Covenant*. 2 vols. New York: Putnam, 1923.

Miller, E. M. "Legal Aspects of the United Nations Action in the Congo," *American Journal of International Law,* LV (January, 1961), 1–28.

Moore, John Bassett. *A Digest of International Law.* Washington, D.C.: Government Printing Office, 1906.

Munro, Sir Leslie. "The Case for a Standing UN Army," *The New York Times Magazine,* July 27, 1958.

O'Ballance, Edgar. *The Sinai Campaign of 1956.* New York: Praeger, 1959.

O'Donovan, Patrick. "How the U.N. Troops Were Mobilized," *The Reporter,* XVI (January 10, 1957), 30–32.

Pearson, Lester B. "Force for U.N.," *Foreign Affairs,* XXXV (April, 1957), 395–404.

Penn, William. *An Essay Towards the Present and Future Peace of Europe by the Establishment of an European Diet, Parliament or Estate.* London: Peace Committee of the Society of Friends, 1936.

Possony, Stefan T. "Peace Enforcement," *Yale Law Journal,* LV (1946), 910–49.

Report of Committee on Study of Legal Problems of the United Nations. "The Establishment of the United Nations Emergency Force," in *Proceedings of the American Society of International Law,* 51st Annual Meeting, Washington, D.C.: American Society of International Law, 1958, pp. 206–29.

Rosenne, Shabtai. *Israel's Armistice Agreements with the Arab States; A Juridical Interpretation.* Tel Aviv: Published for the International Law Association, Israel Branch, by Blumstein's Bookstores, 1951.

Rouse, J. H., and G. B. Baldwin. "The Exercise of Criminal Jurisdiction under the NATO Status of Forces Agreement," *American Journal of International Law,* LI (January, 1957), 29–62.

Rousseau, Jean-Jacques. "Extrait du Projet de paix perpétuelle, de M. l'abbé de Saint-Pierre," *Oeuvres Complètes,* Paris: Hachette, 1877.

Rowan-Robinson, G. A. "An International General Staff, Lessons from the Past," *The New Commonwealth,* IX (September, 1948), 127–31.

Saint-Pierre, Abbé de. *A Project for Establishing the General Peace of Europe by a More Equal Partition than Has Hitherto Been Proposed.* London, 1712.

Scheuner, V. "Eine Internationale Sicherungsmacht in Dienste der Vereinten Nationen," *Zeitshrift für öffentliches Recht und Volkerrecht,* XIX (August, 1958), 389–415.

Schwartz, Murray L. "International Law and the NATO Status of Forces Agreement," *Columbia Law Review,* LIII (1953), 1091–113.

Schwebel, Stephen M. "The International Character of the Secretariat of the United Nations," *British Yearbook of International Law.* XXX (1953), 71–115.

Servais. "Les Forces de police des Nations-Unies," *Revue militaire générale,* I (January, 1957), 130–36.

Sohn, L. B. "Authority of the UN to establish and maintain a permanent UN force," *American Journal of International Law,* LII (April, 1958), 229–40.

Spry, Graham. "Canada, the United Nations Emergency Force, and the Commonwealth," *International Affairs,* XXXIII (July, 1957), 289–300.

Stoessinger, John G. "Financing the United Nations," *International Conciliation,* No. 535 (November, 1961).

Stone, Julius. *Aggression and World Order.* Berkeley and Los Angeles: University of California Press, 1958.

—— *Legal Controls of International Conflict.* London: Stevens and Sons, 1959.

Strange, Susan. "Suez and After," *The Yearbook of World Affairs 1957,* New York: Praeger, 1957.

U.S. Congress. House. *United Nations Emergency Force. Hearings before the Subcommittee on International Organizations and Movements of the Committee on Foreign Affairs House of Representatives.* Eighty-fifth Congress, July 24 and 25, 1958.

U.S. Department of State. *United States Policy in the Middle East. September 1956–June 1957. Documents.* Department of State Publication 6505, Near and Middle Eastern Series 25, August, 1957.

Walters, Francis P. *A History of the League of Nations.* 2 vols. London: Oxford University Press, 1952.

Wambaugh, Sarah. *The Saar Plebiscite.* Cambridge: Harvard University Press, 1952.

War Obviated by an International Police. A Series of Essays Written in Various Countries. The Hague: Martinus Nijhoff, 1915.

Weissberg, Guenter. *The Internation Status of the United Nations.* New York: Oceana, 1961.

Wright, Quincy. "Intervention, 1956," *American Journal of International Law,* LVII (1957), 257–76.

INDEX

Abu Suweir, 124, 126

Adams, Sherman, quoted on crisis, 19, 25, 229n8

Administration of UNEF, 129, 132, 137, 139, 142, 154, 202, 252n33

Administration units, 120, 122, 128

Administrative Tribunal, UN, 234n27

Advance preparations, *see* Permanent force for UN

Advisory Committee, UNEF's, 34, 35, 52, 57, 90, 96, 102, 132, 133-34, 138, 142, 192, 236n52, 253nn39, 40, 41, 42, 254n4

Advisory Committee on Administrative and Budgetary Questions, 152-53, 154, 160, 161-62, 183, 261n59

Afghanistan, 119, 235n44, 245n60

Afro-Asian nations, 132-33; views on crisis, 18, 26; and withdrawal of Israel, 84

Agreement on Status of Force, *see* Status of Forces Agreement of UNEF

Aide-memoire, Egypt-UN, 52-53, 57-58, 237-38n66

Aimon, Archbishop of Bourges, 207

Albania, 109, 197

Alexander, H. T., on powers of ONUC, 104-5

Algeria, 6, 13, 15, 24, 226n36

American League of Free Nations Association, 210

American League to Enforce Peace, 210

Angelis, Virgil de, 139

Apportionment of UNEF expenses, *see* Financing UNEF

Arab States: relations with Israel, 6, 7-11, 62, 78-79, 188, 223-24n7, 224n10, 247n88; and boycott of Israel, 7, 8-9; and permanent peace settlement, 8, 95, 113; views on crisis, 19, 26, 32, 113, 118; and functions of UNEF, 91; and financing UNEF, 165

Arbitration, *see* Peaceful settlement

Argentina, 249n127

Armistice Agreements: violation of, 7, 10-11, 98-99, 225n22, 243n40, 249n136; establishment of, 8, 99; compliance with, 10-11, 28, 36, 66-67, 80-81, 84, 85, 91, 97-99, 111, 243n43; and UNEF, 61-62, 67, 80-82, 97-98, 200, 237n64; denial of, 71, 98-99; and Gaza, 78, 80-82, 200; and Gulf of Aqaba, 95; provisions of, 97-98, 247n93

Armistice demarcation lines: raids, 7, 10, 78-81, 225n22; infiltration across, 10, 98, 100, 102, 103, 246n75; withdrawal behind, 48, 71, 76, 80, 81; and UNEF, 62, 81, 83, 84-85, 86, 90, 91, 98, 100-3, 106, 114, 127, 186-87; and deployment of UNEF, 62, 84-85, 100, 128, 237n64, 240n90, 244nn45, 50, 253n49; *see also* Withdrawal of invading forces

Armstrong, Hamilton Fish, reporting on Gaza, 85, 88-89, 92; on peace settlement in Middle East, 111-12

Aswan High Dam, 13, 226n35

Australia, 14, 23, 31, 75, 82, 178, 229n14, 246n85; *see also* Commonwealth

Austria, 178

Belgium, 178

Belligerent rights, 7, 8-9, 62, 111, 114, 188, 242n28, 243nn35, 40, 249n36

Ben-Gurion, David: reprisals against Egypt, 10; negotiations with Secretary-General, 11, 202; and deployment of UNEF, 62; and negotiations with U.S., 87; on Armistice Agreement with Egypt, 99

Bokhari, Ahmed S., 131

Boxer Rebellion, 208

Brazil: deployment of contingent, 101, 127, 128; evaluation of UNEF, 107; contributions to UNEF, 119, 122,

DATE DUE

MY 5 '64	DISPLAY	
OC 6 '64		
NO 12 '64		
NO 30 '64		
DE 16 '64		
FE 4 '65		
FE 10 '65		
MY 5 '65		
MY 18 '65		
JA '66		
MR 18 '68		
AP 15 '70		
AP 29 '70		
MY 13 '70		
DE 19 '72		
JA 9 '73		
JA 30 '73		
GAYLORD		PRINTED IN U.S.A.